Rumors in Financial Markets

Rumors in Financial Markets

Insights into Behavioral Finance

Mark Schindler

John Wiley & Sons, Ltd

Copyright © 2007   John Wiley & Sons Ltd, The Atrium, Southern Gate, Chichester,
West Sussex PO19 8SQ, England

ML

Telephone   (+44) 1243 779777

Email (for orders and customer service enquiries): cs-books@wiley.co.uk
Visit our Home Page on www.wiley.com

Other Wiley Editorial Offices

John Wiley & Sons Inc., 111 River Street, Hoboken, NJ 07030, USA

Jossey-Bass, 989 Market Street, San Francisco, CA 94103-1741, USA

Wiley-VCH Verlag GmbH, Boschstr. 12, D-69469 Weinheim, Germany

John Wiley & Sons Australia Ltd, 42 McDougall Street, Milton, Queensland 4064, Australia

John Wiley & Sons (Asia) Pte Ltd, 2 Clementi Loop #02-01, Jin Xing Distripark, Singapore 129809

John Wiley & Sons Canada Ltd, 6045 Freemont Blvd, Mississauga, ONT, L5R 4J3

Wiley also publishes its books in a variety of electronic formats. Some content that appears in print may
not be available in electronic books.

Anniversary Logo Design: Richard J. Pacifico

Library of Congress Cataloging in Publication Data

Schindler, Mark.
   Rumors in financial markets : insights into behavioral finance / Mark Schindler.
     p. cm.
   ISBN-13: 978-0-470-03196-4
   ISBN-10: 0-470-03196-4
   1. Investments—Psychological aspects. 2. Investments—Decision making. I. Title.
   HG4515.15.S35 2007
   332.601'9—dc22

                                     2006032510

British Library Cataloguing in Publication Data

A catalogue record for this book is available from the British Library

ISBN 978-0-470-03196-4

Typeset in 10/12pt Times by Integra Software Services Pvt. Ltd, Pondicherry, India
Printed and bound in Great Britain by Antony Rowe Ltd, Chippenham, Wiltshire
This book is printed on acid-free paper responsibly manufactured from sustainable forestry
in which at least two trees are planted for each one used for paper production.

Contents

List of Symbols

$t = 0, 1, \ldots, T$ time periods
$s = 1, \ldots, S$ states of the world
$l = 1, \ldots, L$ lotteries
$x = 1, \ldots, X$ outcomes
$c(s)$ consequence of state s
$\Theta(p(s))$ second-order probability of occurrence of state s
$u(c(s))$ utility of consequence c in state s
$p(s)$ probability measure of occurrence of state s
$E(p)$ expectation with respect to the probability measure
$SEU(x) = \sum_{s \in S} p_s u(x_s)$ subjective expected utility
q_t stock price at time t
d_t dividend at time t

Preface

More than three years ago the rumor started to spread among my acquaintances that I was considering writing a PhD thesis. Jointly responsible for the fact that the rumor turned out to be true and that this book could be completed on the basis of my PhD thesis during my employment at the Institute for Empirical Research in Economics at the University of Zurich are a number of people whom I would like to thank.

First, I would like to thank my dissertation advisor Professor Thorsten Hens for his continuous guidance throughout my studies. Because of his critical challenges and numerous suggestions, he helped to bring the quality of this work to a level that I could never have reached on my own. He has encouraged me and my work far more than average and given me extensive freedom, so that I could work most efficiently. Despite all his other tasks and responsibilities, Professor Ernst Fehr agreed to act as a second referee for my thesis, and I would like to thank him very much. His expertise in experimental economics has helped to ensure the highest quality standards for the experiments performed.

In addition, this work could never have been done without the financial support for the European Science Foundation Project on 'Behavioral Models on Economics and Finance' provided by the Swiss National Science Foundation. It is therefore gratefully appreciated. In this regard, I would like to thank Professor Klaus Reiner Schenk-Hoppé for his support.

There are many people to thank at the University of Zurich who provided generous support of all kinds. Specifically I would like to highlight Thomas Bamert for the creation of the online survey as well as Sascha Robert and Omar Pennacchio for the programming of all the experiments. Concerning the in-house distribution of the online survey I would especially thank Philipp Dodds from UBS.

Furthermore the creative and inspiring atmosphere within our chair has led to many excellent discussions with Kremena Damianova, Dr Anke Gerber, Dr Stefan Reimann, Rina Rosenblatt-Wisch, Marc Sommer, Sven-Christian Steude, Andreas Tupak, Dr Peter Wöhrmann and Martin Vlcek. Thank you for all your critical and encouraging comments.

During my studies I had the opportunity to discuss my research with many people at numerous congresses, seminars and meetings, benefiting from their suggestions and comments. Special thanks go to Peter Bossaerts from CalTech, Werner Güth from the Max Planck Institute Jena, José Manuel Gutierrez from the University of Salamanca, Manfred Nermuth from the University of Vienna, Joerg Oechssler from the University of Bonn and Shyam Sunder from Yale University.

I definitely could not have finished this work without the motivation from my personal environment. Many friends have again and again encouraged me in my work, giving me countless valuable comments and providing their help. Thank you in particular to Mike Andres, Pascal Botteron, Anne Bourgeois, Mathias Bucher, Christian Bührer, Barbara Eberle-Haeringer, Gabi Kellenberger, Larissa Kihm, Christopher Koch, Nick Mihic, Marco Ruch, Alexandra Schaller, Philipp Sigrist, Stephan Skaanes, Ralph Villiger and Marc Wydler.

Finally, I would like to thank Caitlin Cornish (Senior Commissioning Editor) and Emily Pears at John Wiley & Sons for their help and assistance in bringing this project to completion.

By far the greatest thanks go to my parents Joan and Hans, and to my sister Christine, who have supported me during my long period of education in every respect and with all of their hearts. This work is dedicated to them.

1

Introduction

*A trader may, when it comes to rumors on
stock exchanges, not even trust his own father.*

ANDRÉ KOSTOLANY (own translation)

A rumor can be everywhere, at any time, at any place. It is perceived as something mysterious, almost magical. A rumor frequently produces a hypnotic effect. It fascinates, overwhelms, entraps and stirs up people's minds. Rumors are the oldest mass medium in the world and their nature is still difficult to grasp. What is so special about rumors, that people get so excited, anxious and nervous? Why do companies release press bulletins stating, 'We don't comment on rumors'? People do not know too much about this important social phenomenon, especially from a scientific point of view. Where does it start, how does it develop, where and when does it end? How does it differentiate itself from gossip, legends and just ordinary information? How are rumors spread, when are they believed and what kind of an impact can they have? Everyone believes they are able to recognize a rumor when they are faced with one, but no one can give you a satisfying definition of it. The longer people think about rumors, the more they realize how difficult it is to set limits on what they are and what they are not. Why is it so difficult to capture the exact content and functionalities of a rumor? There are at least two possible explanations for that. The first explanation is that a rumor is not observable from the beginning to the end. When people start studying a rumor, it is usually already dead or in the final phase. In many cases it will be very difficult to find out its starting point and development process. The second possible explanation is that rumors, at least until a few years ago, have included a moral aspect. This prejudice has made people think more about the moral entitlement of a rumor than of actual functionalities.[1]

One of the most central elements of the Theory of Finance is the economics of information and how new information is updated to reallocate scarce resources. Rumors are a special form of information and their special characteristics have to be accounted for when applied to the Theory of Finance. Since rumors involve not only financial but also psychological and sociological elements, it is necessary to apply an interdisciplinary approach when analyzing rumors in financial markets. While the individual behavior when faced with rumors in financial markets is one aspect to be analyzed, probably the more interesting one is to search for behavioral mechanisms on an aggregate level. One of the goals of this work is to evaluate whether rumors lead to systematic behavioral patterns when trading assets in a financial market.

Unfortunately, from a scientific view, not too much is known about rumors, in particular in financial markets. This is somewhat astonishing, since rumors on the one hand have a very long history and are known to be a very efficient mass media communication channel, and on the other hand appear almost on a daily basis in technical newspapers and magazines.

One of the difficulties about research on rumors is their complexity in nature. A second argument for the poor research so far can be found in the difficulty of gathering sound quality data on rumors, in particular in financial markets. This work is an attempt to gain more insights into the topic.

The overall aim of the book is to provide insights into various aspects of rumors in financial markets. How can this be achieved? Since the subject is not easy to address and just about everyone has a different opinion on it, first of all it has to be clarified what exactly a rumor is and how it fits into other notions such as information, news and gossip. Secondly, since this is an investigation on rumors in financial markets, rumors have to be set in context to the existing finance literature. This includes aspects such as how rumors, as a quite special form of information, are used to allocate scarce resources from a Behavioral Finance point of view. In addition, many people claim that market participants act irrationally when rumors evolve in financial markets. This question has to be addressed as well. Furthermore, since rumors, in particular in relation to financial markets, are at the edge of being legal, the aspects of insider trading and market manipulation have to be clarified as well. However, to really get more insights on the topic, further research is necessary. As a first step, a survey was conducted in the financial marketplace to find out what the questions and hot topics are that market participants are faced with when rumors evolve. From the results of the survey, it became clear that certain aspects discussed were not very relevant to further analysis, while with other aspects more questions seem to have arisen than been clarified. The next step was to analyze the most suitable research methodology to try and answer these open questions. Research methodologies such as theoretical modeling, empirical analysis, field studies and experiments were considered. A review of that literature is discussed in Chapters 3 and 6. In the end, the choice fell on conducting financial experiments, for many reasons. The detailed arguments in favor of that research methodology are discussed at the beginning of Chapter 6. The overall goal of those financial experiments was to gain insights on why we observe what we observe when rumors evolve in financial markets. Why is it that stock prices all of a sudden perform wild swings, volatility rockets to the sky and market participants simply shake their heads because they aren't able to explain what is going on? Exactly these kind of questions the experiments try to find an answer for and discover what is going on in people's minds and whether there are any theoretically sound explanations for these phenomena. Therefore that chapter of this book is more devoted to theory and describes the financial experimental setup and results of the experiments conducted. The conclusions of all the results are drawn in Chapter 7, what open issues still remain and what kind of future research could be performed to better understand the fascinating happenings in financial markets, in particular when rumors appear.

1.1 OBJECTIVES OF THIS BOOK

From the statements above, five main objectives for this book were identified:

1. The first objective is to present an *overview* of the nature of rumors. This includes the definition and structuring of rumors in comparison to other terms such as information, news and gossip.
2. The second objective is to provide an overview of *rumors in relation to the Theory of Finance*. This includes how rumors can be related to Behavioral Finance and how they link to the concept of rational behavior. In addition, the second objective includes how rumors

and the existing studies can be classified and categorized. Concerning how rumors are modeled, the first category of models focuses on the determining factors for the intensity of a rumor. The second category models the rumor transmission process, while the third focuses on applied market microstructure settings.

3. The third objective focuses on the *legal aspects* of rumors in financial markets. The links from rumors to insider trading and market manipulation are analyzed in detail and the implications thereof are drawn up.

4. The fourth objective focuses on gaining *insights from industry experts*. Since up to now not very much is known about the appearance of and individual dealing with rumors in financial markets, a survey among practitioners should provide insights into various aspects thereof.

5. The fifth and last objective is to gain *experimental insights* into aggregate behavior when rumors are spread in financial markets. The goal is to find theoretical explanations for various empirically observable effects, such as a strong increase in price volatility and apparently unfounded movements in traded asset prices. In addition, whether the often-heard claim of herd behavior is legitimate when rumors appear in financial markets is also investigated.

1.2 STRUCTURE OF THIS BOOK

Reflecting on the main objectives formulated above, the book is structured into seven chapters:

Chapter 2: Definitions and Characteristics of Rumors begins with the various definitions and structuring of the notions of news, information, gossip and rumor. This is followed by a historical background to studies on rumors.

Chapter 3: Rumors and the Theory of Finance discusses how rumors can be integrated into the new theoretical approach of Behavioral Finance. Furthermore it analyzes how rumors can be applied to the concept of rational behavior. The various empirical studies of rumors in financial markets are reviewed, including a meaningful classification and categorization thereof. The different model categories are presented and put into structure. In addition, the limitations of the various models are analyzed and specified.

Chapter 4: Legal Aspects of Rumors in Financial Markets analyzes the links between rumors and both insider trading and market manipulations. They are put into structure to distinguish them clearly from one another, including several examples. Furthermore the chapter provides a discussion of the academic controversy about the regulation of insider trading. Models and implications thereof are also provided for insider trading as well as for market manipulation.

Chapter 5: Survey of Rumors in Financial Markets empirically surveys how industry experts, such as traders and sales people, perceive, value and trade on rumors. The focus of the study is the development of rumors, the speed of their transmission, what the factors are for believing them, how personal networks are of value and how they are traded on. The results are summarized and used as a basis for experiments performed and discussed in Chapter 6.

Chapter 6: Rumor Experiments describes the experiments performed and analyzes the results in detail. The experiments start by testing basic hypotheses of rumor characteristics and proceed to more complex experimental settings. Altogether four stages of experiments are performed. The first stage focuses on the question of ambiguity aversion, the second on varying informational contents, the third tests the hypothesis of herd behavior and the fourth stage analyzes the communication behavior of market participants.

Chapter 7: Conclusions and Outlook summarizes the results and considers the future role of rumors in financial markets.

1.3 RESEARCH METHODOLOGY

The research methodologies applied vary according to the different parts of the book.

The first part (Chapters 2 to 4) is of a more descriptive nature. Therefore the research methods included gathering information from various books, articles and papers in journals, as well as speaking to people in the field such as traders, sales people and regulators, and attending conferences.

For the survey (Chapter 5), two methods were used to access both quantitative and qualitative data – online survey and personal interviews. The online survey was sent by e-mail to professional traders and sales people dealing with all asset classes (stock, bonds, FX and commodities) and financial instruments including derivatives. Personal interviews were held with selected traders and sales people.

The third and experimental part (Chapter 6) of the book uses the data raised from the experiments performed. All experiments were performed at the Institute for Empirical Research of the University of Zurich during the time period between May 2003 and January 2005. The details on exactly how the experiments were designed and why an experimental approach was chosen can be found at the beginning of Chapter 6 and in the appendices.

2
Definitions and Characteristics of Rumors

Fama crescit eundo

Latin saying, by VERGIL, Roman poet, 70–19 BC

2.1 DEFINITIONS

According to the Merriam-Webster dictionary, a rumor is

1. Talk or opinion widely disseminated with no discernible source.
2. A statement or report current without known authority for its truth.

Allport and Postman (1947), two of the pioneers in rumor research, were influenced by the events of World War II when they defined a rumor as 'first of all unauthenticated bits of information in that they are bereft of "secure" standards of evidence'.[1] Knapp (1944) defines a rumor as 'a proposition for belief of topical reference disseminated without official confirmation'.[2] Peterson and Gist (1951) see it as 'an unverified account or explanation of events, circulating from person to person and pertaining to an object, event or issue of public concern'.[3] Although all the definitions are not the same, they contain elements differentiating a rumor from information. The different characteristics are that a rumor is: (a) not verified, (b) of local or time-limited importance or interest, and (c) intended primarily for belief.[4]

1. A rumor is a piece of information that has poor authenticating data. A rumor can either be confirmed as true or be found to be false at a certain point in the future. The important difference from information is that information is always confirmed immediately, while rumors are never confirmed immediately, but may or may not be confirmed sometime in the future.[5]
2. The local or time-limited importance or interest of the rumor refers to its 'public'. The 'public' of the rumor are the people who are confronted with it.[6] Rumors pertain to topics of consequence or significance. People inquiring not only want to know about the consequence of the rumor, but also need to know what other people think about it to prepare further actions.
3. Rumors are statements intended primarily for belief; they might be true or they might be false. One should possibly act upon them, depending on what others believe. In that sense they don't differ from verified information. Because rumors are primarily for belief, this characteristic distinguishes them from other informal information like gossip, folklore or legends. Gossip is primarily meant to entertain people[7] while folklore and legends are stories that do not necessarily claim to be true, but aim to convey important truths. Rumors, in contrast, insist upon being taken literally.

What exactly is an unverified piece of information? In daily life people hardly verify information that has been given to them. When people read an article in a newspaper, they usually trust the people who wrote the article and that the content is true. They do not have proof that it's actually true, yet they assume that it has been verified. As a result, the verification of the information is inseparably linked to the person from whom they received the information and who is assumed to have verified it. If they don't trust the person who has provided the information, they will doubt that it has been verified. Therefore the criterion of verification always implies a strong subjective element. As a result, every definition of a rumor that is based on 'unverified information' leads to a logical dead-end and can't be differentiated from other orally communicated information by any mass media.[8] Is then every orally communicated piece of information a rumor? This does not make a lot of sense. If people are asked: 'What are the latest rumors?', then they don't want to hear the latest official information released from a news agency. A reasonable definition of a rumor has to exclude the oral transmission of a piece of official information. The first definition of a rumor integrating a dynamic point of view stems from Shibutani (1966).[9] He defines a rumor as 'a recurrent form of communication through which men caught together in an ambiguous situation attempt to construct a meaningful interpretation by pooling their intellectual resources'. In his view rumors are like improvised news that results from a collective distribution process. According to Shibutani, a rumor is at the bottom of an important and ambiguous event observed by people. The rumor is the résumé of the people's intellectual resources to achieve a satisfying interpretation of the event. Therefore a rumor is a process of information processing as well as a process of interpretation and annotation. A rumor is a collective act to give unexplained facts a sense or meaning. The people gather and comment on the news, resulting in one or two explanations. The development of the rumor's content thus cannot be ascribed to the adulterant effectiveness of the memory, but to the development and contribution of the comments given during the rumor's process. Where the public wants to understand but does not receive any official answers, there are rumors. Rumors are the black market of information.[10] At the same time Shibutani's definition refers to its formation and development. It concerns the rumors evolving immediately after an event. This definition seems too specific. Rumors don't need an event wanting to be explained. Some rumors just happen spontaneously or even create events themselves.

There exists no strict line between a rumor and information. The dividing line between information and a rumor is subjective and the result of one's own belief.[11] People call something information when they consider it true and call it a rumor when they consider it false or not confirmed. If someone is convinced that a rumor is true, then it will be considered as information. When people have doubts, they will consider the same message as a rumor. That's the paradox concerning a rumor. When the public recognizes the rumor as a 'rumor', it will not be spread any further. But if it's not recognized as such, it can still spread. People don't first have a belief about a piece of news and then they call it as a rumor or not. The label is the result of the belief's conviction, which is a purely subjective value judgment. The rumor itself is the belief's visible form.[12] Therefore a rumor can be understood a lot better in its existence than in its character.

Although the question of truth or falsity of a rumor is consistently asked at first, it is not the most important question to be answered in order to understand rumors. The development of a rumor evolves because some people believe a message to be important enough to forward it within their social environment. This action alone does not lead to any conclusion at all on whether the rumor is actually true or not. The dynamics of a rumor are independent of the problem of its truth. That's why Kapferer (1996a)[13] defines a rumor as the following: 'A rumor is an emergence and dissemination of information in a societal organism that has either not yet been confirmed by official sources or denied by them.' He states the reasons for his definition as the following. The content of a rumor is not distinguished by its verification but by its nonofficial source. The verification of the message is inseparably linked to the trustworthiness of the person. This is too subjective a criterion to justify a definition. Instead there exists at a certain point in time a public consensus about the identity of the so-called 'official' sources. Although people possibly don't trust these official sources completely, they are still authorized to release explanations. In comparison, gossip is something already known and doesn't anticipate or contradict official sources.

Kapferer has been criticized[14] for stating that rumors are recognized as 'not yet confirmed from the official sources or are denied by them'. Schlieper-Damrich (2003) argues that in Kapferer's definition mass media could not be considered as official sources. Mass media are capable of spreading rumors, as, for example, the Gulf War in 1991 and the war against Iraq in 2003 have shown, but according to Kapferer's definition official sources are not. Rumors then could only spread orally or via unofficial media such as flyers.

Kapferer's definition is hereby clearly misunderstood. The confirmation or denial of a rumor by official sources relates only to the official sources the rumor is affected by. If the definition is applied in this way, then mass media are certainly capable of initiating and spreading rumors. Kapferer's definition can be modified in the following way to account for Schlieper-Damrich's criticism: 'A rumor is an emergence and dissemination of information in a societal organism that has either not yet been confirmed or denied by official sources affected by it.'

Rosnow and Kimmel (2000) argue for their own definition: a rumor is 'an unverified proposition for belief that bears topical relevance for persons actively involved in its dissemination'. Kimmel argues as well that 'the key is that the rumor may eventually turn out to be true or false, but until that time, the communication is subject to the dynamics of rumor. A story in widespread circulation that has been officially verified as false may nevertheless be considered as a rumor, so long as there is a suspension of disbelief in the story's content.'[15] This is an important difference from the definition by Kapferer. He assumes that the verification of a rumor by official sources is immediately generally accepted, while Kimmel argues this does not have to be the case. The rumor is therefore only no longer considered a rumor when the verification of the rumor by official sources is generally accepted. The second major difference from Kapferer's definition lies in the passage 'for persons actively involved in its dissemination'. Kapferer does not make the distinction between the people involved in the rumor and those who are not. This can lead, as Kimmel argues, to different opinions whether a piece of news is (still) to be considered a rumor or has entered the stage of a verified piece of information. Only people actively involved in the dissemination of the rumor can perceive it as a rumor, since where there is no dissemination, there is nothing to be spread, and the spreading is an essential ingredient of a rumor.

2.1.1   Structure of the Categories, News, Information and Rumor

The three different categories can be structured as in Table 2.1. News includes any kind of message, whether it is verified or not. A rumor is a piece of news. When rumors evolve, news or messages are disseminated in a societal organism. At some time they will be confirmed

Table 2.1   Structure of the notions, news, information and rumor

Private vs. public signal — Validity of the signal	News	
	Information	Rumor
Private Signal	Private Information	Private Rumor
Public Signal	Public Information	Public Rumor

as true or denied as false. Information on the other hand is always confirmed immediately. It is assumed to be true by definition. Therefore information does not need to be verified.

An unverified piece of news that has not entered the stage of a rumor is called a communicated thought. The communicated thought can be of a speculative nature, can be an interpretation of existing information or originate from any other kind of creative process.

Signals can be received privately or publicly. If signals are received privately, then information asymmetries emerge. Some people know at a certain time more than others. If signals are received publicly, then everyone receives the signal at the same time (information symmetry). This distinction is, with regards to rumors, important. Signals affect the value of an asset and can be analyzed accordingly. The impact of a news signal can be divided into three different dimensions:

- Magnitude: News has value. The value of the news determines the signal's magnitude (Figure 2.1).
- Precision: The degree of heterogeneity of beliefs and interpretations determines the precision of the news (Figure 2.2).
- Dissemination: Dissemination refers to the time span until the value of the news is fully reflected (Figure 2.3).

According to the three dimensions, magnitude, precision and dissemination, information vs. rumors can be analyzed as follows:

- Magnitude: There is no difference concerning information vs. rumors. A rumor is not characterized by the fact that it has a different magnitude than information.

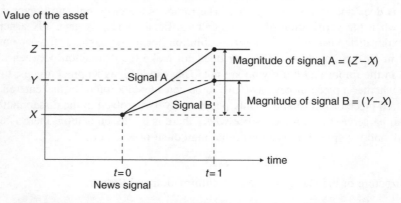

The difference of the signal's magnitude between signal A and B is $(Z-Y)$.

Figure 2.1   Magnitude of a news signal

- Precision: A rumor is a less precise signal than information. The validity of a rumor in comparison to information is uncertain.
- Dissemination: A rumor is characterized by the fact that it is spread and communicated, while with information this is not necessarily the case. The 'speed' of the rumor determines the length of the dissemination process.

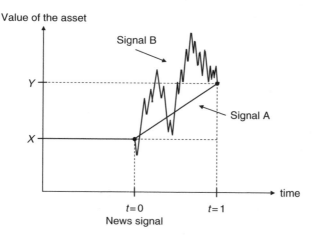

Signal A is interpreted homogeneously. Signal B is interpreted heterogeneously. The precision of signal A is higher than that of signal B.

Figure 2.2 Precision of a news signal

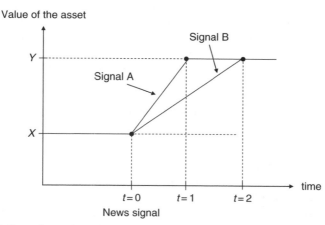

Signal A disseminates from $t=0$ to $t=1$ until the value of the signal is fully reflected, signal B from $t=0$ to $t=2$.

Figure 2.3 Dissemination of a news signal

Table 2.2 Properties of rumor, information and gossip[16]

Property	Rumor	Information	Gossip
Significant	Yes	Yes	No
Supported by truth	Yes or No	Yes	Yes or No
Is spread	Yes	No	Possibly
People oriented	Yes or No	Yes or No	Yes
Association	Negative or Positive	Negative or Positive	Negative

Source: A.J. Kimmel, *Rumors and Rumor Control: A Manager's Guide to Understanding and Combating Rumors* (2003). Reproduced with permission of Lawrence Erlbaum Associates.

2.1.2   Rumors versus Gossip

Rumors are also distinguishable from gossip or nonessential small talk. Informal chat which is mostly about people, is often speculative and creates a blurred line between being a rumor or gossip. Interpersonal talk flowing through an organizational grapevine will probably more accurately be referred to as gossip rather than as rumor. Gossip and rumors are often used interchangeably. According to Hannerz (1967), rumors and gossip show clear differences, especially in communication situations. Gossip refers with no exception to people, while this is definitely not a precondition of rumors. In addition, gossip may be supported by facts which are actually true, while with rumors the content's validity is never known in advance. Rosnow (2001) argues that the nature of gossip in comparison to rumors is more amorphous and superfluous, and is identified by the context in which it occurs more directly. Gossip is meant to entertain and typically evolves spontaneously in informal social situations. Although the attitude of the parties involved in the discussion towards the content might be indifferent or even contemptuous, their ulterior motives may be substantial.

2.1.3   Summary of Rumor Characteristics

Rumors, information and gossip can be distinguished by the properties they possess (Table 2.2). The properties include significance or interest in the message content, whether the message is supported by the truth, whether the communication is people oriented and the association of the message. The first and last two properties can differentiate a rumor from gossip, while the second and third properties can distinguish a rumor from information.

2.2   HISTORICAL BACKGROUND TO STUDIES ON RUMORS

Rumors have a long history. At some times they even had their own goddess. In Greek mythology there was a distinction between the goddess of rumor and that of popular rumor. While *Ossa*[17] personified the goddess of rumor and was called the messenger of Zeus, *Pheme*[18] was the goddess of popular rumor. She announced whatever she heard, first to only a few, then louder until everyone had heard. She was represented by a winged, gentle figure holding a trumpet. In Roman mythology it was *Fama* who personified the goddess of rumor.[19] She is said to have had many eyes and mouths. She traveled around the world, first whispering her rumors to only a few, then becoming louder and louder until the whole world knew the news. She lived in a palace with a thousand windows, all of which were always kept open so she could hear everything that was said by anyone on earth.

The public has been intrigued by rumors for centuries, but it took a long time until the scientific community started to study rumors as a separate subject. It was around 1900 when psychologists, sociologists and psychiatrists started to apply scientific methods to human behavior. These methods included how people dealt with rumors in their daily life. Rumors at that time were almost always of a negative sort, typically about crises, conflicts and catastrophes. Shibutani[20] lists 60 documented rumors, 38 of which are war-related, 13 to a catastrophe and 8 to social and personal crises.[21] The 60th rumor is quite an extraordinary one concerning the appearance of a Virgin Saint in Puerto Rico. Rosnow and Fine (1976) include rumors on deaths of celebrities, on catastrophes, wartime rumors and rumors related to races. Racial and wartime rumors seem to have been the most common and obvious kind of rumor people dealt with a few decades ago.[22] Koenig[23] adds to Shibutani's classification another category called commerce. In recent years commerce-related rumors were predominant in comparison to wartime or race-related rumors.

Early studies of rumors have to be criticized for their prejudice towards rumors as something ethically condemnable and to be prevented as much as possible. The rumor definitions used at the time as in Allport and Postman[24] define a rumor as an unverified piece of information. However, in all their examples the rumors turn out to be false. Therefore it is nothing but logical that Allport and Postman conclude that a rumor leads only to an error. Allport and Postman at the time were engaged by the American Office of War Information, which among other things had the task of controlling the development process of rumors during World War II. That is the reason for their special efforts to discredit that form of communication. Although the notion 'rumor' itself is neutral, they carefully chose examples of rumors that were in accordance with their line of argument. The study by Knapp[25] gives advice on how to prevent rumors spreading. The advice is the following:

1. Assure good faith with the regular media of communication, so that you are not tempted to inform yourself elsewhere.
2. Develop maximum confidence in your leaders and your government, who do their best to manage the problems evoked by crises and war. 'They can better abide the frustrations of censorship and inadequate information than when their attitude is poisoned by suspicion and distrust.'
3. Issue as much news as possible, as quickly as possible. Rumors evolve from partial facts or spontaneous questions of the public where no answers have been given. They satisfy the need to understand the event if it's not crystal clear.
4. Make information as accessible as possible. Even when reliable information is released, it has to be ensured that it reaches the public in a positive and general way. All information gaps have to be filled and all measures 'are vital in the fight against rumor'.
5. Prevent laziness, monotony and personal disorganization, because they can cause a strong appetite for rumors. Therefore it is important to keep the population from idleness through suitable work or leisure occupation.
6. Campaign deliberately against rumor-mongering since 'rumor may be shown as a trick of enemy propaganda used to destroy morale', and 'rumor may be exposed for its inaccuracies and falsehood, and thus discredited generally'.

Under the conditions of World War II, Knapp's advice may have been legitimate and accurate in order to strengthen the efforts of the American nation. However, in peaceful times it appears as a self-portrayal of a totalitarian regime. The advice reveals unintentionally why rumors are unwanted at all times. Therefore the definitions of a rumor based on 'unverified' or, even worse, 'false' information are ideological definitions, because they are biased towards rumors as something morally disturbing. Knapp's advice reads like a caricature in peaceful times, but serves as a great example for showing the prejudice towards rumors. Rumors wouldn't be popular if they were all false. They are so popular just because in some cases they become true. However, rumors may appear disturbing, since they are pieces of information not controllable by a central institution.

Allport and Postman (1946) created a formula to measure the intensity of a rumor. It states that 'the two essential conditions of importance and ambiguity seem to be related to rumor transmission in a roughly quantitative matter. A formula for the intensity of rumor might be written as follows:

$$R \approx i \times a$$

R: Intensity of the rumor, i: importance, a: ambiguity

In plain words this formula means that the intensity of the rumor in circulation will vary with the importance of the subject to the individuals concerned *times* the ambiguity of the evidence pertaining to the topic at issue. The relation between importance and ambiguity is not additive but multiplicative, for if either importance or ambiguity is zero, there is *no* rumor.[26] Koenig comments that 'given the nature of the crises, with matters of personal or national survival occupying people's minds (importance) in a context of confusion, censorship, or conspiracy (ambiguity), this formula and the points of view it represents seem appropriate in wartime'.[27] However, Koenig states at the same time he is not sure 'that it is applicable to all rumor situations, any more than is occurrence of media failure always applicable. All of which is to say that the limitations on these types of studies place a limit on the generalizations that can be derived.'[28] Rosnow (1980) reviews Allport and Postman's theory of rumor extensively. He concludes concerning the tenability of their assumptions, that 'their conceptual definition fails to account for the longevity of symbolic representations in rumor themes that wax and wane but never disappear; it also tends to slight the media's gatekeeper role in the perpetuation of rumor'.[29] Rosnow recognizes the moral bias in Allport and Postman's definition and notes that 'a more liberalized working definition would be that rumor is a proposition for belief that is unverified and in general circulation'.[30] Allport and Postman additionally assume a purgative effect of rumor telling. Rosnow[31] agrees on the plausibility of that assumption in reference to a report by the National Advisory Commission on civil disorders. The report warns that 'rumors significantly aggravated tensions and disorders in more than 65 percent of the disorders studied by the commission'.[32] A third assumption by Allport and Postman[33] that Rosnow reviewed is the process of leveling, sharpening and assimilation. He states that 'there is evidence that intellectual pressures and the natural porosity of human memory can cause rumors to become simplified and ordered in the retelling but that cognitive reorganization can also cause rumors to become more diffuse and complex'.[34] Rosnow additionally reviews Allport and Postman's theoretical assertions. He recognizes 'that there are variables besides importance and ambiguity that influence the origins and perpetuation of rumors'.[35] Allport and Postman secondly theorized that rumor-mongering would be curtailed when a population is under close surveillance or subject to negative sanctions for engaging in rumor. Rosnow concludes that 'it is possible to predict the opposite effect, however, as reactance theory would imply a boomerang effect under these circumstances'.[36]

In his 1991 paper, Rosnow lists variables beyond or as substitutes for the basic law of rumor developed by Allport and Postman that influence the origins and perpetuation of rumors: general uncertainty, outcome-relevant involvement, personal anxiety and credulity.

By analyzing different studies on the variables influencing the intensity of a rumor,[37] Rosnow concludes that the largest evidence of influencing the intensity of a rumor stems from the anxiety studies. The studies on credulity and uncertainty revealed moderate to small effects on the intensity of a rumor.[38]

Rosnow develops three general principles for rumor control.[39] His goal is to 'envision a more expeditious route of effective rumor management when false rumors erupt and damaging consequences are foreseen'.[40]

1. *Prevention strategy:* Anticipate events in which anxiety and uncertainty might be optimum for threatening rumors to take hold, and defuse the situation before damaging consequences develop.
2. *Failure of the prevention strategy:* Try to keep the gun from going off repeatedly. It is important to pay heed to what specimen rumors can reveal about the sources of people's anxieties and uncertainties.
3. *Failure of preventing the gun from discharging:* Minimize the damage that such a burst can do. If the source can be identified (and presumably the rumor is false), then legal action against the rumor-mongers to enjoin and call attention to their malicious behavior might be considered.[41]

Rosnow himself recognizes that 'it is important not to paint an overly optimistic picture of what can be accomplished in combating damaging rumors, because the art of rumor control is still largely based on common sense rather than on both data and theory'.[42] It has to be commented that Rosnow focuses only on the question of intensity and control of a rumor. His approach fails to draw an overall picture for the cause of rumor development, its spreading and belief as well as people's actions. In 1987, Kapferer published his original version of *Les Rumeurs: Le Plus Vieux Média du Monde*, which has served as benchmark for rumor theory since then.

3

Rumors and the Theory of Finance

Nothing moves as fast as a rumor

TITUS LIVIUS Roman historian, 59 BC–17 AD

3.1 RUMORS AND BEHAVIORAL FINANCE

Finance is the study of how humans allocate scarce resources over time. Within the traditional Theory of Finance, two paradigms have evolved over time. Until a few years ago, they were considered as almost axiomatic:

1. *Agents' behavior is perfectly 'rational'*: Perfect rational behavior means that new information is correctly interpreted for the update of one's own beliefs as in the law of Bayes. Secondly, if the individual's beliefs are viewed as given, then they should make decisions that are, from a normative perspective, acceptable in the sense that they are consistent with the notion of Subjective Expected Utility (SEU) introduced by Savage. Section 3.2 provides an overview of the concept of rationality beyond the SEU concept.
2. *Efficient markets*: The Efficient Market Hypothesis (EMH) states that prices will fully and instantaneously reflect all available relevant information. If the hypothesis is correct, then 'prices are right' and there is 'no free lunch'. Therefore there exists no investment strategy that can earn systematic excess risk-adjusted average returns.[1]

3.1.1 Theoretical Excursion: A Formal Definition of the Value of Information

Economic Theory has developed a precise definition of the value of information. A message about various events possibly to happen may be defined as an information structure. The message may have various values to different people depending on

1. whether or not they will base any actions upon it, and
2. what gains or losses of utility will result from the action taken.

Example: The possibility that it might rain today may have completely different values to an owner of a tourist restaurant in comparison to a farmer. While the farmer might be looking forward to rain, because the ground has been dry over the last few weeks, the owner of the restaurant will have a lot fewer guests.

The concept above of the value of an information structure can be formalized as follows:

$$V(\eta) \equiv \sum_m q(m) \, \text{MAX}_a \sum_e p(e|m) U(a,e) - V(\eta_0) \tag{3.1}$$

where

$q(m)$ = the marginal probability of receiving a message m

$p(e|m)$ = the conditional probability of an event e, given a message m

$U(a,e)$ = the utility resulting from an action a if an event e occurs. This is called the benefit function

$V(\eta_0)$ = the expected utility of the decision-maker without the information

According to equation (3.1) a decision-maker will evaluate the information structure at arrival and choose his or her action to maximize his or her expected utility. It is possible to determine the optimal solution for each information structure.

Mathematically, the solution looks as follows:

$$\text{MAX}_a \sum_e p\,(e|m)U(a,e) \tag{3.2}$$

The next step is to weight the expected utility of each optimal in response to all possible messages by the corresponding probability $q(m)$, receiving them and leading to action. Then the decision-maker knows the expected utility of the entire set of messages. This is typically called the expected utility of an information set $V(\eta)$.

3.1.2   The Relationship between the Value of Information and Efficient Markets

One of my favorite contrasts is that when market rises following good economic news, it is said to be responding to the news; if it falls, that is explained by saying that the good news has already been discounted.

BARUCH FISCHHOFF (1982)

Equation (3.1) is applicable to evaluate any information structure. It highlights implicit ideas in the definition of efficient markets. Fama (1976) defines an efficient capital market as one in which the joint distribution of security prices, $f_m(P_{1t}, P_{2t}, \ldots, P_{nt}|\eta^m_{t-1})$, given the set of information the market uses to evaluate security prices at $t-1$, is identical to the joint distribution of prices that would exist if all relevant information available at $t-1$ were used, $f(P_{1t}, P_{2t}, \ldots, P_{nt}|\eta_{t-1})$. This implies, that

$$f_m(P_{1t}, P_{2t}, \ldots, P_{nt}|\eta^m_{t-1}) = f(P_{1t}, P_{2t}, \ldots, P_{nt}|\eta_{t-1}) \tag{3.3}$$

If an information structure is of value, then it must accurately provide us with information we have not known until now. If the distribution of prices in time period t (which was accurately predicted at time $t-1$ based on the information structure available at the time) is no different from the prices predicted by using all the relevant information from the previous time period, then there must not be any difference between the information the market uses and the set of all relevant information. This is the essence of an efficient market; it instantaneously and fully reflects all relevant information. Important to state here is, that this is calculated net of costs, since the search for information can be quite costly. In this case, the utility gain of the ith individual receiving the information must be zero:

$$V(\eta_i) - V(\eta_0) \equiv 0 \tag{3.4}$$

Fama (1970, 1976) developed three different forms of capital market efficiency. They differ in the notion of exactly what type of information is understood to be relevant in the phrase, that 'prices reflect all relevant information'.

1. *Weak-form efficiency:* No investor can earn excess returns by developing trading strategies based on historical price or return information.
2. *Semistrong-form efficiency:* No investor can earn excess returns from trading rules based on any publicly available information.
3. *Strong-form efficiency:* No investor can earn excess returns using any information, whether publicly available or not.

In the weak-form efficiency, the relevant information structure η_{ii} is defined as the historical prices of all assets. When capital markets are efficient in the weak form, then equation (3.3) states that the distribution of prices today has already been incorporated in the history of past prices. This implies that no trading rule based on the development of past prices is able to generate any excess returns. In addition, according to equation (3.4), no one would pay anything for the information of historical prices.

This concept has become one of the cornerstones of the Theory of Finance. Literally hundreds of articles have been published testing whether capital markets are indeed efficient. The corresponding hypothesis has become famous as the Efficient Market Hypothesis (EMH).

3.1.3 The Criticisms of Behavioral Finance

If the brain were so simple we could understand it, we would be so simple we couldn't.
LYALL WATSON

The framework of the traditional Theory of Finance is of remarkable simplicity, and it would be more than satisfying if the forecasts were confirmed by the data. Unfortunately, after years of research, it has become evident that basic facts about financial markets, such as cross-sectional causes of average stock returns and individual investor behavior, cannot be explained in this context. However, the debate in the literature about the foundation and application of other theoretical approaches still continues.[2]

Behavioral Finance is a relatively new approach to the Theory of Finance, at least partly as an answer to the difficulty of the traditional paradigm to explain empirically well-proven effects. In a wider sense it is argued that certain observable phenomena can be better understood with non-perfect rational behavioral models. In particular, these approaches analyze what happens when one of the two or both fundamental assumptions of individual rational behavior are relaxed.[3] In one type of Behavioral Finance model, individuals are not able to update their beliefs correctly. In other types of models, Bayes' law is applied correctly; however, they make decisions that are normatively not compatible with the notion of subjective expected utility.

One of the objections against Behavioral Finance is that even when a few individuals do not act rationally, then a majority of rational agents will prevent traded asset prices from moving too far from their 'true' value.[4] One of the achievements of Behavioral Finance as of today is a number of scientific contributions showing that in an economy where rational and irrational individuals interact, irrational behavior can have a significant and substantial impact on the prices traded. These contributions, known in the literature as limits to arbitrage, are one cornerstone of the research area of Behavioral Finance.[5]

Allowing clear predictions to be stated, behavioral models have to be able to specify the kind of irrational behavior. How do the behavioral patterns deviate from Bayes' law and the maximization of the subjective expected utility? So that these questions can be

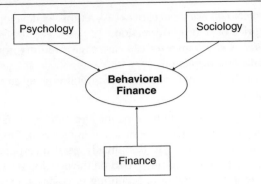

Figure 3.1 The underlying sciences of Behavioral Finance[6]
Source: V. Ricciardi and H.K. Simon: What is Behavioural Finance?, *The Business Education and Technology Journal* **2**(1): 26–34 (2000). Reproduced with permission of Golden Gate University.

answered, economists have consulted the experimental evidence of cognitive psychology. That research area has demonstrated that certain biases systematically occur while individuals determine their preferences and, given their beliefs, while they make their decisions. Psychology therefore is a second cornerstone of Behavioral Finance. A third cornerstone of Behavioral Finance, sociology, is often neglected, but is of great importance when individuals interact on markets, in particular, financial markets. Until now it has been implicitly assumed that the individuals' decisions are made without any interaction and are accomplished without any other individual's influence. However, particularly actions on financial markets are not undertaken in an isolated fashion, but are often and to a great extent socially influenced.

Figure 3.1 shows the interdisciplinary approach of Behavioral Finance. Traditional Finance, however, stays at the heart of Behavioral Finance conceptual studies, yet integrates behavioral aspects from psychology and sociology. The uniqueness of Behavioral Finance lies in the integration and foundation of these different scientific research areas.

3.1.4   The Link between Rumors and Behavioral Finance

The valuation of information, and how new information should affect the allocation of scarce resources, is one of the fundamentals the Theory of Finance is based on. Since rumors are a special form of information, it stands to reason that rumors should be analyzed from a financial point of view. Secondly, rumors are heavily influenced by psychological and sociological factors. Rumors implicitly contain a social element, since without communication of the rumor it would not spread. Psychology also plays a role when rumors evolve, since they can lead to emotions like fear and anxiety. In such cases people might not make decisions as rationally as they otherwise would do.

These characteristics make rumors predestined to be analyzed by Behavioral Finance, since it covers elements of all the sciences mentioned above. Behavioral Finance takes up two perspectives. The first one is the individual level, where an investment decision process is analyzed, while the second is on an aggregate or market level. Within the first approach, Behavioral Finance analyzes under what circumstances and how individuals make investment decisions that deviate from perfect rational behavior postulated by the traditional Theory of Finance. Within the second approach, Behavioral Finance claims that among other factors, non-perfect rational behavior is responsible for the failure of the Efficient Market Hypotheses (EMH).[7] In this work, the focus is clearly on the second approach. Chapter 6, 'Rumor Experiments', analyzes effects on a market level such as price movements and price fluctuations from the performance of market experiments.

3.1.5 Financial Markets as a Fruitful Ground for Rumors

Financial markets have always had a flair for rumors, because on the trading floor all action is based on news. Knowing more than other market participants can lead to real money profits. As one trader stated, 'the traders' jungle drums are amongst the most sensitive in the world'.[8] They may gamble if they believe the rumor reflects the truth, but even if it's not the case, it can lead to financial consequences. Rumors in financial markets are seen as a substitute for news. News in financial markets is absolutely critical. Therefore in the absence of news, something is simply invented. In a tense, stressful working atmosphere, all traders operate with high-powered antennas. The fear that other people may know something they don't know leads to stress and anxiety. In these situations the traders need confirmation of their views and positions. Gaps in information are often filled with speculative thoughts. The communication of speculative thoughts is a classical form of rumor development. Rumors can only evolve when the content is interesting and relevant. Merger or takeover talks are an example of an event in favor of rumor development. Statements such as 'We are always interested in reasonable and beneficial acquisitions' or 'We decline to comment on that issue' open the door to rumors and fantasies.

Are rumors in financial markets different from other rumors? No, but there are factors that make financial markets especially sensitive to rumors:[9]

- The number of participants is limited. The size of the potential public of a rumor is limited and the traders have an efficient communication network.
- The traders are experts in their field and have a high credibility. They know the market well and are specialized in certain financial products or instruments. Traders don't believe all the fresh they receive.
- Time is crucial. Traders are under constant time pressure. The tense and nervous atmosphere is an excellent breeding ground for the spread of rumors. Traders don't have time to verify the news or to assess its accuracy. They have to decide what to do despite the uncertainty involved. The necessity of fast decisions keeps the hunger for fresh news (and thus for rumors) alive.
- In comparison to other rumors, those in financial markets always involve a financial risk. A trader could be wrong in assessing the market's belief. If he doesn't trade, he risks missing a profit if the rumor is proven true. In general, the trader is not concerned about the source of the rumor. He doesn't have the time to think about it. The rumor is there, that's enough for him. Many traders don't even care if the rumor is going to be true (see Section 5.5 'Belief in rumors').
- Financial markets are a place where decision-makers are flooded with news. It is well known that rumors evolve in the absence of news. The same holds for news overflow. What news is believed when one receives too much? One is likely to work with the most secure news received and rely on factors supporting one's own views.

3.1.6 Six Types of Rumors

The apparent variety of rumors can be reduced when rumors are classified according to source and type of emergence. An analysis regarding these two factors leads to six types of rumors (Table 3.1):

1. Whenever the public hasn't received quick and satisfying answers to open questions, it forms its personal and collective view of the circumstances leading to a rumor. The process of emergence is spontaneous and evolutionary. The public creates and chooses those hypotheses that generate the highest satisfaction and the highest subjective probability of being true.
2. In comparison to (1), the hypotheses are deliberately provoked to profit from a certain event.

   Example: The rumor of the merger of two airlines, Swiss and Lufthansa. In a newspaper interview, the Swiss CEO failed to give satisfying answers concerning the future direction of Swiss. His statement, 'If airlines wanted to be profitable, the inevitable solution is to merge and use synergies among the different parties,'[10] provoked rumors concerning a merger with Lufthansa.
3. In this type, a hardly noticed detail or signal triggers the rumor. For such a signal to be perceived, a small group of people must pay special attention to that detail. The public then reacts instantaneously and in an extremely sensitive manner to it.
4. As in case (3) it's possible that certain interpretations of a detail are spread deliberately.

   Example: There exist several fundamental religious communities that strongly believe in the 'incarnation of the devil'. They search for every possible sign supporting their view. Procter & Gamble was a 'victim' in the mid-1980s of a rumor that the hidden numbers of Satan could be found in their logo.
5. The fifth type of rumor is characterized by the fact that it has an uncertain point of origin. In its analysis, no fact, symptom, sign or detail can be found. It is a product of fantasy. Typically, such rumors are known to create emotions of fear, feelings of health or happiness, and spiritual experiences.
6. In comparison to case (5) fantasy rumors are more likely to be deliberately provoked.

   Example: The rumor of the appearance of a Virgin Saint managed to cause more than 100,000 people to flock to a place in Puerto Rico in 1953. She was supposed to bring health and heal diseases in all witnesses.[11]

Spontaneous rumors originating from an event or a detail may be assumed to form the majority of rumors in financial markets. In general, fantasy rumors are not believed in

Table 3.1 Six types of rumors[12]

Type of emergence		Source of the rumor		
		From an event	From a detail	Pure fantasy
	Spontaneous	1	3	5
	Deliberately provoked	2	4	6

Source: J.N. Kapferer: *Gerüchte: Das älteste Massenmedium der Welt*, published by Gustave Kiepenheuer Verlag. Leipzig (1996). Reproduced by permission of Editions Du Seuil.

Table 3.2 Categories of rumors in financial markets[13]

Type of emergence	Domain of the rumor		
		Public	Market
	General	1	3
	Specific	2	4

Source: F.W. Koenig: *The Social Psychology of Commercial Hearsay*, published by Auburn House (1985). Reproduced with permission of Greenwood Publishing Group. Inc. Westport. CT.

the market and therefore not very realistic. It's likely that some rumors are deliberately provoked (see Section 5.3.1).

3.1.7 Classification of Rumors in Financial Markets

The six different types of rumors as stated previously apply to any kind of rumor. Rumors in financial markets can be further classified into two dimensions and four categories (Table 3.2):

1. Example: Saddam Hussein will go into exile. The rumor that Saddam Hussein might go into exile is a *general* rumor and related to the *public*.
2. Example: OPEC agrees on raising oil production. This rumor is one concerning the *public*, since the general population notices the price change immediately at the gas station. At the same time the rumor concerns a *specific* industry.
3. Example: Financial institutions may face additional regulatory requirements. Such a rumor is relevant to the financial community; thus it's a *market* rumor and of *general* interest.
4. Example: Novartis is in merger talks with Roche. A rumor with regards to merger talks between Novartis and Roche is a *market* rumor concerning one *specific* industry.

3.2 RUMORS AND RATIONAL BEHAVIOR

People often speak of unexplainable price movements, caused by irrational market participants, when rumors evolve in financial markets. Since rationality is a key concept within economics and the Theory of Finance, it is necessary to deal with the subject in the context of rumors to evaluate whether the statement above is justifiable.

The term rationality, the historical roots of which are in Latin, originates from the word '*ratio*' which means reason. A rational behavior is therefore to make reasonable decisions. However, what is understood by a reasonable action is still open and can be judged individually. In economics, by rational behavior it is understood to make decisions that maximize the individual's personal utility and this corresponds to the classical picture of a 'Homo economicus'. However, we humans don't always act as 'Homo economicus' in reality. So this kind of definition does not really help us to discover what rational behavior is. Maybe it would help to go the opposite way and to define what irrationality means. According to the Brockhaus-Encyclopedia, irrationality is defined as 'by the mind not comprehensible'. In comparison to the definition of rationality here, the mind is set in relation to reason. If an action is not comprehensible by the mind, it is obviously not reasonable. Just as with a reasonable action, it is a subjective evaluation whether an individual's action is considered not reasonable. The historical context therefore is not able to deliver insights into which definition of rationality actually is rational and reasonable respectively. Therefore, different concepts of rationality are presented and reviewed for their 'reason'.

3.2.1 Rationality in the Classical Theory of Finance

In the classical Theory of Finance the concept of rationality has become known as a goal-oriented action under side conditions.[14] Rationality is therefore always connected to human action. There exist two prominent views of a rational action: (1) the concept of preferences: consistent decisions in situations with different possible alternatives are made; (2) the concept of expected utility: your own expected utility is maximized.

1. *The concept of preferences*: Making consistent decisions implies that you have a preference relation and your choice is made according to the respective best alternative according to that preference relation. Under a preference relation it is understood that you are able to state whether you find an alternative A at least as good as an alternative B. The concept of preference relations therefore relies on a relative valuation. Thereby it is demanded that the preference relation possess certain plausible properties. Those properties are, however, not explained here in further detail, since they are quite technical (for the formal illustration of preference relations, please refer to Appendix I.1).
2. *The concept of expected utility*: The simple idea behind the maximization of the expected utility is that preferences ('I prefer alternative A to alternative B') of individuals can be separated from the payoff's probabilities and their level. While the preferences are in every case subjective, a distinction has to be made concerning the arrival of the probabilities and the level of those payoffs. Probabilities can either be objectively predetermined or based upon subjective evaluation. This difference will be further illustrated. It is furthermore important to know that you don't even have to know your own utility function or even undertake a valuation of the alternatives with their expected utility, to be able to maximize your own utility. As long as the preference relation fulfills certain properties, it can be presented by an expected utility function (for the formal illustration of expected utility, please refer to Appendix I.2). According to this concept a rational action therefore is therefore a choice of an alternative action, when you maximize your own expected utility within the expected utility function.

The maximization of your own expected utility implies making consistent decisions as described under (1). However the inverse does not hold, i.e. whoever makes consistent decisions does not automatically maximize their own expected utility:

There exist several preconditions that have to be fulfilled so that every individual can calculate his expected utility:

1. An action to maximize the expected utility always contains a time dimension. The individual therefore has to know all states after the taking of the action.
2. All individuals have to be able to evaluate the probability distribution for the arrival of the states with their consequences after the taking of the action.

Comment: The common literature still does not apply a unified definition of various notions in relation to the theory of expected utility. In particular, the notions, certainty, risk, uncertainty and ambiguity are not always treated in the same manner. Section 6.4.1 explains in detail the different notions.

What is important for this chapter is that an individual has to be able to derive a probability distribution for all states and their consequences. This probability distribution can either be purely subjective or objectively given. For the purposes of illustrating the difference between the two, consider the following example:

- Objective probabilities orient themselves typically at physical laws that are given by nature and generally accepted. For example, you should be able to assume that when rolling a dice with six sides, the 'objective' probability is one to six that when rolling the dice once a six will appear. In this regard it is also spoken of a 'fair' dice.
- Intersubjective probabilities can be passed from one individual to the other, hoping that these will be persuaded and will take over the estimation of the other's individual probability distribution. These probability distributions don't necessarily have to do anything with the true distribution. However, if a sufficiently high number of individuals come to the same estimation of the probability distributions, then that can turn into quasi-objective probabilities.
- Subjective probabilities direct themselves to imaginations of belief, perceptions and personal evaluation of each individual. Assume I am being asked what the probability is that the sun will shine tomorrow. What will I answer? I don't know for sure if the sun will shine or not. I can try to follow from today's weather what tomorrow's weather will look like. Or I could look at the weather forecast to find out what the models of the meteorologists predict. As a third alternative I could build simple rules regarding when in the past the sun has shone and derive my own prediction thereof. From that I will come up with a personal evaluation, based on my perception and interpretation, of how probable I believe it is that tomorrow the sun will shine. I will, however, never be able (not even the best meteorologists can) to say with certainty with what 'objective' probability tomorrow the sun will shine or not.

What type of probabilities are now necessary to answer economic questions? This question cannot be answered consistently. For the application of the expected utility theory to the capital asset pricing model (CAPM), objective probabilities of the arrival of the future states have to be assumed. The difficulty with subjective probabilities lies therein, that they are in their form completely arbitrary and no belief concerning their regularities exists. Since every individual has his or her own imagination of how probable the arrival of a certain state is, the allocation of a probability is a pure matter of belief and does not have anything to do with the reality. In addition, with this concept most decision situations are then mathematically no longer applicable. Because this is a very unsatisfying situation for traditional economists, it is argued that the individuals are able to transform subjective probabilities into equivalent objective probabilities. An example, therefore, of how this could work according to the classical Theory of Finance in a rational world is 'Bayesian updating'.

An example concerning 'Bayesian updating': A newborn child (let it be assumed that this newborn child is very intelligent) observes its first sunrise. It asks itself whether tomorrow the sun will rise again or not. Then it allocates both events the same past probabilities. The child does that by putting a white and black ball into an urn. The next morning, when the sun rises again, it puts another white ball into the urn. The probability, that a randomly drawn ball from the urn is a white one (i.e. the child's 'degree of belief' that tomorrow the sun will rise again) has risen from one-half to two-thirds. After the sunrise the next day the child adds another white ball into the urn and the probability rises to three-fourths. And so on. Over time the original estimation, that the sun will rise with the same probability as the sun will not rise, will move to an almost certainty, that the sun will always rise.

Is 'Bayesian updating' realistic? The literature at least agrees that probabilities as objective measures are only allowed under a number of preconditions. There have to be a large number of events that have been realized under the same conditions and their frequencies are measurable as well as relative. These preconditions, however, are practically not observable in the real world. In addition, it shows that the concept of objective probabilities is a relative concept, since it is dependent on the individual's pre-information. This insight has extensive implications. If the individual is able to improve his or her decision situation by the gaining of additional information and can come closer to the true objective probabilities, then with the existence of objective probabilities all individuals have to be fully informed. If these assumptions cannot be held, then the question arises what information the individuals must have in order to assess all future events and how decisions are realized. This does not imply that individuals are still not able to maximize their expected utility with the information they have. Though are they capable of interpreting the information available to maximize their expected utility or are they satisfied with a non-maximal solution? These questions lead to the concept of bounded rationality.

3.2.2 Bounded Rationality

The notion of bounded rationality is in large part associated with the contributions from Herbert Simon (1982) who has influenced this concept to a large extent. It is due to him that the concept of bounded rationality has become an integral part of economics.[15] The theory of bounded rationality emphasizes disclosing the discrepancy between perfect rational behavior, as postulated by the classical Theory of Finance, and real human behavior in the economic reality as can be observed for everyone. Such a discrepancy does not imply that humans act irrationally. It is rather understood that individuals are not able to give perfect predictions nor does their knowledge enable them to reach the optimum as postulated by the classical theory.

Simon has analyzed the differences between the unrealistic assumptions of the classical theory and the insights from the view of cognitive psychology. Cognitive psychology explains that humans make decisions in a state of bounded knowledge and limited capability to make predictions. Simon's model explains the processes in a consistent manner with cognitive psychology, through which different alternative actions under uncertainty are formulated, compared and evaluated. According to the principle of bounded rationality the human capabilities of cognition and interpretation are limited. As a result individuals are not capable of making the best possible choice for themselves, since (at least in most cases) these are very complex.

These ideas had during their development a difficult task to win recognition. At the time, formal optimization models were widely advanced and were accepted as effective, however complex methodology for decision making. What was neglected in the optimization models is the fact that it takes time and high perception and interpretation capabilities to make optimal decisions. Furthermore such optimization models – unlimited capabilities of information perceptions and processing – are analytically not consistent with traditional economic theory. The activities of information gathering and processing are assumed as free of charge and without time costs. This, combined with the unlimited capabilities of information perception and processing, is an evident violation of the principle of scarce resources.

Simon formulated his theory upon the fact that the human being itself is the limiting factor within the decision process. He refers in particular to the limit of the internal environment of the human being. He understands, for example, the human brain as a resource with a limited capacity in a world full of new information. As a consequence humans are not capable of making optimal decisions but have to make rational decisions to achieve specific goals within existing states and restrictions. Such restrictions can be perceived characteristics, objective characteristics of the surrounding environment as well as characteristics of the organism itself which views the restrictions as a given and not changeable.

Simon defines the rationality of the classic Theory of Finance as objective rationality, rationality due to its own limits as subjective or bounded rationality. In the case of objective rationality the decision-maker is asked to formulate all possible alternative actions and their consequences. He argues, however, that it is impossible for a single individual to achieve a sufficient level of objective rationality. This is because the individual's capability to formulate alternative actions is limited and the consequences thereof are not fully predictable. Future consequences can by no means be precisely formulated, but only estimated. In addition, an individual can only formulate and compare a few alternative actions; the human brain will never be able to consider all the relevant aspects for every decision. In addition, various processes are being analyzed that aim at finding a possible solution for a certain problem (the problem-solving process). Summarizing, according to the concept of bounded rationality, it is sufficient to make a decision with the limited information available, and with the human brain's limited processing and interpretation skills, to achieve a satisfying aspiration level. If no alternative actions fulfill a satisfying aspiration level, another alternative action is sought until one is found that satisfies the aspiration level defined. The individual therefore does not need either to have all information in the beginning or to know all possible alternative actions to make a rational decision.

3.2.3 Procedural Rationality

After psychological studies found how humans typically make decisions, it became evident that they spend most time in the formulation of the alternatives and in the evaluation of the resultant consequences. The actual action does not take much time at all, once the alternatives have been formulated and chosen. The core of the analysis therefore shifts from the 'what' to the 'how' of decisions are made. John Dewey (1997), for example, has provided valuable insights in his work into how this process takes place. The starting point for the decision-making process is the existence of a complex situation. A phase of self-doubt follows while attempts are made to formulate an action plan. The effectiveness of the plan is compared and evaluated to one's own experiences and observed facts. If additional difficulties evolve, then new possible solutions on the basis of new data are developed. This process continues until a satisfying action plan is developed. Procedural rationality is based on this decision-making process.

To understand whether rational behavior in the sense of the classic Theory of Finance exists, it is sufficient that individuals maximize their expected utility upon the predetermined, objective situation. Bounded rationality stays at a static description of the individuals' perception and interpretation limitations vis-à-vis themselves and their surrounding environment. In the definition of bounded rationality it is sufficient to know the individual's goals and the objective characteristics of the situation. If the individual's goals are known, then rational behavior is the result of the given objective characteristics of the individual's environment and is completely predetermined. These assumptions lead to an economic behavior that is completely independent of psychology. In the context of procedural rationality, it is, however, essential to know how individuals process and conceptualize perceived reality as well as how they use their brain capabilities to reach the right conclusions from the information available. Procedural rationality, therefore, is not a static approach, but it combines the individual's limiting elements with a dynamic, learning process not restricted in time. In the sense of procedural rationality, rational behavior concerns a functional choice to achieve a certain result. The rationality in such a behavior concerns the process of generating such a choice. The approach of procedural rationality distinguishes itself from other approaches, in that a time dimension is explicitly integrated into the decision-making process. The search for a functional choice, therefore, always costs time. Moreover, the approach of procedural rationality is a dynamic process, because the individual is assumed to be capable of learning from his experiences and observations of his environment and to redefine his choice after a new evaluation.

The concept of procedural rationality is also related to the previously mentioned approach of Bayesian updating. In Bayes' theorem, individuals collect information from different sources. They have to, for example, combine new information with already existing information as well as with their own information or information from their environment. Rational individuals integrate the new information according to Bayes' theorem, i.e. the information is integrated into the existing information set with a weighting proportional to its precision. As in the approach of procedural rationality, the individual's capability to process information is limited as well. As a result of this, an individual will apply ad hoc rules for the combination of the different sources of information. In this process the individual will without doubt make mistakes. It is only assumed that on average these ad hoc rules are a good approximation of Bayes' theorem as long as there is no systematic bias in the mistakes made. If these assumptions are fulfilled, then an action according to Bayes' theorem is rational. Of course, these assumptions concerning the ad hoc rules can be challenged. It is not at all clear why these ad hoc rules should on average result in a good approximation of Bayes' theorem. Bayes' theorem implies a one-time, complete and error-free learning process and excludes further learning processes. It is doubtful whether an individual acts irrationally simply because, due to limited learning skills, he is unable to make systematic errors and requires repeated learning processes to eliminate his mistakes.[16]

3.2.4   An Action is Always Rational

An even more forceful approach to the notion of rationality is postulated by the economist Ludwig von Mises (1996). He is of the opinion that human action always has to be rational. Hence the notion 'rational action' is a pleonasm and as such has to be rejected. His argument is that the ultimate goal of an individual's action is always to satisfy certain needs. Since no one can translate his own valuation measures to other people, it is useless to judge the actions, the goals and the will of others. No one can judge whether an alternative action would have made another person more happy. Von Mises argues that an irrational action is typically related to the abandonment of material advantages in comparison to the fulfillment of ideological, non-physical values. However, striving for the fulfillment of non-material, ideological values is neither more rational than other human needs nor irrational.

In comparison with other animals, the human being is able to control his drives. He can control both his sex drive and his will to live. This is a principle of his free will, ie he can give up his own life under conditions he assesses as intolerable. An individual can die as the result of an external cause or he can kill himself. To live is for the human individual a question of choice and is a personal, subjective valuation. According to von Mises the opposite of a rational choice is not irrational behavior, but a reaction to stimuli on the part of the sense organs and instincts that cannot be controlled by the human will. Emotions such as laughing or crying are this kind of stimuli. Crying and laughter are barely under conscious control. Most people probably would agree that you cannot cry or laugh to order. This insight is central to the understanding of which actions are controllable and which are not. Robert Provine, professor of psychology and neuroscience at the University of Maryland, is of the opinion that explanations for such actions after the event are simply attempts to rationalize an irrational, unconsciously guided action of instinct, i.e. to give a veneer of sense and rationality. Then it is also intuitively comprehensible that an action is to be considered irrational, if the stimuli for the trigger of that action cannot be controlled.[17]

3.2.5 Rationality in Financial Markets

Postulating that market participants in financial markets act at least in a procedural rational way, past price movements in particular on equity markets over the last few years have to be entirely reassessed.[18] Market participants act rationally in a way as their actions are intended to be to their advantage and are taken with the information available and in coordination with the actions of the other market participants. The actions are taken to achieve their own defined goals. Let us assume in addition for the analysis of rational behavior in financial markets that investors are price takers. This is not a critical assumption. At least for large capitalized, liquid stocks it does not seem possible for a single market participant to steer and control the traded price over a longer period of time.

The price, which is the unintended result of the sum of all intended actions, is obviously what interests the market participants most. They are therefore forced to adjust their positions to the unintended result. This can happen, for example, if they adjust their portfolio relative to a benchmark or if they respond to fresh news, such as rumors. As a result of the evaluation of their own positions with respect to the new, unintended price, the positions have to be reviewed and adjusted. The reason why this doesn't happen simultaneously is information-processing asymmetries. With these kinds of information-processing asymmetries it is not meant that a few market participants know more than others, but that the available information is processed and interpreted differently. It is when the positions are adjusted to the new, unintended result, that the largest capital flows occur. In that sense the behavior of the single market participant is rational and 'socially influenced'. The positions are then adjusted to the market development, which is an expression of the actions of an anonymous, but in general not at all irrational, mass of people.

Why does the impression now emerge that, in the light of the price developments on equity markets over the last ten years, financial markets have been acting irrationally? One explanation might be that irrational behavior is always mentioned when prices fall or rise in a very short period of time. These short-term price movements reveal that market participants have no economic explanation for such price movements. Therefore financial markets have to have been acting irrationally during that time. The irrationality of financial markets serves then as the only possible explanation for the happenings on financial markets. If large price movements happen over a longer period of time, no one will speak of irrational behavior. This creates the crucial link to rumors. It is often argued that market participants act irrationally when rumors in financial markets evolve and when all of a sudden strong price movements are observed in a very short period of time. If there is no solid ground for an explanation of all the emotion and excitement going on, and people are stunned because of the price movements and volatility observed, then irrationality can be the only explanation. Is this reasonable? As stated above, people don't like an event or price movement to happen without having an explanation for why it happened. An unsolved issue cannot be left unsolved. There must always be an explanation for what has happened in the past. Irrational behavior then has to fill the gap.

Another often-heard statement is, that when market participants act irrationally, this implies that the financial market is not efficient. This is definitely not the case. Rationality always refers to actions of single individuals, while in an efficient financial market the instantaneous and full appreciation of all relevant information is reflected in the asset's price. Of course, the actions of all individuals lead to price movements according to the information flow. However, while rational actions always refer to the individual level, the efficiency of a financial market is measured on an aggregate market level.

Example of how the market can be efficient with irrational market participants: The last traded price of the stock Novartis was at 10:42 a.m. on February 11, 2003, at CHF 50.00. The bid–ask was at CHF 50.00 to CHF 50.05. Suppose a market participant wanted to sell his Novartis shares at CHF 40.00 without any fresh news coming in (and he has no insider information), then you would probably call him a pretty stupid market participant. Indeed this kind of behavior would be pretty 'unreasonable', i.e. in this sense irrational, however, not completely impossible. What would now happen? Of course, immediately a trade for the Novartis share would take place at CHF 40.00, since the market values it at CHF 50.00. If the market supposes there is no piece of information in the transaction itself, then the price of the Novartis share will immediately afterwards rise to CHF 50.00 again. The market has behaved extraordinarily efficiently, although there has been an irrational market participant active on the financial market.

Wouldn't the market be inefficient if just enough market participants were to act irra- tionally, as they did, for example, during the New Economy Bubble between 1998 and 2000, so that such a bubble could evolve in the first place? Not necessarily. If again pro- cedural rational market participants are assumed, then they perform their actions for their advantage and in coordination with the actions of the other market participants. Applying this statement, even when a share is bought at a high price, this action can be viewed as rational, so long as the price of the share further continues to rise and another par- ticipant is found who buys the share back. With this kind of view it is not difficult to see that a bubble on financial markets can evolve without the market participants acting irrationally. The participants are probably fully aware that the potential for gain as well as the potential for loss during a bubble is quite high. However, this says nothing con- cerning the rationality of an action. Taking an action with high risk is not necessarily irrational.

Another interesting phenomenon that the classical Theory of Finance traditionally has great difficulty in explaining is the high traded volume on equity markets. Excessive traded volumes are in a meaningful way only explicable by the concept of procedural rationality.

Then it is also comprehensible why, after news with a high information content (such as yearly earnings of corporations or interest rate decisions of the Federal Reserve), high traded volumes are observed. Obviously there is a process that market participants follow to interpret the information received and to value it accordingly.

3.3 EMPIRICAL STUDIES OF RUMORS IN THE STOCK MARKET

In an early study, Rose (1951) analyzed the short-term influence of rumors on stock prices in a sample of U.S. stocks over a period from 1937 to 1938 and from 1948 to 1949. In order to measure the effect of rumors on stock prices, he calculates a so-called stickiness factor. He finds support for the hypothesis that if a 'rumor affects the stock market over several days, it will do so by creating an unidirectional trend in stock prices over these days'.[19] By 'unidirectional' Rose means that the price will move in a single direction (up or down) over some short period of time. Pound and Zeckhauser (1990) investigate the effects of takeover rumors on stock prices. They use a sample of rumors published in the *Wall Street Journal*'s 'Heard on the Street' (HOTS) column. In their sample are takeover rumors from every edition on a daily basis from January 1, 1983 to December 31, 1985. Their main findings are the following. Firstly, the market reacts efficiently to published takeover rumors, correctly assessing the average probability that the rumor will be followed ultimately by a takeover bid. They conclude that there are no excess profits to be made on average from either buying or shorting the stocks of firms that are the subject of widely circulating rumors. Some market participants who are very close to the market may profit from rumors as they begin to diffuse through the investment community. Secondly, in the period before the publication of rumors in the national press, there has typically been a significant price run-up for the takeover targets, while no reaction to the rumor on the date of its publication could be found. Thirdly, rumors seldom predict imminent takeover bids. In less than half of their sample, rumors correctly predicted a takeover within one year, and just two out of 42 within 50 days of publication. These results are supported by two recent, though less scientific studies conducted by fool.com and SmartMoney. The fool.com study was performed in the fall of 1998[20] and analyzed the weekly *Business Week*'s 'Inside Wall Street' column by Gene Marcial. For both years 1996 and 1997 they find poor results for rumored takeovers published in the *Business Week* column. Less than half of the targeted rumor takeovers, at least within the next two years, actually took place and sometimes not by the companies that were presumed to be the buyer. Kimmel (2003)[21] also lists a number of rumored takeovers that never happened, taken from a study by SmartMoney in 1999. He states that 'in most cases, the speculation generated by these unfounded stories never pans out, which does not mean that they do not cause a market reaction'. He does not come to any clear conclusions, but rather notices that investors might rely more on takeover rumors than on following patterns for a takeover target.

Zivney et al. (1996) take an approach similar to that of Pound and Zeckhauser, but consider both the HOTS and the 'Abreast of the Market' (AOTM) column. They argue that rumors initially appear in the AOTM and then days or weeks later are repeated in the HOTS column. In addition they argue that the one-year holding period proposed by Pound and Zeckhauser should be reconsidered due to overreaction observations from other new information. There is, meanwhile, a considerable amount of evidence for overreaction to other new information.[22] Zivney et al. cover the period from 1985 until 1988, when takeover rumors were especially numerous in 1988. Altogether the authors gathered 871 rumors to be examined. It has to be mentioned here that the HOTS column has been applied to other studies not related to rumors, but to insider trading[23] as well as securities recommendations of analysts.[24] Their results are similar to those of Pound and Zeckhauser in the sense that the market reacts efficiently to rumor publication. However, for the AOTM subsequent rumors they find a clear overreaction in the market, which gives rise to profitable investment opportunities. The overreaction persists in spite of adjusting for target firm size, percentage of institutional ownership and market risk (beta). Like Pound and Zeckhauser, they also observe a significant price run-up during the 20-day period before the publication of the rumor. Basically the same study was conducted by Kiymaz (2001) for the Turkish market at the Istanbul Stock Exchange. The results of his study are in line with the other studies mentioned. He discovers a positive, significant abnormal return in each of the four days prior to the publication date, but insignificant negative abnormal returns in the post-publication period.

A recent empirical study has been performed by Gorodsinsky (2003) for the German stock market. He uses a database from the VWD-Newswire, which delivers information upon important rumors. The rumors are selected in a standardized manner from the editors. In the year 2002, 136 rumors of DAX-100 stocks were spread from the VWD-Newswire. The year 2002 was quite special, not only for the German stock market. The DAX fell altogether by 40%. Therefore, the majority of rumors are concerned with events that suggest a further drop in prices. The author finds that on average, the daily excess returns of those stocks exposed to a rumor is 2.8% with a standard deviation of 6.4%. However, the result is strongly influenced by one outlier. Without the outlier, the figures would have been 2.3% and 3.5% correspondingly. With 18 out of the 136 rumors analyzed, the daily return moved in the opposite direction than the rumor intended. This would indicate that other news in addition to the rumor was responsible for the price development of that day. In that case, the analyzed results should be treated with great care or even doubted. Though, as the author notes, in most of the 18 cases the circumstances were complex or the corporations immediately published denials to move the stock price back up.

As with other empirical studies, the one mentioned above experiences some drawbacks not to be ignored. The first drawback is the rumor selection process. The editors of VWD-Newswire observe a significant price movement and inquire in the market about its cause. If a rumor is mentioned, then they verify the explanation with other market participants. If other market participants also have heard the rumor, then it is published. One consequence of this selection process is that only rumors are published that actually have influenced the price significantly. All the rumors that do not influence the stock price are not included in the database. Therefore it is not surprising that the author finds daily excess returns of the stocks exposed to rumors. The author states that many empirical studies are not able to discriminate between false reports and true events, while all rumors analyzed from the VWD-Newswire database represent actual false reports.[25] An inquiry at VWD revealed that for obvious reasons they are not able to know which rumors turn out to be true. Many of their rumors published in fact turned out to be true. If the author has only analyzed false rumors from the VWD-Newswire database, then there is another strong bias included in the selection of the rumors.

The conclusion is that, with all empirical studies, there are significant drawbacks included in the analysis. This suggests that empirical studies are possibly not the most suitable approach to developing a good understanding of the market's reaction to a rumor.

3.4   REVIEW OF MODELS ON RUMORS

Owing to the complexity of the nature of rumors, it is a difficult task to model rumors as a whole. As a consequence, researchers have focused on partial aspects of rumors. Essentially two different aspects have been differentiated, namely the transmission process and the intensity of the rumor. Most models developed so far have focused on the transmission process and the consequences thereof. A second set of models have put rumors into a market microstructure setting and analyzed the consequences of strategic behavior thereof. The first attempt to model rumors stems from Allport and Postman (1946)[26] mentioned in Section 2.2, 'Historical background to studies on rumors', where it is discussed and analyzed in depth.

The rumor theory of Bruckner (1965) focuses on the transmission mechanisms when rumors evolve. He tackles the question of whether and how rumors become more or less accurate as they are passed on. Exploring several joint conditions on the accuracy of a rumor, he comes up with the effects to be expected shown in Table 3.3. The patterns refer to the number of interactions when rumors spread. In the first type, a *serial chain*, the rumor moves from one person to another in a serial manner in a series of single interactions. In the second type, a *multiple network*, many people hear the rumor from more than one source. The critical set refers to the critical ability of an individual judging, evaluating and passing on the validity of a rumor. The *uncritical set* does not distinguish between a true or false rumor. The individual lacks the critical ability to evaluate the validity of rumors and passes them on in any case. When among individuals multiple interactions take place in a transmission set, this should overcome the individuals' faulty memory and the rumor will come through unchanged.

Bruckner then analyzes the group involvement and structure and their expected effects on rumor transmission (Table 3.4). He differentiates between a close and a diffuse group structure as well as high and low involvement of the group involved. He states as a conclusion that 'the two variables . . . seem to form a natural ranking in their effects on the frequency of rumor transmission and repetition. This ranking could also be seen as a ranking of motivation and opportunity.'[27]

Table 3.3   Rumor patterns and orientation and their expected effects on transmission of the rumor.[28] (Reproduced, with permission, from Bruckner (1965))

Pattern	Critical set	Uncritical set	Transmission set
Serial chain	Slight decline in accuracy through memory flaws. Truth/falsity ratio remains high.[a]	Slight decrease in distortion. Truth/falsity ratio drops at each interaction.	Rapid decline in information. Leveling, sharpening, assimilation.
Multiple-interaction network	Increasing accuracy as rumor moves through net. Truth/falsity ratio rises rapidly.	Great increase of distortion as accurate rumor is lost in false ones. Radical drop in truth/falsity ratio.	(Hypothetical.) Very slow decline in information. Rumor stays intact.

[a] Truth/falsity ratio is arrived at by dividing the number of true items by the number of false items in the message. *Source*: H.T. Bruckner: A theory of rumor transmission, *Public Opinion Quarterly* **29**(1) 54–70 (1965). By permission of Oxford University Press.

Table 3.4   Group involvement and structure and their expected effects on transmission of the rumor.[29] (Reproduced, with permission, from Bruckner (1965))

Involvement	Group structure	Tellings	Repetitions	Pattern
High	Close	Many	Many	Intense network
High	Diffuse	Many	Sporadic	Largely chains, a few small nets
Low	Close	A few	Almost none	A few small chains and nets
Low	Diffuse	Almost none	None	Very short chains

Source: H.T. Bruckner: A theory of rumor transmission, *Public Opinion Quarterly* **29**(1) 54–70 (1965). By permission of Oxford University Press.

After the early study of Allport and Postman not much happened in the area of formal rumor modeling, until Banerjee (1993) revived the idea of information transmission processes. The distinctive features of the processes he models are that the information transmission takes place in such a way that the recipient does not quite know whether to believe the information. Additionally, the probability that someone receives the information depends on how many people have already heard it. In particular, he studies an example in which there is an investment project whose returns are known only to a few people. The project is costly and the amount of the cost is private information. What the other investors observe is only whether the other agents have invested in the project or not. They do not know if the others knew the potential returns or if they too were acting just on the observation of others. The individuals use a Bayesian updating approach to obtain a stochastic process describing how the rumor develops over time.

Banerjee provides a comparative statics analysis of his model. The dynamics of his model are approximated through a system of differential equations used for epidemic models known from the epidemiological literature. Then the comparative statics of the model are obtained from an analysis of the approximated deterministic system. Therein changing the speed of the rumor does not have any welfare effects, while increasing the amount of information in the system as well as giving higher productivity has ambiguous effects on the overall welfare.

Kosfeld (2005) takes a simplifying step and models rumor transmission as a purely mechanical act. His model combines standard microeconomic theory and particle system theory in order to analyze the spread of a rumor through word-of-mouth communication, and the rumor's impact on demand and prices of goods in a competitive market. By modeling the rumor as a purely mechanical act, Kosfeld is able to analyze the stochastic process directly and does not have to approximate the process to obtain results on the rumor's evolution. The second distinction in his model refers to the communication of the rumor. He argues that for the rumor dynamics it is reasonable to assume that rumor communication is restricted only to local neighborhoods. Banerjee in comparison allows for the agents to meet and communicate with all other agents. While other models of word-of-mouth communication[30] focus more on the question of social learning and efficiency measures, Kosfeld concentrates on the effects of market outcomes and asset prices. One of his main ideas is that the agents who are infected by the rumor are also the ones who spread the rumor to their local neighbors. He models the rumor dynamic as an interacting particle system, the latter being a continuous-time Markov process on the state-space of all configurations of beliefs in the economy. One of the assumptions made is that every neighbor who communicates the rumor increases the probability of an agent becoming infected by the rumor and as a consequence also starts spreading the rumor himself. The result is a rumor dynamic similar to an infection process. The economy is modeled as a two-states, two-good exchange economy with two Arrow securities, each paying a return of one if the corresponding state of the world occurs, and zero otherwise.

With this approach Kosfeld is able to provide an analytical foundation for the empirical findings on price run-ups after rumor occurrences in financial markets. Since in his model the rumor contains positive information about the likelihood of one of the two states, it induces those agents affected by the rumor to shift part of their demand to the corresponding security. In addition, in his model there exists no finite upper bound for the relative price run-up for the security positively related to the rumor, if communication and reactions to it are extreme.

Physicists have also been attracted by processes of information transmission. Eguíluz and Zimmermann (2000) propose a model for stochastic formation of opinion clusters. They do so by modeling an evolving network and include herd behavior to account for the empirically observed fat-tail distribution of financial asset returns. The only parameter they use in their model is the rate of information dispersion per trade as a measure of herd behavior. They find that for the parameter to be below a critical value, the system displays a power-law distribution of returns with an exponential cutoff. If, however, the parameter is above the critical value, then they find an increasing probability of large negative and positive returns. The authors note that these may be associated with the occurrence of large crashes.

In another physics journal, Liu, Luo and Shao (2001) consider a rumor's transmission quantitatively. They introduce a spin chain to describe the rumor's transmission along different channels mathematically. The spins represent the operations. The result of a rumor's transmission is then the chain's spin sum. The authors argue that their model is favorable for social prognostication and can determine quantitatively how competition among various opinions can affect the exaggerating behavior due to a rumor.

While information transmission covers one important characteristic of a rumor, two recent studies have focused more on optimal strategic behavior when receiving a signal prior to others. Brunnermeier (2003)[31] analyzes the effects of information leakage on market efficiency. In his model, a trader receives an early but imprecise signal about a forthcoming news announcement, e.g. in the form of a rumor. The new element Brunnermeier offers is that the stock-price reflects unrelated long-run information held by other traders as well as the early-informed trader's short-run signal. The features of the informed agents' strategy are firstly to exploit his private but imprecise information twice, once before the public announcement and a second time after it. Secondly, he builds up a large position which he intends to unwind partially after the public announcement, because he predicts that the market will overreact to the news. Thirdly, he trades aggressively prior to the announcement in order to make it more difficult for other market participants to learn from past price movements.

In his discussion of the results and implications of his model, Brunnermeier points out the following: when the leaked signal becomes less precise, the inefficiencies disappear. This seems obvious since the early-informed trader knows less precisely than before what the true signal is going to be. When the early signal error limits infinity, it coincides with no information leakage. In the opposite case, when the short-term information is perfect, the trader has no informational advantages and does not trade in the second period. The second conclusion drawn from the paper is that the kind of trading behavior the early-informed trader follows reduces the long-term informativeness of prices, and hence provides a strong argument in favor of the SEC's Regulation Fair Disclosure.

Van Bommel (2003) provides a study combining insider trading with the spreading of rumors. In his model, a trader or small investor first receives private information about a security's true value. Since his trading capacity and therefore his price impact are negligible in comparison to the overall trading volume, there is information left to be exploited. A rational expectations model shows that the informed trader is able to enhance his profits by spreading informative yet imprecise trading advice to followers to manipulate the market prices. Van Bommel's statement, that 'the equilibrium presented ... is played within the law'[33] must, however, be firmly rejected. The illegality of the trading action is performed by the informed trader and is a clear case of insider trading.[33] However, the spreading of rumors by the informed trader is itself not illegal and cannot be treated as a form of illegal market manipulation. After the trader is informed, he has three possibilities. He may be honest, bluff or cheat. When he is honest about the private information he received, he spreads rumors in the same direction as the actual signal. When the trader bluffs, he stays honest when receiving a clear signal maintaining a reliable source of valuable information. However, when he does not receive any clear signal, the trader takes a random position and subsequently spreads a rumor corresponding to the position taken. The third possibility is that the trader is cheating. In this case he has no scruples against spreading false or bluffing rumors and takes a market position opposite to the information he possesses. Before revelation of the true information the trader unwinds the position, making a profit. The problem with the 'cheating' strategy is that the public will not believe the rumors spread. This is due to a moral-hazard cost imposed on the strategy. If the followers know that an informed trader has the incentive to cheat, they will not believe any rumors. Van Bommel analyses the model with repeated games and finds that under relatively weak conditions that the equilibrium from the 'honest' strategy can be supported. The other two will eventually refrain from bluffing or cheating, since they may lose their reputation and hence the ability to manipulate prices.

3.5   ETHNOGRAPHICAL STUDIES

Market participants in financial markets have also been studied from an ethnographical point of view. Ethnographical studies describe and interpret the culture of a population or a cultural group. Brügger[34] describes the world of foreign currency traders and their way of communicating with each other. Rumor communication belongs to their daily life. Brügger states that personal networks are viewed as very important for traders for receiving valuable information from other traders, such as rumors. Usually rumors are communicated to other traders whom the person knows well and trusts. It does not matter if the other trader works for a competitor or not. Certain relationships among traders are purely informative with no business relations. In that case, however, it is important that both parties provide the other one with valuable information so that a certain balance is assured. The relationship is therefore reciprocal. Goldinger[35] analyses the rituals and symbols of the exchange from a broader point of view. He states that rumors as an information process potentially influencing the market allow for a special status, since from their indeterminacy, their ambiguity and their mostly anonymous origin there seems to be a special fascination with them. In his view this could have something to do with the 'playful atmosphere of the focused assembly called the stock exchange'[36] and the fact that the uncertain outcome of the game is the primary reason for the fun and excitement. In addition, the high potential relevance stemming from the indeterminacy and ambiguity of a rumor can also be a reason for its special status. Goldinger refers to Watzlawick (1985), who shows that relevance produces the social and cultural reality in which phenomena such as money, securities and trading on stock exchanges are possible. If relevant information (for stock exchanges) is objective, verifiable and reliable, then it loses the potential of relevance and mutates from ambiguous to non-ambiguous. All market participants will react in the same manner to such a piece of information. Only if there is a spark for different interpretations, then the information is interesting and a competition arises for the 'right' or profitable behavior. The game with rumors is then like the salt in the soup.

Goldinger[37] performed a small empirical study over three months in which rumors induced large price movements, and analyzed how many of the movements turned out to be correct. He admits that the study has some subjective element to it and the data are not suitable for statistical preparation. His results are the following: from 89 rumors, 58 turned ex post to be true. So would a strategy be profitable to simply buy every time a rumor evolves? In one-third of the cases one would be wrong, but in two out of three cases one would be right. Goldinger says that the strategy is not systematically profitable, since from his observation the rumors initiating fast and large price movements were mostly those turning out to be false. It gets even more complicated when converse rumors start alternating. The confusion is then complete for both professional traders and lay investors, but at least the professionals are able to buy or sell a lot faster than the lay investors.

4

Legal Aspects of Rumors
in Financial Markets

Let your tongue not be a flag,
that in the wind of each rumor starts to flutter

IMHOTEP, Egyption architect and doctor,
advisor of King Djoser, 3. Dynasty around 2650 BC

4.1 RUMORS IN FINANCIAL MARKETS AND INSIDER TRADING

4.1.1 Introduction

Insider trading is illegal. According to the SEC,[1] insider trading generally refers to 'buying or selling a security, in breach of a fiduciary duty or other relationship of trust and confidence, while in possession of material, nonpublic information about the security. Insider trading violations may also include "tipping" such information, securities trading by the person "tipped" and securities trading by those who misappropriate such information.' Insider trading liability is ordinarily based on a violation of Section 10(b) of the Securities Exchange Act of 1934 and Rule 10b-5 thereunder. Liability for trading on inside information is usually premised on Rule 10b-5's prohibition on fraudulent acts and practices. 'Under the "traditional" or "classical" theory of insider trading . . . Rule 10b-5 [is] violated when a corporate insider trades in [that corporation's securities] on the basis of material, non-public information.'[2]

With regards to rumors, the question of insider trading has to be posed in relation to the nonpublic availability of the information. Fleming states that 'trading on material, inside information is prohibited only if that information is truly non-public'.[3] 'To constitute non-public information under the [1933 Securities Exchange] Act, information must be specific and more private than general rumor.'[4] Violation of the securities laws is not found where 'the disclosed information is so general that the recipient thereof is still undertaking a substantial economic risk that his tempting target will prove to be a "white elephant"'.[5] 'However, an insider's confirmation of rumors that a company is in actual merger discussions, even if no specific details of the merger are provided, constitutes a tip of material non-public information.'[6]

Examples of insider trading cases that have been brought by the SEC are cases against corporate officers, directors, and employees who traded the corporation's securities after learning of significant or confidential corporate developments. In addition, cases have been raised against friends, business associates, family members, and other 'tippees' of such officers, directors and employees, who traded the securities after receiving such information. Further cases involve employees of law, banking, brokerage and printing firms who were given such information in order to provide services to the corporation whose securities

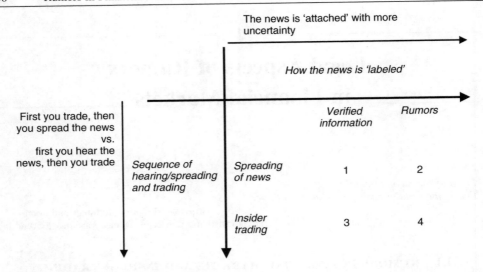

Figure 4.1 Rumors and insider trading

they traded. The list also includes government employees who learned of such information because of their employment by the government, and other persons who misappropriated, and took advantage of, confidential information from their employers. The SEC has treated the detection and prosecution of insider trading violations as one of its enforcement priorities, because insider trading undermines investor confidence in the fairness and integrity of the securities markets.

Rumors can be categorized in relation to insider trading as follows (Figure 4.1):

1. *Spreading 'verified' false information:* Spreading 'verified' false information is clearly illegal. The Emulex case falls into this category. A young hacker created a false press release, and he knew at the time that the content of it was false. The time sequence is as follows: the hacker first sold the stock short and waited until after the news had spread to realize his gain.

2. *Spreading rumors:* Spreading rumors as such is not illegal, although it is sometimes clearly in the deep gray zone. In the years 1999 and 2000, 15-year-old Jonathan Lebed earned between USD 12,000 and USD 74,000 daily over six months for a total gain of USD 800,000.[7] The SEC reported that he would buy blocks of microcap stocks and then post messages and rumors over the Internet about the company to increase traded price and volume. His aim was to influence people to buy the stocks and therefore pump up the traded price. The messages seemed to be more or less credible, but no one considered it necessary to verify the messages posted before buying the stock. The SEC initially wanted to force Lebed to return all his gains for stock price manipulations, but he fought the ruling and was shown to be at least partially right. Richard Walker, at the time director of enforcement of the SEC, stated on March 1, 2001, when the SEC accused 23 companies and individuals of using the Internet to defraud investors, that 'on the Internet, there is no clearly defined border between reliable and unreliable information'.[8] It must be said that the media itself does not determine whether a piece of information is reliable or not, but the Internet is especially vulnerable to the spreading of unreliable news.

Legal discussion: Section 17(a) of the Securities Act and Section 10(b) of the Exchange Act and Rule 10b-5 thereunder prohibit acts, transactions, practices or courses of business that operate as a fraud or deceit in connection with the offer, purchase or sale of securities, including misrepresentations and omissions of material fact. Section 10(b) and Rule 10b-5 thereunder expressly prohibit the use of any manipulative or deceptive device.

Comment: The SEC found that Lebed violated Section 17(a) of the Securities Act and Section 10(b) of the Exchange Act and Rule 10b-5 thereunder, however, obviously not to a full extent. Why otherwise would he have been allowed to keep part of the money gained?

3. *Insider trading with verified information:* Insider trading is by definition done with verified information, meaning the information received before others is certainly going to be true. This is one important factor that differentiates insider trading from trading on rumors. Another important characteristic of insider trading on verified information is the sequence in which the information is received and is traded on. (See also Section 4.3 'Rumors in financial markets and price manipulation'.) With insider trading the information is received first and then it is traded on, and not the opposite.

4. *Insider trading labeling the inside information as a rumor:* Inside information does not necessarily have to be 'labeled' as such. People with inside information try to deny that their inside information was in fact inside information, but call it something else, e.g. a rumor. In practice there have been several cases that point out the fine line between insider trading and dealing with rumors. The case of the SEC vs. Lohmann[9] is a good example of such a borderline between inside information and rumors. Lohmann received insider information of a forthcoming merger between the Williams Companies and MAPCO. He traded for himself and phoned a friend of his, who traded as well. During the investigation Lohmann based his defense on an article published by Reuters News Service citing 'vague takeover rumors' and 'speculation that there's going to be some sort of a deal' involving MAPCO. However, the SEC could prove that the Reuters article was published after Lohmann had tipped his friend and traded for himself. The SEC clearly stated that Lohmann possessed information that was more specific and more private than any market rumors. Even if Lohmann had spread rumors about the merger before he had traded, he still would have possessed private information he based his trading on. Therefore he would have traded upon superior information, since he would have been the only one to know for sure that the rumor was going to be true and his action would be illegal.

Interestingly enough, in Switzerland the Swiss Federal Banking Commission (SFBC) has recently issued for comment proposed guidelines on market abuse.[10] It has an explicit section on the spreading of inside information as rumors and states the following: 'The spreading of rumors before an intended abuse of information, in order to free oneself subsequently at best from the allegation in reference to those rumors abusing confidential and price sensitive information, is illegal.'[11]

The regulator's weapons:

1. The SEC has civil enforcement authority only, though it works closely with various criminal law enforcement agencies throughout the country to develop and bring criminal cases before the law, when the misconduct warrants more severe action. It obtains evidence of possible violations of the securities laws from many sources, including its own surveillance activities, other divisions of the SEC, the self-regulatory organizations and other securities industry sources, press reports and investor complaints.

2. All SEC investigations are conducted privately. Facts are collected and developed by their authorization of investigation such as: the obligation to disclose information about the institutions and people supervised (in writing or consultation), testimonies of people not supervised, informal inquiry, examination of brokerage records, review of trading data and additional evidence such as records of telephone calls of traders etc.

4.1.2   Review of Scientific Literature on Insider Trading

The scientific literature on insider trading has grown considerably over the last ten years. It is seen as one of the most controversial aspects of securities regulation. The controversy derives from the question of whether insider trading should be deregulated or not.[12] One set of scholars favors the deregulation of trading with inside information. In contrast, another set of law and economics scholars take the position that the property right of inside information should stay at the corporation level. The law of insider trading rules the allocation of property rights produced by a firm. Early common law in the United States allowed for the trading on inside information without having to disclose inside information. In recent decades, however, a number of more and more complex federal prohibition laws against insider trading have emerged. It is seen today as one of the most central features of modern securities regulation. Many other countries have followed, although enforcement levels still vary substantially from country to country.

4.1.2.1   The arguments for deregulation

There is general agreement for an accurate pricing to be beneficial for both firms and society. Manne (1966a) argues that insider trading causes the market price of the affected security to move towards the 'correct' price the security would command, if the inside information were publicly available. Therefore firms and society would benefit from accurate market prices. In theory, the effect of insider trading should have only a minimal impact on the affected security's price. However, as Gilson and Kraakman (1984) have pointed out, derivative forms of market efficiency can cause significant market price effects in two ways. The insiders start to trade on their material nonpublic information. At first their trading has only a small price effect. Now though, some uninformed traders become aware of the insider trading through observation, hints or leakage of information sources. They start to trade as well, causing an increasing price effect of the security. At last the market reacts to the price effect and drives the price towards the 'correct' price including the inside information. One of the issues with derivative trading is its inefficiency (Figure 4.2).[13] While the market efficiency[14] argument would hold for an immediate and direct price effect, derivative trading takes more time and causes excess volatility, leading to an undesired reallocation of the capital distribution. In that sense it can be compared to rumors spreading slowly within the trading community and adjusting slowly to the market price movements. When these inefficiencies of derivative trading are accounted for in the argumentation of insider trading deregulation, the market efficiency justification loses much of its force. The same arguments can be put forward for rumors. Rumors can lead to derivative trading as well and therefore to market inefficiencies in comparison to trading upon verified information. Trading on rumors should therefore not be prohibited, because in comparison to insider information the validity of the rumor's content is not known and therefore no certain profit is possible.

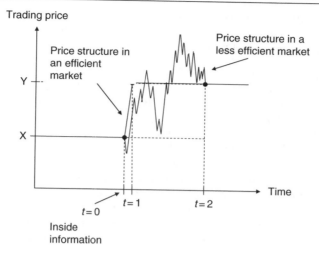

Figure 4.2 Market inefficiency of derivative trading. A trader receives inside information at time $t = 0$. In an efficient market, the inside information should be incorporated into the traded price instantly (or in the graph at $t = 1$). But if the market is less efficient, then the price movement is more volatile and it takes until $t = 2$ for the inside information to be incorporated into the traded price. The inefficiencies stem from two sources: first, it takes longer for the information to be incorporated into the traded price and, second, the price structure is more volatile

Other arguments for insider trading deregulation focus on the efficient compensation scheme[15] and the entrepreneurial compensation.[16] Dooley (1980) explains that the SEC's desire to enlarge its jurisdiction, enhance its prestige and make strong efforts to federalize corporation law, is one of the drivers for further regulation. Another argument brought up by Haddock and Macey (1987) is that market professionals, who are a cohesive and powerful community of interest, are the drivers and strong supporters of insider trading prohibition.

4.1.2.2 The arguments in favor of regulation

Prohibiting insider trading is usually justified on the grounds of fairness or justness. As could be predicted, such arguments do not fall on fruitful ground in the economic and law community. Those in favor of regulation respond to the deregulators' efficiency argument, that either efficiency is not a suitable measure, or regulation is justifiable on efficiency grounds as well. Efficiency arguments for regulation, in opposition to arguments based on fairness or justice grounds, can be structured into three main categories:[17]

1. Insider trading hurts investors and thus undermines the general confidence in financial markets.
2. Insider trading hurts the issuer of affected securities.
3. Insider trading is regarded as theft of property rights possessed by the institution and should be prohibited in either case, no matter if any investor or corporation has been hurt or not.

1. *Insider trading hurts investors and thus undermines the general confidence in financial markets*: Insider trading is said to hurt investors in two ways: investors trade at the 'wrong' price and are misled to make poor transactions.

   (i) *'Wrong' price:* An investor who trades an asset with an insider having access to material nonpublic information will claim that he has been deceived and traded at the 'wrong' price. The term 'wrong' price refers to the price at which the undisclosed information has not been incorporated yet. If, for example, a stock trades at USD 50, but after the disclosure of the new information (which before was inside information) trades at USD 75, then the shareholder selling at USD 50 will claim a missed opportunity of selling the stock for USD 25 more. Of course the investor is not able to know if he trades with an insider or not. What therefore happens is a reallocation of the gains from the stock price movement from the investor to the insider. Bainbridge states that 'unless immediate disclosure of material is to be required . . . , there will always be winners and losers in this situation. Irrespective of whether insiders are permitted to inside trade or not, the investor will never have the same access to information as the insider. It makes little sense to claim that the shareholder is injured when his shares are bought from an insider, but not when they are bought by an outsider without access to information.'[18] He concludes that the 'injury thus is correctly attributed to the rules allowing corporate nondisclosure of material information, not to insider trading'.[19] The argument of Bainbridge would be very valid, if the SEC had not meanwhile released new rules on selective disclosure and insider trading taking effect on October 23, 2000.[20] The regulation FD (fair disclosure) 'provides that when an issuer, or person acting on its behalf, discloses material nonpublic information to certain enumerated persons (in general, securities market professionals and holders of the issuer's securities who may well trade on the basis of the information), it must make public disclosure of that information'.[21] Bainbridge's argumentation therefore no longer holds. With these new regulations in place, the shareholder has a valid argument claiming to be injured by insider trading.

   (ii) *Misled to make poor transactions:* It can be argued that insider transactions affect traded prices in the sense that this induces derivative trading. However, it is difficult to find cogent arguments why this should be the case. If trading decisions are purely induced on previous price movements, then the investors would have traded irrespective of the presence of insiders in the market.[22]

2. *Insider trading hurts the issuer of affected securities*: Information is an intangible property able to be used by more than just one person without potentially lowering its value. When a manager concludes a major new deal and trades the firm's stock upon that, it is more than doubtful that by this behavior he will lower the value of the firm. However, as Bainbridge[23] states, there are circumstances where the value of the firm is lowered by insider trading:

   (i) It may delay the transmission of information or the taking of corporate action.
   (ii) It may interfere with corporate plans.
   (iii) It gives managers incentives to manipulate stock prices.
   (iv) It may harm the firm's reputation.

3. *Insider trading as theft of property rights*: The consensus is increasing among scholars that the protection of property rights in information is most easily justified for the prohibition

of insider trading.[24] Property rights in relation to information can be viewed either to allow the owner to enter into transactions without disclosing the information or to prohibit others from using the information.[25] The existence of property rights for intangibles, including information, is common and well established, such as trademarks, copyrights and patents. The reason for prohibiting insider trading has the same logic as for prohibiting patent infringement or theft of trade secrets. It is to protect the economic incentives of producing socially valuable information. As Padilla states, 'one of the most overlooked aspects in the literature on insider trading is the control function of property rights'.[26] One of the characteristics of property rights is to allow the owners to control what they own. Therefore the owners or the shareholders of the corporation have the ultimate rights of the means of production and of control over the corporation, not the managers of the corporation. The owners can, if they wish, delegate some or all of the control function to managers who decide on their own about the day-to-day operations of the firm, although 'the ultimate decisions concerning the use of their property and the choice of the men to manage it must therefore be made by the owners and by no one else'.[27] The critical issue therefore is 'whether one can justify assigning the property right to the insider'.[28] Due to this conclusion, the arguments that the property rights should be assigned to an insider instead of to the corporation, if not to the shareholders, lose much of their weight. The economic theory of property rights in information cannot justify transferring the right in the information from the shareholder to the insider.

4.2   REVIEW OF MODELS ON INSIDER TRADING

Models of insider trading have attracted many legal and economic scholars to debate about and study it since the Securities and Exchange Act in 1934. Much of the debate has been over the benefits and drawbacks of prohibiting insider trading. However, more literature on insider trading has evolved related to other areas. The areas include market linkages and informed trading by the market microstructure literature, trading by registered insiders, insider trading and competition and more recent information transfers as well as finance and product market competition. The models discussed in this work relate only to regulation and profitable insider trading issues.

4.2.1   Models of Insider Trading Regulation

When insiders trade, the traded prices reveal more information than if no insiders had traded. Therefore insider trading may be beneficial. Manne (1966a) was the first to argue that, if inside information is socially valuable, then permitting insider trading may lead to more efficient prices in a rational expectations model. George (1989) demonstrated how in such a model the prices may be processed more efficiently. Leland (1992) shows in a rational expectations model with endogenous investment level that, when insider trading is permitted, the following effects will result: stock prices better reflect information, expected real investment will rise, markets are less liquid, owners of investment projects and insiders will benefit, and outside investment and liquidity traders will lose. Fishman and Hagerty (1992) point out that under certain circumstances, allowing insider trading does lead to less efficient prices. Their argument builds on two adverse effects on the competitiveness of the market. Due to the increasing competition among inside traders, the incentive to buy costly information may be reduced.

The early models finding arguments that insider trading is socially costly are based on unfairness to the uninformed investor, such as the one by Brudney (1979). Glosten (1989) builds a model where insider trading leads to imperfect risk-sharing. This occurs because the market makers' response to the traders with inside information is to reduce the market liquidity. This implies additional costs for liquidity traders. Manove (1989) argues that insider trading discourages corporate investment when outsiders are aware of its general presence in the marketplace. Ausubel (1990) presents a model in which insider trading may effect a Pareto improvement. In his general equilibrium environment, he incorporates an investment stage followed by a trading stage. If the uninformed traders expect the inside traders to take advantage of them in the trading stage, the uninformed traders will reduce their investment. Bernhardt et al. (1995) introduce insider trading in a dynamic general equilibrium economy with rational and informed traders. These traders invest in assets with different levels of adverse selection or inside trading. Depending on the value of the insider information, the overall effects can either be welfare increasing or decreasing. Estrada (1995) studies the insider trading regulations on securities markets and social welfare under risk aversion. He finds, in terms of securities markets, that insider trading regulation can be shown to have both beneficial and detrimental effects. In terms of welfare, insider trading regulation made insiders and workers worse off, outsiders and liquidity traders better off, and society as a whole worse off. DeMarzo et al. (1998) model a trade-off between regulating insider trading and allowing it in order to facilitate efficient price discovery. An optimal enforcement policy must balance these benefits against the costs of enforcement. They find that the optimal policy involves allowing for small information-motivated trades and imposing penalties for large trades.

4.2.2   Models of Trading by Registered Insiders

There exists a large literature on market microstructure examining whether informed traders such as insiders are able to trade profitably.[29] Laffont and Maskin (1990) study the question whether the efficient market hypothesis still holds with a large trader and private information. The hypothesis states that even in markets with significant information asymmetries, equilibrium prices should aggregate information effectively. This implies that a trader can derive all he needs to know about the information of others simply by observing the prices traded. With their model, the authors conclude, that if there is imperfect competition and the informed trader is large enough to affect prices, then the efficient market hypothesis may well fail.

Fishman and Hagerty (1995) suggest a trading strategy for corporate insiders who are required to disclose their trades. The requirement to disclose decreases the inside traders' profits due to a more rapid price impact, although it gives them the opportunity to bluff that they are trading on relevant information when in fact they are not. The authors show that occasional bluffing can increase the inside trader profits in comparison to those disclosed and purely based on information-based trading. John and Narayanan (1997) extend the model of Fishman and Hagerty. They show that when good and bad news are asymmetric, insiders also manipulate when they are required to disclose. Huddart et al. (2001) study the topic in a Kyle (1985) setting and find that insiders add noise of random traders in order to hide their true intentions.

Empirical studies have focused mostly on the investigation of abnormal returns to insider trades in order to test hypotheses on market efficiency. Studies of these kinds are found in Allen and Ramanan (1995), Chakravarty and McConnell (1997, 1999), Cornell and Sirri

(1992), Damodaran and Liu (1993), Finnerty (1976), Jaffe (1974), Meulbroeck (1992) and Seyhun (1986, 1992, 1998). Papers focusing on cross-sectional differences in returns of insider trades are Aboody and Lev (2000), Huddart and Ke (2004), Rozeff and Zaman (1998) and Seyhun (1986).

4.3 RUMORS IN FINANCIAL MARKETS AND PRICE MANIPULATION

Stock market manipulations have a long history and go back to the most ancient financial markets. Joseph de la Vega writes in his book *Confusion de Confusions* on the Amsterdam stock exchange from 1688:

> The greatest comedy is played at the exchange. There, . . . the speculators excel in tricks, they do business and find excuses wherein hiding places, concealment of facts, quarrels, provocations, mockery, idle talk, violent desires, collusion, artful deceptions, betrayals, cheatings, and even tragic end are to be found.[30]

At the time market manipulations were common and de la Vega describes several techniques for tricking naive investors. For the understanding of today's markets it is, however, important to be aware that price manipulation and insider trading are not the same thing. The SEC considers them both to be illegal. The literature often confuses the two terms: insider trading and price manipulation. The SEC defines manipulation as an 'intentional conduct designed to deceive investors by controlling or artificially affecting the market for a security. Manipulation can involve a number of techniques to affect the supply of, or demand for, a stock. They include: spreading false or misleading information about a company; improperly limiting the number of publicly-available shares; or rigging quotes, prices or trades to create a false or deceptive picture of the demand for a security.'[31] With regards to Figure 4.3, one of the elements differentiating insider trading from price manipulation is the order of when information is received/spread and when action is taken. Market manipulation therefore belongs in the row 'spreading of news'. However, market manipulation is a subgroup of

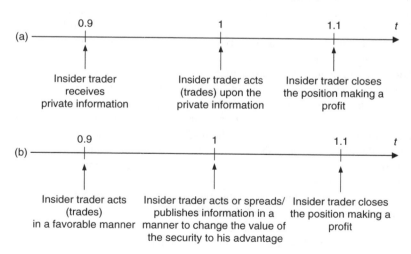

Figure 4.3 The reversed sequence of information and action concerning insider trading and price manipulation. (a) Insider trading. (b) Price manipulation

the row 'spreading of news', since not every spreading of news has to be considered manipulative.

With insider trading the trader receives a verified piece of information first. A necessary condition to classify the action as insider trading is the fact that the action the information is based on is known to be true. If the information is not necessarily going to be true, then the trader is not sure whether he will make a certain profit. A rumor is by definition not known to be true or false at the time of emergence, so trading based on rumors cannot be classified as insider trading. After the trader receives the verified information, he trades in a favorable fashion to make a certain profit.

With price manipulation the sequence of trading and receiving/publishing information is reversed. First, the trader takes a position in the financial market. Then he takes action or publishes information, so that his position will turn out to be favorable for him. Depending on what he does, Allen and Gale (1992) differentiate between action-based manipulation and information-based manipulation.[32] By their definition, action-based manipulation is 'manipulation based on actions that change the actual or perceived value of the assets'.[33] It seems reasonable to assume that only corporate insiders are able to perform action-based price manipulations. Information-based manipulation is defined as 'releasing false information or spreading of false rumors'.[34] This definition does not make a lot of sense. Like many others, Allen and Gale fall for the idea that rumors necessarily turn out to be false. The Emulex case is one where it was clear that information published was false and therefore clearly illegal. The case of Jonathan Lebed (see Section 4.1 'Rumors in financial markets and insider trading') is much less clear. He did not publish or spread any information that was false. Instead he praised the companies he had invested in to the skies, including the spreading of rumors. Does his action fall into information-based manipulation because of this? The answer is: partly. From the total gain of USD 800,000 he had to repay USD 285,000, so just a bit over a third of the total gain. Information-based manipulation, as defined by the SEC, includes the 'spreading of false or misleading information about a company . . . to create a false or deceptive picture of the demand for a security'.[35] So the crucial question to be answered from a regulator's point of view is: when is information misleading so as to create a deceptive picture of a company? Do rumors fall into such a category? No matter if rumors fall into this category, it is more sensible to define information-based manipulation as manipulation based on releasing and spreading *any* kind of information.

Allen and Gale make a third distinction in price manipulation that in their view is much more difficult to eradicate: trade-based manipulation. 'It occurs when a trader attempts to manipulate a stock simply by buying and selling, without taking any publicly observable actions to alter the value of the firm or releasing false information to change the price.'[36] This definition is significantly different from the other two in that there is no action or spreading/publishing of information after the trading. The price movement upon the trading in the past is therefore the only determining factor for price manipulations in the future. Traditional finance scholars would argue that such a strategy cannot be profitable. 'When a trader tries to buy up a stock, he drives up the price. When he tries to sell it, he drives down the price. Thus, any attempt to manipulate the price of a stock by buying and selling requires the trader to buy high and sell low. This is the reverse of what is required to make a profit.'[37]

There follow two examples of rumors and price manipulation.

1. 'And then I first took from Larry ten thousand IBM, so that he believed I was buying. . . . So Larry approached me and asked me if I was up to something, but I was just

cool and spread the rumor that a ground-breaking innovation is becoming apparent. He wanted to know how good the information was and as a proof I bought another ten thousand from him. That was enough. Larry went to the specialist, bought ahead and pushed up the price. Five points further up I started to sell my babies. I made thirty grand on it. Great trade.'[38]

Analysis: Is this kind of behavior illegal? The SEC defines manipulation as '. . . spreading of false or misleading information about a company . . . '.[39] Is the spreading of rumors false or misleading? First, rumors are by definition not false, but their validity is uncertain by nature. Are they misleading? Possibly. Do they 'create a false or deceptive picture of the demand for a security', as written in the definition by the SEC? The answer is a matter of interpretation. Definitely the trader quoted above is operating in a gray zone. There are other important aspects to be addressed from this example:

(i) It makes a difference whether the trader above is the first to spread a rumor or is somewhere along the spreading process when hearing a rumor. If he claims to be the first, then his behavior definitely becomes illegal, since he knows that the rumor is not true. Then his action would be declared as the spreading of false information and therefore illegal. If, though, he claims to be somewhere along the spreading process, he can always refer to an unknown, reliable, credible source that he had heard the rumor from. The transition of position in the line of rumor spreading allows the trader to shift the responsibility and the rumor's credibility to the unknown source and to take him out of the line of legal fire. He will claim that he innocently just had passed on a rumor he had heard and that the rumor's content sounded credible. Therefore there is no way to argue that false information was spread. Secondly, it seems credible to argue that it was not misleading, since the rumor's content is known (ground-breaking innovation) and it is up to the receiver if he believes the rumor or not.

(ii) In comparison to other places, in financial markets the rumor's credibility can be measured directly by the price movement it creates (compare the results of the survey in Section 5.5.1). So when Larry asked the trader about the credibility of the rumor, the trader simply bought another ten thousand IBM, and by that action the credibility was high enough for Larry to buy for himself. So in financial markets the rumor's credibility can be influenced by trading correspondingly, which is quite a unique feature. At the same time it creates a positive feedback effect, since the other participants will have to react to the price movement and take a position for themselves. In the end, the market's reaction is like a 'self-fulfilling prophecy', although the rumor's content is perhaps more than doubtful.

2. On January 19, 2005, the *Wall Street Journal Europe* published a story entitled: 'Fining Analyst for Rumor Sends Wrong Message'.[40] What is the story? On Friday, January 14, 2005, the U.S. National Association of Securities Dealers (NASD) levied a fine of USD 75,000 on Walter Piecyk, an analyst for the independent firm Fulcrum Global Partners for spreading 'sensational negative rumor' about RF Micro Devices. He claimed that RF Micro Devices' largest customer, Nokia, was going to delay equipment from the company and shorted RF Micro Devices stock. Mr Piecyk received the fine, because he 'did not conduct a reasonable inquiry into whether there was a basis for the rumor'.[41] This allegation stands on shaky grounds, since they did not blame him for making up a false rumor and spreading it while knowing it to be wrong. They fined him for circulating

it. The stock fell on the day of the rumor spreading about 5%, despite the company denying it on the same afternoon. The next day, the stock fell another 8% and during the next weeks fell even further. This strongly suggests that investors were generally worried about the company's valuation and not just because of the rumor.

As the *Wall Street Journal Europe* mentions, eye-catching about this incident is that the rumor was negative. Would RF Micro Devices also have complained to the NASD if the rumor were positive? Would the NASD have acted the same for positive though false rumors? Possibly, though companies don't usually angrily deny false rumors that make their shares more valuable.

4.4 REVIEW OF MODELS ON MARKET MANIPULATION

The papers on and models of manipulation are numerous and still growing. Jarrow (1992) shows under what conditions of equilibrium price processes market manipulation strategies are to exist. The answer is shown to depend critically on the properties of the price process as a function of the speculator's trades. The existence of market manipulation trading strategies is then related to the time asymmetry in the sensitivity of the price changes to the speculator's trades.

Allen and Gale (1992) provide in addition to a classification scheme a model of strategic trading in which some equilibria involve manipulation as well. Important to state in this context is that they only consider uninformed traders in comparison to informed traders, which is actually one of the distinguishing characteristics of insider trading. In their model, trade-based manipulation of an uninformed trader is profitable in the presence of certain restrictions on the strategy of the informed trader. Otherwise the manipulation strategy of an uninformed trader is regarded as being unprofitable.

Allen and Gorton (1992) consider a model of pure trade-based uninformed manipulation, in which the price asymmetry of buys and sells of noise traders creates the possibility of manipulation. However, in every equilibrium of their model the uninformed manipulator does not make any profits.

There are a number of models focusing on non-trade-based price manipulations. As an example, Benabou and Laroque (1992) consider an information-based model of price manipulation based on reputation. The manipulator thereby sometimes tells the truth to gain and increase his reputation and sometimes lies to profitably manipulate prices. Bagnoli and Lipman (1996) present a model of action-based manipulation, where the manipulator pools his sources with a market participant, who is able to take action altering the value of the firm. The manipulator initially takes a position, then announces a take-over bid and, while the price rises, unwinds his position to make a profit.

Many other papers examine price manipulations theoretically in a number of different settings. Kumar and Seppi (1992) investigate the vulnerability of futures markets to price manipulation. Gerard and Nanda (1993) examine the potential for manipulation in seasoned equity offerings. Jarrow (1994) studies the impact of the derivatives security markets on market manipulation. Kyle (1984) and Merrick et al. (2004) examine manipulation involving delivery squeezes of future contacts.

Finally, Goldstein and Guembel (2003) show that when prices have an allocational role, there can be opportunities for market manipulation. When prices affect resource allocation, then they also affect the true value of the underlying asset. This feedback of prices to asset values enables an uninformed trader to generate self-fulfilling expectations by selling the asset short. The price impact distorts the asset allocation and reduces the value of the asset even further. The manipulator is able to close out the short position to make a profit. The authors show that this type of manipulation is only possible on the downside. The varieties of allocational implications of buy and sell side speculation are therefore not negligible. Zhou and Mei (2003) demonstrate that smart money can strategically take advantage of investors' behavioral biases and is able to make a profit when manipulating price processes. Other literature related to the latter two are studies by Chakraborty and Yilmaz (2000) and Drudi and Massa (2002). Aggarwal and Wu (2004) study what happens when a manipulator can trade in the presence of other traders who seek out information about a stock's true value. Information seekers buy on information and are the ones who get manipulated by potentially informed parties such as corporate insiders, brokers, underwriters or market markers. The authors empirically test their model using a dataset of the SEC and find the results consistent with their model. They conclude that stock market manipulation may have important impacts on market efficiency and is relevant for securities fraud in general.

5

Survey of Rumors in Financial Markets

Rumor is a pipe blown by surmises, jealousies,
conjectures, and of so easy and so plain a stop
that the blunt monster with uncounted heads,
the still-discordant wavering multitude, can play upon it.

WILLIAM SHAKESPEARE,
from *King Henry the Fourth*, Part II
(Rumor in induction)

5.1 THE SURVEY AND ITS INTENTION

Up until now the first chapters have provided a good overview of various aspects concerning rumors that has been mostly based on theoretical considerations. However, when relating the insights of those chapters to what is actually observed in the marketplace, one probably receives the impression that an essential part of the whole subject is still missing. Still many open questions remain: Why do rumors so often appear in financial markets? Where do they come from and what is their role? How are they interpreted and spread? More questions follow: When are rumors believed in such a context, when are they traded upon and what role do personal networks play? Does it really matter in financial markets whether you trade on verified information or on a rumor? To all those questions the theory presented does not have, or only scarcely has, answers. As a consequence, let's ask the practitioners to find out what they consider important and what they believe deserves further attention to be analyzed. This is the objective of this chapter, to find out from practitioners how rumors evolve, spread and are traded on in financial markets. A survey was considered a good method to achieve the objective set and to provide new insights into the subject based on real observations of practitioners frequently exposed in the marketplace. Since the answers stated are to a certain extent indicative rather than perfectly accurate, a degree of caution should be maintained. For that reason the results of the survey are used as a basis for rumor experiments conducted and discussed in Chapter 6.

5.2 PARTICIPANT PROFILE

5.2.1 Survey Parameters

To assess the professionals' current practice towards rumors in financial markets, over 200 professionals in the field were surveyed in the spring of 2003. Two methods were used to access both quantitative and qualitative data – an online survey and personal interviews. The online survey was sent by e-mail to professional traders and sales people dealing with all asset classes (stocks, bonds, FX and commodities) and financial instruments including derivatives.

Personal interviews were held with selected traders and sales people. All participants were asked questions on the following topics:

- *Development of rumors:* How do rumors evolve and what is their origin?
- *Spreading of rumors:* Why do rumors spread and how long does it take for the entire trader community to know them?
- *Belief in rumors:* How do you determine if the market believes the rumor? How does that correspond with your own judgment? Do you actually know the probability of the rumor being true and do you care?
- *Network formation:* When rumors spread, do information networks evolve? How important are these networks for you to stay on top of the news flow?
- *Trading on rumors:* Do systematic price patterns evolve and if so, how can you profit from them?
- *Rumors vs. information:* In financial markets, what is the difference between rumors and information? Do you trade differently on rumors than on information, and if so, why?

In addition, those participants interviewed were asked their perception and views on rumors. Had they seen any trends lately when dealing with rumors? The qualitative data are incorporated throughout this chapter. For reasons of confidentiality, individuals or institutions they represent are not disclosed. Moreover, it must be stressed that the quantitative data of this report are 'indicative' rather than 'representative'.

5.2.2 Survey Participants

The online survey was sent to over 200 professionals in regional, private, and investment banks. In addition, several interviews were held with selected traders and sales people who are faced with rumors in financial markets on a frequent basis; Some 141 answers were received. This represents an answer rate of almost 70%. Some 91% of respondents were male, reflecting the current status in the business. Participants in the study included professionals from institutions of all sizes (Figure 5.1). As can be seen from Figure 5.2 the participants on average have a considerable amount of working experience in their profession. Most of the participants work in their profession either as traders or sales people (Figure 5.3). The distinction between traders and non-traders is important for the analysis of further results.

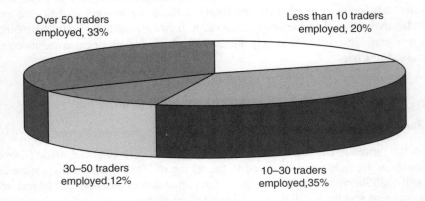

Figure 5.1 Number of traders employed at your branch

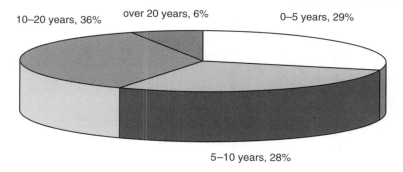

Figure 5.2 Years of working experience in the profession

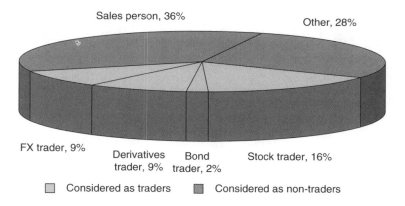

Figure 5.3 What is your profession? Among the many 'other' professions are investment advisors, portfolio managers and strategists.

5.3 DEVELOPMENT OF RUMORS

5.3.1 How Rumors Start and Why

The public is always very keen to determine the source of rumor and why it evolves. The search for the source usually takes high priority, since still many believe the rumor to be provoked on purpose. This view of the world is on the one hand comfortable and on the other useful at the same time. Imagination starts to blossom and a fantasy world of conspiracy, manipulation and disinformation as in the best of movies is able to develop. A rumor is said to be useful, as it can be used as proof for a negative incident or development and to repress the emergence of rumors of all kinds. While it is argued that in most cases a rumor is a spontaneous social product following no purpose or strategy, what do the participants of the survey believe? (See Figure 5.4.).

Some participants follow the mystery path (one can make money on it) and others follow the spontaneous path (there is no reason, it just happens). The answer of all respondents 'because it's in their interest' received the highest percentage. Daniel Vasella, CEO of the large pharmaceutical company Novartis, made an interesting comment in this regard in a newspaper interview: 'Rumors are selectively being used by certain banking circles for their

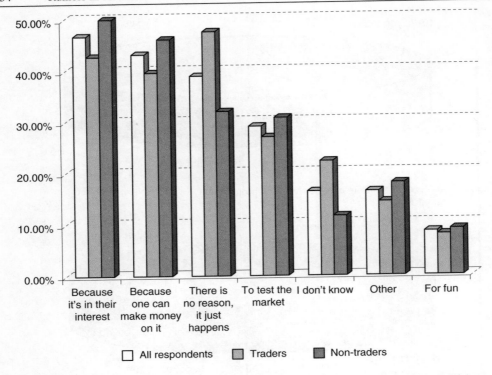

Figure 5.4   Answer to the question: Why does a rumor evolve? (Several answers are possible)

own purposes. The earlier they are launched, the more they have a function as a bellows. If the rumors appear only in the end, then the sole purpose is to move the price or the exchange ratio in the direction desired.'[1] An astonishingly high number of participants marked 'because one can make money on it'. If that were true, everyone would create and spread as many rumors as possible to make money. This is definitely not what is observed in the market (Figure 5.5).

Traders as well as non-traders on average receive rumors of professional relevance 'a few times a week'. It is logical that traders receive on average rumors more often than others. To systematically make money, the frequency of rumors would have to be much higher. There is a contradiction to the argument of systematically making money. Traders recognize the contradiction themselves and state, 'there is no reason, it just happens'. This answer from traders received the highest percentage and is clearly higher than that of non-traders (48% vs. 32%, see Figure 5.4).

In spite of this, many traders believe there is a magic force behind a rumor leading to systematic profits. This is amazing. Interestingly enough, six traders marked 'because one can make money on it' as well as 'there is no reason, it just happens'. Their beliefs are contradictory. Although they believe rumors evolve spontaneously, they also believe that there is something mysterious about them and that money can be made.

When people hear rumors in financial markets, how do they receive them? Oral communication and information services are the most common form of receiving rumors. The

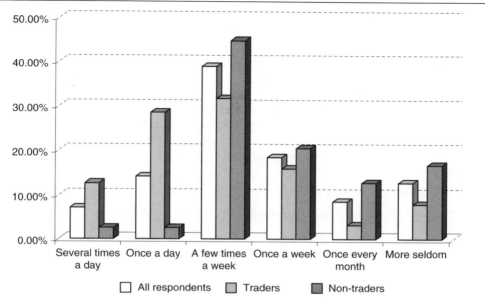

Figure 5.5 Frequency of hearing a rumor of professional relevance

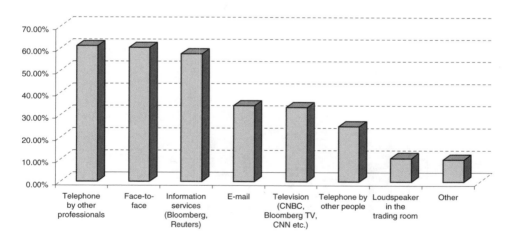

Figure 5.6 Means of communicating rumors. (Several answers possible)

bar chart (Figure 5.6) shows the answer of all respondents only because they are essentially independent of the participant's profession. Typically one receives a phone call from another professional saying something like, 'I have heard from another fellow that company XY may release a profit warning.' Or, the Bloomberg news ticker reports, 'According to industry sources, company ABC may have to raise new equity capital.' Characteristic of such rumors is the fact that the source is never explicitly named. To enhance the credibility of the rumor the term 'well informed' is frequently added. With such a formulation it becomes clear that someone is interested that the rumor should be believed. Though it is actually astonishing how many times you can read in newspaper 'due to takeover rumors the stock price of company XYZ has gained so and so much for day', because there is no other news to explain the price movement. One sales person interviewed mentioned: 'People don't want price movements to be left unexplained, so they either have to invent something, or they will look for a rumor. In hindsight everything has to make sense or has to be at least explainable. I have to make up a story when a client calls and asks me for advice on a certain stock. I can't tell him that I don't have clue why the stock price has fallen or risen.' What is almost more astonishing though, is that when rumors appear, hardly anyone will ever perform additional research to assess or verify the rumor. It is then simply regarded as a given – end of story.

5.3.2 Correlation between Market Volatility and Frequency of Rumors

It is sometimes claimed that in volatile markets the market participants are confronted with more uncertain news such as rumors. Possibly the volatile price movements themselves trigger speculation and rumor evolvement in the market. The participants answer the question, 'Do you hear more rumors in volatile markets?' as shown in Figure 5.7. What stands out is that the participants definitely hear more rumors in volatile markets. Thus the intuitive response of most people, 'I hear more rumors in volatile markets', seems to be true. This leads to another question: Is the volatility the cause and the rumor the effect or vice versa? One opinion is that rumors are the trigger for volatile markets while others would argue that volatile markets are the cause for the evolvement of rumors. The answer to this question is clear-cut only in very few cases and is to a large part a matter of perception. One trader said: 'With a few exceptions it is very difficult to exactly say why what happened. When markets

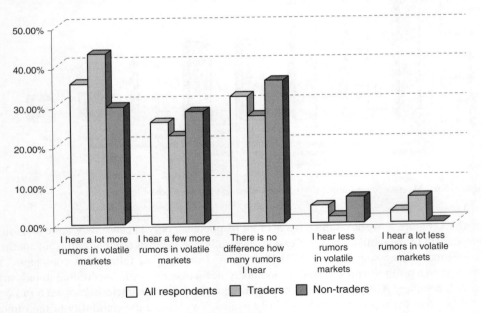

Figure 5.7 Frequency of rumors and market volatility

get nervous and volatility rises, everyone is desperate for news. The price movement itself then sometimes is "news" enough so that people start talking and rumors start to evolve. In my opinion, two things have to be separated. The first scenario is that a rumor evolves and the price starts to move. In this case, the news was clearly first. But then there is the second scenario where the wild price movements trigger the news. So there is no single answer to what comes first.'

5.3.3   What Is the Source?

The search for the hidden, strategic operating source survives, persistently allowing the public to justify believing a 'false' rumor. Not having to admit that one was wrong is an easy way out. The source is then blamed as having deceived the public. The public and the market participants in particular are able to shrug off their true responsibility. Innumerable signals and messages are sent by innumerable potential sources without having any effect on the traded prices. Only when traded prices move is the question of source raised. It is therefore not of great significance. On the contrary, much more important is to find an answer to the question of what are the factors that trigger a corresponding price movement. Therefore all the excitement and commotion going on is a result not of the source, but of what the public makes of it.

Since the public is very interested in the source of the rumor, participants were asked, 'How often do you know the source of the rumor?' The results are intriguing (Figure 5.8). There is a clear distinction between the distribution of answers of traders and non-traders. In addition, non-traders claim more often than traders that they know the source of the rumor. This is surprising. Traders are closer to the market and should know the source more often than non-traders. One may conclude that non-traders overstate their belief in knowing the source of the rumor, which is a sign of overconfidence. This basically doesn't matter since

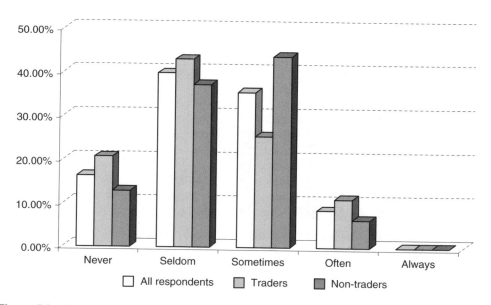

Figure 5.8 Frequency of knowing the source of the rumor

the source itself is not a relevant feature. Nevertheless, it's interesting to note that the source of rumors is assessed quite differently among the various professionals. One investment advisor pointed out: 'These messages when a rumor is mentioned all sound very similar, they all refer to well-informed industry or market source, which you have no clue about what to think of. Therefore the medium that publishes the rumor takes over the credibility for the source behind it. That's why I trust a message from the *Wall Street Journal* a lot more than an unknown internet source.'

5.3.4 First Actions on a Rumor

What do people do first when they hear a rumor? Over 50% of all respondents state that 'they watch and see if the price moves' (see Figure 5.9). The price movement is the leading indicator of the market regarding the rumor as significant. The answer 'calling and asking other people' is highly favored and stated by over 66% of all respondents. One has to keep in mind that traders desperately seek views supporting their own. On the other hand only a small minority (18%) admit that they spread the rumor. Where exactly is the difference between spreading a rumor and calling or asking other people what they think of it? Certainly that is a form of spreading the rumor as well. It is likely that many people fear admitting they spread rumors because there might be something objectionable to it.

One trader commented on his action strategy as follows: 'There are two factors that make me think about taking action on a rumor: If can tell anything about the source, that's good, but not a precondition. The more recognized the medium is that comes out with the message, the better. Though the second factor is more important. The people have to think that this message is a good story, that it has news value, meaning there has to be something new, refreshing in it. That's what people are looking for and are spontaneously willing to bet on it. If the same rumor is heard all over again, it gets to be boring and not much will happen. Then I watch and see if the price moves and look at the traded volume, that is important. That's when I go for it. I have sometimes been lucky, sometimes not.'

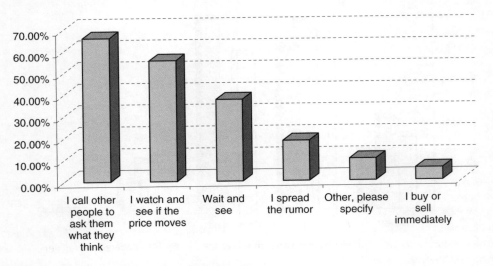

Figure 5.9 First actions on a rumor. (Several answers possible)

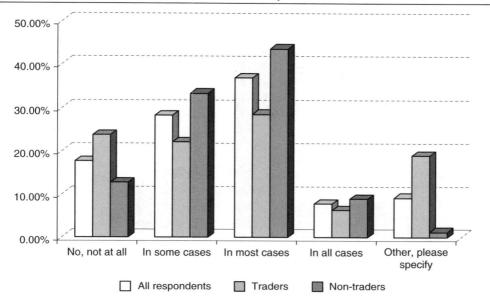

Figure 5.10   Answer to the question: Is the market reaction more sensitive to *specific* than to *general* rumors?

5.3.5   Action on Specific versus General Rumors

This section analyzes the reaction of the market to specific versus general types of rumors. The classification of *general* vs. *specific* rumors follows the same definition as in Section 3.1.7 'Classification of rumors in financial markets'.

The answers to the question, 'Is the market reaction more sensitive to *specific* than to *general* rumors?', provide interesting results (Figure 5.10). While non-traders in general react often in a more sensitive way to specific rumors, the same doesn't hold for traders. The frequency of the first three possible answers 'no, not at all', 'in some cases' and 'in most cases' among traders is almost equal. Furthermore, many traders responded with 'other, please specify'. These traders don't consider the classification of *specific* versus *general* as a differentiating factor. They rather focus on 'depends on the potential impact' of the rumor. That supports the view that traders are only interested in the price impact of the rumor and nothing else.

5.4   SPREADING OF RUMORS

5.4.1   To Spread or Not to Spread?

The participants were asked if they spread a rumor and, if yes, why or under what circumstances. Their answers are shown in Figure 5.11. On average over 60% of the participants admit that they spread the rumor either in any case or at least when they believed that it was significant. Independent of profession, about 20% don't spread the rumor in any case. Among the 'depends' answers there were many statements like, 'Only if I can verify it to a reasonable degree or when I need help verifying it', or, 'I only tell the rumors in-house'. It is reasonable to assume that most market participants spread the rumor in some form.

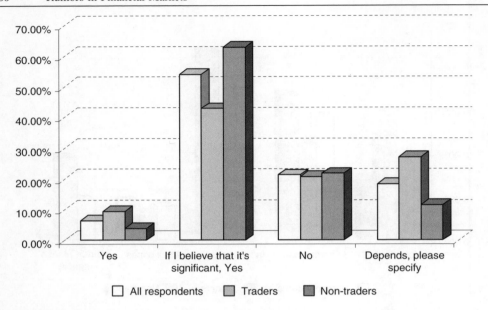

Figure 5.11 Answer to the question: Are rumors spread when they are heard?

However, they restrict themselves either to a significant rumor or to a limited audience so as not to be heavily exposed. A trader commented as follows: 'It's important to have your personal network out there. If I am unsure what to think, what I should believe, and not quite happy what I hear in-house, then I call up trustworthy contacts and ask them about it, but not other people.'

5.4.2 First or Last in the Row?

It's extremely important for participants in financial markets to be on top of the news flow. If they receive relevant information ahead of other participants, they have a good chance of turning this headstart into real money profits. Regarding rumors, this conclusion is not necessarily valid. The individual can't be sure of how the market will react to the rumor. Nevertheless, if one is on top of the news flow, one is able to participate in and influence the development process of the rumor. The first ones to hear the rumor therefore have a better chance of anticipating the market reaction to the rumor. How do the participants rank themselves in the order of hearing a rumor in the financial market? Are they overconfident in believing that they are always on top of the news flow? Figure 5.12 shows the answers to these questions.

The results provide interesting insights into the self-estimation of the participants. The answers of all respondents are astonishingly symmetrically distributed around the mean 'about in the middle'. Therefore it can't be presumed in general that they overestimate their ranking in the order of hearing a rumor. However, as the results are split between traders and non-traders they look a bit different.

A far higher percentage of traders (28%), in comparison to 10% of non-traders, believe that they are 'one of the first' to hear a rumor. Only 11% of traders, in comparison to 24%

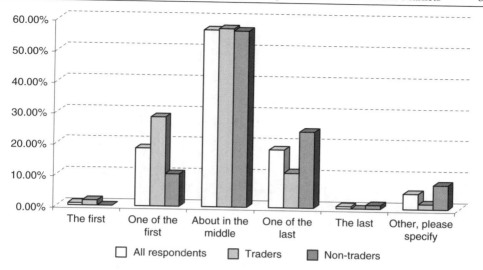

Figure 5.12   Answer to the question: Are you thought to be one of the first or last to hear a rumor?

of non-traders, say that they are 'one of the last'. This leads to the possibility of a certain degree of self-overestimation among traders. An alternative explanation is that traders are actually 'one of the first' and non-traders 'one of the last', which indeed could be true. While one interviewed sales person mentioned, 'I always have the feeling as if I'm one of the last', another trader claimed, 'If as a trader you're not one of the first, you're simply a loser.' One respondent actually claimed he was 'the first'. The interpretation of this statement is to each his own.

   An important question with regard to being 'one of the first' or 'one of the last' is how long it takes for the rumor to be known by the entire trader community. A considerable length of time for a rumor to reach the whole trading community leads to information asymmetries among the market participants. If, however, the rumor is spread to all participants at high speed, this won't lead to information asymmetries, but to information processing asymmetries. All the participants receive the information at the same time but they process it in a different way. This statement holds, however, for any kind of news, whether it's a confirmed piece of information or 'just' a rumor.

5.4.3   Spreading Time: How Long it Takes

Over 70% of traders state that within minutes the rumor is known within the entire trader community, while only 41% of non-traders state the same (Figure 5.13). The analysis of the answers leads to the conclusion that traders are closer to the market than non-traders (Figure 5.14). Second, rumors appear to spread at high speed through the trading community. This is fully in line with a statement from an interviewee that, 'All of a sudden there is rumor around and everyone knows about it. I don't know exactly where it came from, but that doesn't matter really.'

   It is easy to understand that rumors spread very quickly in financial markets. Time is crucial. The results from this question are consistent with the statement that many participants receive the rumors from the media, such as information services or television. Since everyone

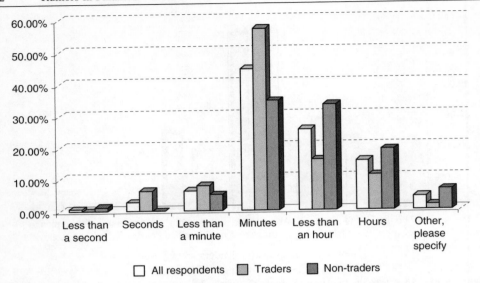

Figure 5.13 Answer to the question: How long does it take for the entire trader community to know about a rumor?

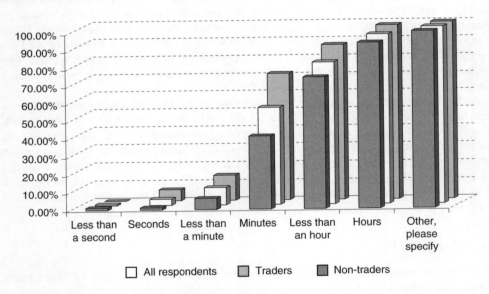

Figure 5.14 Cumulative distribution of Figure 5.13

follows the same television stations and has the same information service providers, they all receive the rumor at the same time. This is probably not the case for all evolving rumors but certainly for a good part of them. If it only takes minutes or less to let a rumor spread within the entire community, this implies rumors don't create any information asymmetries among the participants. As with verified information, only information processing asymmetries are caused by the rumor. However, these different interpretations have to be adjusted depending on the market's belief and the traded price of the asset. The following section shows the exact relationship between the belief in the rumor and its traded price.

5.5 BELIEF IN RUMORS

5.5.1 Why Rumors are Believed

The participants were asked what factors are important to them in believing a rumor. Figure 5.15 shows the determining factors for the survey participants' belief in a rumor. Consistent with the available evidence, the participants indicate 'the person or source one hears the rumor from' to be the greatest determining factor (over 50% of all respondents) for believing a rumor. Another determining factor indicated by over 40% of the participants is 'if the price moves on the rumor'. The price movement is an indicator of the belief of all participants in financial markets and is an expression of the reaction of the market as a whole. It can be viewed as the combination of plausibility and desirability of the news. Over 30% of the traders state that they don't care 'if the rumor is going to be true'. This is a clear indication that to those people it doesn't matter what happens to the rumor as such. It is important is not what the person believes but only how the market values it. Their attitude towards the credibility of the rumor is neutral in that their opinion doesn't count. Only the one who can anticipate the market's belief in the rumor can make money on it. A classic statement from interviewees to that question was: 'If I want to be longer-term invested in that security, I better want to know very much what the chances are of the rumor becoming true or not. However, if I am a short-term investor just interested in a quick profit, I don't care at all what happens in the end.' Figure 5.16 shows the relationship between the belief of the market and price movement.

Figure 5.15 Determining factors for a person's belief in a rumor. (Several answers possible)

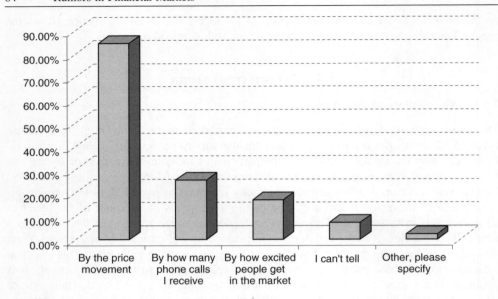

Figure 5.16   Determining factors for the market's belief in a rumor. (Several answers possible)

The results show how strong evidence of the price movement is the determining factor for market belief. Almost 85% of all respondents say 'the price movement' indicates the market's belief. 'By how many phone calls I receive' is mentioned by 25% of the respondents, all other answers receive noticeably less than 20% of the responses.

The results clearly lead to one conclusion: The market can be viewed as a 'Keynes beauty contest':

> professional investment may be likened to those newspaper competitions in which the competitors have to pick out the six prettiest faces from a hundred photographs, the prize being awarded to the competitor whose choice most nearly corresponds to the average preferences of the competitors as a whole; so that each competitor has to pick, not those faces which he himself finds prettiest, but those which he thinks likeliest to catch the fancy of the other competitors, all of whom are looking at the problem from the same point of view. It's not a case of choosing those which, to the best of one's judgment, are really the prettiest, nor even those which average opinion genuinely thinks the prettiest. We have reached the third degree where we devote our intelligences to anticipating what average opinion expects the average opinion to be. And there are some, I believe, who practice the fourth, fifth and higher degrees.[2]

As a result, the only thing that really counts is the anticipation of the other market participants' expectations. The consequence is an infinite regression of the interpretation of the validity of a rumor as well as information processing. So from that perspective, are rumors any different from verified information?

The following quotation describes the situation nicely: 'Ninety percent of what we do is based on perception. It doesn't matter if that perception is right or wrong or real. It only matters that other people in the market believe it. I may know it's crazy, I may think it's wrong. But I lose my shirt by ignoring it.'[3]

5.5.2   Does it Matter What You Believe?

If the market can be viewed as a Keynes beauty contest, the following question is crucial: How difficult is it to estimate the average belief of other market participants? As a basis for the estimate of this average belief is the participant's own personal belief. The question therefore arises, how difficult it is for the individual to estimate the rumor's validity.

The results (Figure 5.17) lead to the conclusion that the participants 'sometimes' are able to estimate the rumor's validity. Therefore it should 'sometimes' be possible to estimate the average market belief. Figure 5.17 also shows that over 20% of traders don't care whether the rumor becomes true (this agrees well with the data of Figure 5.15).

It is quite likely that a number of participants overestimate their ability to predict the rumor's validity. If that were true, then the true distribution would be even more shifted to the right. Because of the difficulty of estimating a rumor's validity, most people simply look at the price movement as the indicator of the average market belief.

Does it really matter if the rumor is going to become true in the end? Why should one care? Is there any personal involvement? One is only personally involved if one has traded upon the rumor and real money profits are one of the consequences. Therefore it shouldn't matter in the end if the rumor becomes true. A portfolio manager commented on that question as follows: 'Sometimes it's almost like a game for me. When a rumor evolves, I just for fun write down spontaneously what I think of it. Will it become true or not? My judgment has gotten a bit better over time, though that's maybe mainly due to the fact that most rumors have turned out to be false in the end and I have biased my opinion in that direction.'

The responses to the question, 'Do you care in the end if the rumor becomes true?' show an astonishingly high percentage answering 'yes' (over 35%) (Figure 5.18). Why is this the case? The only reasonable explanation is a feeling of responsibility or a personal relationship towards the rumor. For those participants who trade on rumors it is understandable that they

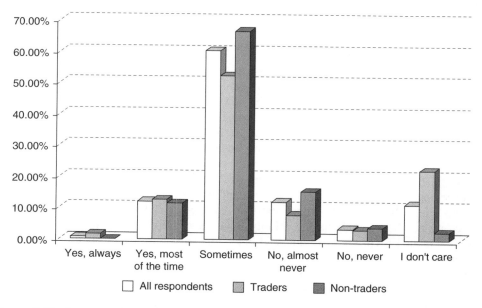

Figure 5.17   Answer to the question: How often can you predict that the rumor is going to be true?

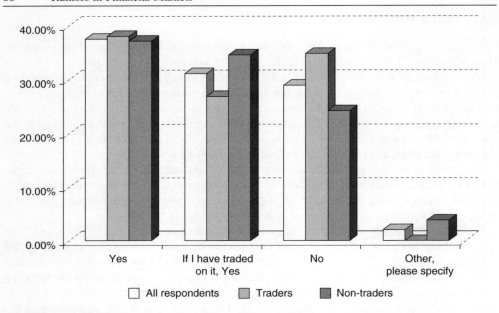

Figure 5.18   Answer to the question: Do you care in the end if the rumor becomes true?

care whether the rumor becomes true. However, it is important to know that many positions generated from trades on rumors are not held until the verification of the rumor. These are speculative positions for money profits based on the short-term price development of the asset. In addition to the respondents answering 'no', the traders mentioned above would not have to care about the verification of the rumor as well.

5.6   NETWORK FORMATION

Personal networks are an important tool for traders. They help to build beliefs, to confirm views from other traders, to exchange news or simply to chat. They can deliver first-hand information, keeping one at the edge of the news flow. The same holds for rumors. How important are information networks when it comes to rumors in financial markets? Can one make systematic profits from them? In order to build up information networks one has to find those persons providing and exchanging valuable information.

Over 70% of the participants keep track of the person who has provided them with rumors (Figure 5.19). This is an important requirement for the formation of information networks. Not everyone will tell you rumors nor will you tell rumors to everyone you know. The people forming information networks know and trust each other and have a closer relationship to each other. These people have a priority status. Because of this close relationship, one expects a mutual exchange of rumors and other first-hand information. Is this observed in the market?

The answers to this question (Figure 5.20) provide clear results. The difference between the 'yes' and 'no' answers among traders and non-traders is very pronounced (70% 'yes' vs. 30% 'no' among traders, 33% 'yes' vs. 61% 'no' among non-traders). This is a clear indication that traders build information networks in comparison to non-traders. Traders

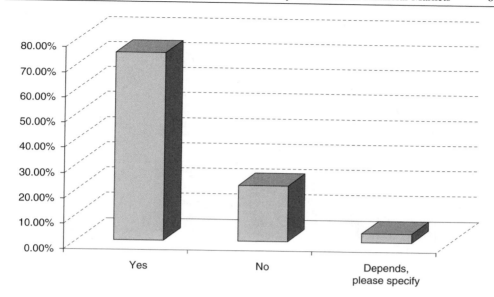

Figure 5.19   Answer to the question: Do you keep in mind which information sources have provided you with rumors?

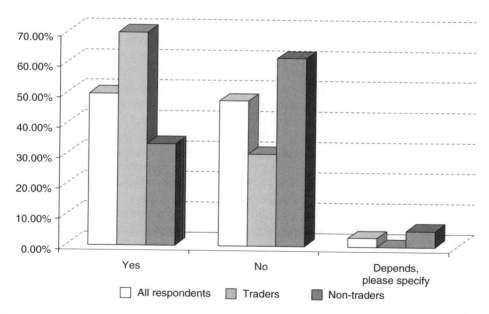

Figure 5.20   Answer to the question: Do you spread a rumor to priority people – hoping they will do the same?

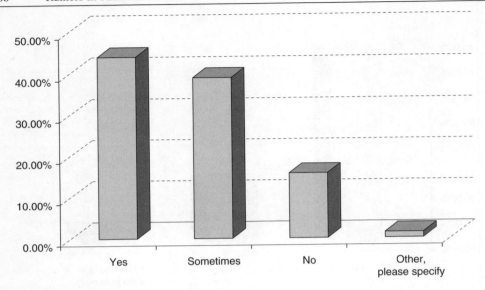

Figure 5.21   Answer to the question: Do information networks evolve such that for a while a group of traders knows more than others?

regard them as important. One person interviewed mentioned, 'This feature is one of the most important ones when dealing with rumors in financial markets. The verification of one's own opinion with that of other people you trust is absolutely crucial.' This is a strong issue among traders, but not among non-traders. The other explanation for the non-traders' response is that they verify their opinion in other ways. However, this is not regarded as very likely.

The most important question with regards to information networks is whether their members know more than others (Figure 5.21). Second, can they profit from them? Over 40% of all respondents state 'for a while a group of traders know more than others' and nearly 40% state 'sometimes'. These statements have to be judged cautiously. In Figure 5.14 over 70% of traders claim 'that within minutes the entire trader community knows about the rumor'. If a headstart actually exists, according to the respondents, it can last only a few seconds, or up to minutes. Making systematic profits from this is questionable. More realistically, the results show some participants may know more than others for a short period of time. The thought of a few mysterious, strategic traders may have shifted the distribution more to the left than in reality. One sales person interviewed commented on the question: 'Of course you have your own personal networks that you use and you are very grateful for. This network can indeed be of great value. However, there many others like us out there, and you don't know what they know. In addition, with today's information economy, information spreads so fast and is almost instantaneously available all over the globe, if an information advantage exists, then only for a very short period of time. Otherwise one would have to assume that the others operate very close to insider trading.' The conclusion concerning information networks is the following: they help the participants confirm their views but they don't guarantee higher profits.

5.7   TRADING ON RUMORS

5.7.1   Systematic Price Patterns?

The question that interests traders most is whether one can systematically make money on rumors. Does a secret formula exist to determine the point in time for getting in and getting out of the market? It is argued, that this is not the case and the price movements from rumors are very similar, if not identical, to those of other news. Do the participants agree with this statement? (See Figure 5.22.) There are several issues to be addressed from the answers. Over 35% of the traders state there exist no systematic price patterns when rumors evolve. Furthermore, over 20% of the traders say 'the price moves immediately to the new anticipated price'. In that case the market would be completely efficient and no systematic profits would be possible. More non-traders than traders say the price moves with swings to the new anticipated level. A fact to be recognized is that swings can occur from reactions to news with high information content as well. When a company releases its annual statement (an event with high information content), high-volume trading is usually observed, combined with corresponding price swings. This is not due to participants receiving information different from that of other participants but due to different or asymmetrical interpretation. It is the asymmetrical information interpretation that causes the corresponding trading behavior leading to high traded volume and price changes. Rumors are in that sense no different from information. It is a rather daring assumption to assume that systematic profits can be made from such price movements.

5.7.2   Rumor Sources and Profits

Can at least the creator of the rumor profit, even though no systematic price patterns evolve? This question is again one to test the belief in the mysterious and strategic operating source

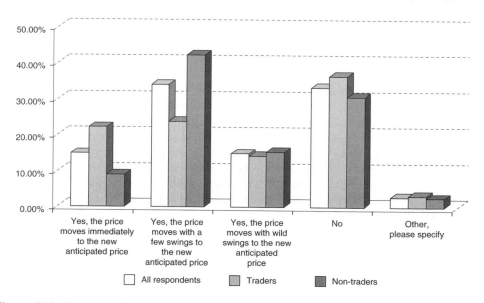

Figure 5.22   Answer to the question: Do systematic price patterns exist when rumors evolve?

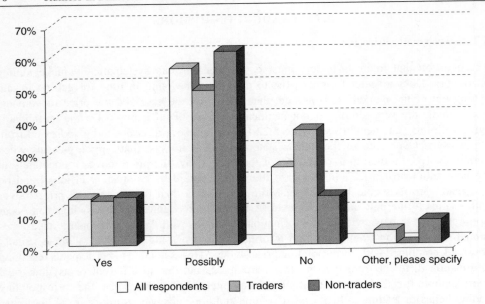

Figure 5.23 Answer to the question: Can the person who has created the rumor profit from it systematically?

able to achieve risk-free profits. Because the impact of the rumor can be assessed only by the people spreading it, not by the source alone, it is argued there is no way for the source to profit systematically. How do the participants assess the same question?

The results (Figure 5.23) are revealing since once more the answers of the traders and non-traders show clear differences. Among all respondents 70% claim the source is, at least possibly, able to profit systematically from the rumor. Yet at the same time many more traders than non-traders believe this is not possible (37% vs. 15%). The idea of the mysterious, strategic source survives persistently in people's minds. It seems, though, that traders have a more sophisticated view. The source cannot foresee the reaction of the market to the rumor. Out of one hundred initiated messages perhaps five will trigger the creation of a rumor. To know which of the five messages and how the market will react to them is impossible. Of course it is always possible to find an *ex post* explanation for a price movement. André Kostolany (1998) has described the situation as follows: 'The news doesn't determine the prices but the prices the news. At the end of the day every market participant looks for arguments to explain a price movement, and that with arguments which he wouldn't have dreamt of two hours ago!'[4] Of course, there exist factors advantageous to the spreading and belief of a rumor. However, to conclude that the source is able to profit from it *systematically* is highly improbable. The people interviewed were asked what their trading strategy would be for making systematic profits as the creator of a rumor. They all answered in the same fashion: 'I have no idea what kind of trading strategy I would have to follow!'

5.7.3 Thoughts Triggered by the Price Movement

What happens first in the participants' minds when they see something going on in the market? Is the view confirmed that people think the price movement is the determining

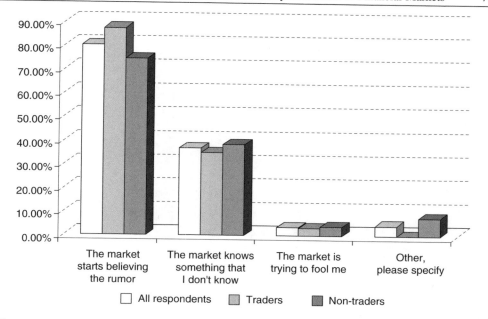

Figure 5.24 Answer to the question: What are your thoughts when the price moves on a rumor? (Several answers possible)

factor for the market's belief in the rumor? See Figure 5.24 for the response to this question. As in Figure 5.16, about 80% of all respondents state 'the market is starting to believe the rumor' when the price moves on it. This is a full confirmation of the results seen so far in this report. It is interesting to note that 35% (traders included) state, 'the market knows something that I don't know'. How can this high percentage be explained? A possible explanation is that these participants feel left out of the spreading process. It is this worrying feeling that others possibly know more than oneself. Figure 5.25 shows the frequency of answers to the question 'Are you thought of as being one of the first or last to hear a rumor?' for the subgroup giving the answer 'the market knows something I don't know'.

Figure 5.25 shows a correlation between those participants believing they are 'about in the middle' or 'one of the last' and those tending to believe 'the market knows something I don't know' (in both cases over 40%, 79 and 25 samples). Very few participants stating they are 'one of the first' to hear a rumor (15%) also believe 'the market knows something I don't know'. The categories 'the first' and 'the last' can be ignored since there is only one response in each case. What kind of conclusions can be drawn from this? Either the participants who believe they hear the rumor first are better informed (which is conceivable but not very plausible) or they exhibit more self-confidence. Why would 35% of the traders claim 'the market knows something that they don't know'? It obviously reflects their feeling and their lack of self-confidence. By considering themselves to be in the middle or late in hearing a rumor they think they miss something when the price moves. As shown, this does not have to be the case. If they are connected to various information services and have a well-established personal network, there is no reason for them not to be on top of the news flow.

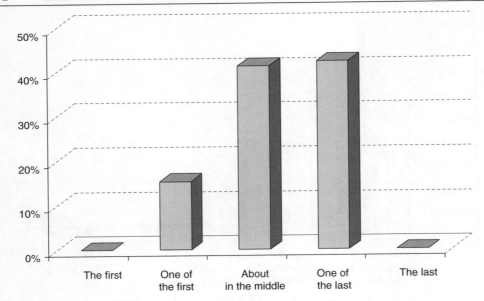

Figure 5.25 Frequency of answers to the question: 'Are you thought of as being one of the first or last to hear a rumor?' for the subgroup giving the answer 'the market knows something I don't know'

5.7.4 Actions Triggered by the Price Movement

What the participants think is one thing, but what do they really do when they see the price moving? People are judged by their actions and not by their words.

The results from the question, 'What are your actions when the price moves on a rumor?', are intriguing: 75% of all traders testify they either 'surely' will or 'might' trade on the rumor, while only 40% of non-traders answer the same (Figure 5.26). Traders show strong signs of herd behavior. They jump on the bandwagon. Even though the price has already moved, they still believe they can make profits from buying. This is a classical form of herd behavior leading to short-term momentum, excess volatility and long-term reversal. This is a frequently observed phenomenon in financial markets. Jumping on the bandwagon works as long as there are more participants pushing the price further up. This behavior creates a trend, signaling the market's belief in the rumor. Whether all the participants trading the asset actually believe the rumor to be true is another question.

How can herd behavior be explained? Herd behavior doesn't have to be an irrational behavior as long as the market participant's expectation is to find another participant buying it for a higher price. The participant has to be aware of the risk involved. A risky behavior does not necessarily imply an irrational behavior. If a rational action is defined as an utility-maximizing Bayesian action in an efficient market, this kind of behavior would be classified as irrational. If, though, an alternative definition of rationality is used, e.g. bounded or procedural rationality, it would not necessarily have to be classified as irrational.

It is sometimes argued in the scientific literature that irrational traders should be driven out of the market because they permanently lose money. This does not have to be case. If so-called irrational traders are overconfident of their ability to forecast the future risk–return profile of an asset, it means they underestimate its risk. If they underestimate its risk, they

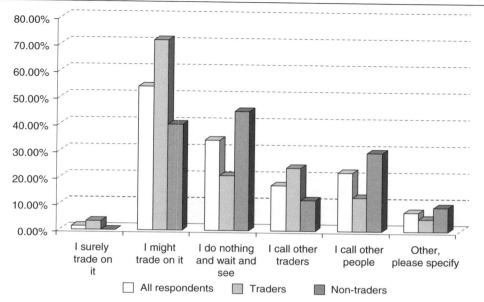

Figure 5.26 Answer to the question: What are your actions when the price moves on a rumor? (Several answers possible)

still are compensated for the true risk taken and earn the corresponding rate of return. So from this perspective it can't be argued that irrational traders should be driven out of market.

The answers received indicate that non-traders are not willing to take the same amount of risk as traders. Considerably more non-traders than traders either do 'nothing and wait and see' or 'call other people'. Nevertheless about 40% of non-traders might trade on the rumor. They seem to be a bit more cautious when trading on a rumor yet are subject to herd behavior as well.

5.8 RUMORS VERSUS INFORMATION

5.8.1 Trading on Rumors versus Trading on Information

The results in this report indicate that trading on rumors versus trading on information should not greatly differ from each other. The participants view this issue differently (Figure 5.27). Over 80% of all respondents answered that they trade differently on rumors than on verified information. Several of those interviewed confirmed the participants' view that they trade differently on rumors in comparison to information. Their explanation is that rumors are usually short-lived and therefore are traded on for much shorter time spans than information. Rumors are good for short-term profits but not regarded as a good basis for long-term investments. Long-term investors rather wait until the rumor is either confirmed or denied by an official source.

Some persons interviewed stated that on principle they never trade on rumors. Why? What is there to rumors that people don't trade on them? Where exactly is the difference between trading on a rumor and trading on verified information? True, a rumor is an unconfirmed piece of news and one could therefore argue there is more uncertainty involved than when trading on information. This fact alone doesn't justify the attitude of not trading at all on

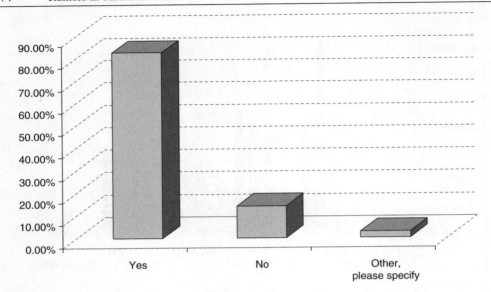

Figure 5.27   Answer to the question: Do you trade differently on rumors than on information?

rumors. There has to be something morally unacceptable or a matter of attitude which keeps people from trading on rumors.

5.8.2   The Difference between a Rumor and Information

If, as in Figure 5.27, rumors are differently traded on than information, how do the participants view rumors differently from information? This question was asked last in order to prevent a bias on answers to further questions.

The participants' opinion is clear (Figure 5.28); 70% of the respondents indicate 'in com-

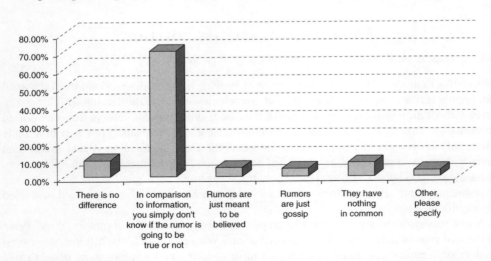

Figure 5.28   Answer to the question: How do you view rumors differently from information for your professional work?

parison to information one simply doesn't know if the rumor is going to be true'. The answers with the next lower percentages are 'there is no difference' with 9% and 'they have nothing in common' with 8%. If what the participants state with regard to their professional work is true, rumors differ from information only in the degree of uncertainty since the level of truth is unknown. Apart from this uncertainty they should not be treated differently. However, the results shown in Figure 5.27 indicate this is not the case. The participants contradict themselves in that they don't act on rumors as if they are just unconfirmed information, but on the mystique of a strategic operating source. Possibly it is time for the actors to take a break and rethink their perception of a rumor. Rosnow and Kimmel (2000) define it as 'an unverified proposition for belief that bears topical relevance for persons actively involved in its dissemination'.[5]

5.9   CONCLUSIONS FROM THE SURVEY

5.9.1   Rumors Follow Logical Rules

Rumors are in no way mysterious or even magical, as many people in financial markets still believe. They follow strong logical rules to be analyzed in detail. Financial markets are a fruitful ground for rumors. This is due to the fact that in such environments a limited number of people, all experts in the field, have to make risky decisions under constant stress and anxiety, while being flooded with news.

These circumstances make financial markets extremely 'vulnerable' to the emergence of rumors. Since rumors are the oldest mass medium in the world, there will be rumors wherever there are financial markets. Many people immediately show a negative reaction when hearing the word rumor. They consider rumors to be something dangerous, difficult to comprehend or even evil and as such they should be banned. This view is not supported. A detailed analysis during the early phase of a rumor permits insight into and better understanding of its specific characteristics.

Rumors do not appear without any reason. There is always something in the background, which can be an event, a detail or pure fantasy. It can be processed spontaneously or deliberately provoked. The source is not as important as many believe. Crucial for the spreading and the impact of the rumor is what the public makes of it.

Although for many people the question of source is the most interesting and often an intriguing question, from a scientific point of view it is not. The idea of a hidden, strategic operating source of a rumor survives persistently and permits the public to justify believing a 'false' rumor. The source can be blamed for everything and the responsibility for its creation can be shrugged off completely. It is argued that the evaluation of the rumor's source in financial markets is almost impossible. The answers given by traders largely confirm this view, while non-traders on average claim to know the source of the rumor more often. This leads to the conclusion that non-traders are highly overconfident concerning their capability of evaluating the source of a rumor.

Rumors in financial markets evolve most often spontaneously and without any intended reason, although many participants think otherwise. They are heard on average a few times a week through media like information services, e-mail or television, or orally by telephone or face-to-face. The intuition of many market participants that the frequency of rumors is considerably higher in volatile than in non-volatile markets, is confirmed. This phenomenon is easily explained by the desire to receive additional news in uncertain times, even if it is less accurate. When participants hear rumors they do two things: they observe the price movement and contact other people to hear their thoughts. Interestingly enough, talking to other people is already a form of spreading the rumor, although it's normally unintended. By approaching other people they signal that they consider the rumor to be important, not to say that they already believe it. They let the rumor spread and become important without being aware of it.

5.9.2 Prices Reflect Beliefs

Rumors are not spread automatically, people have to talk about them. There are several conditions that influence the spread of rumors. These conditions depend partly on the medium through which the rumor passes. In financial markets one talks about rumors to inquire and convince. The market actors are not sure whether others possibly know more than they do. By talking about a rumor it is hoped to receive more accurate, validated news. It's important to realize that by contacting others the person inquiring already exposes himself to considering the rumor to be significant. The people approaching others are already biased and look for views supporting their own. If the person did not consider it to be significant, he would not want to talk about it. Rumors can only spread because they are believed in!

The media are in a very convenient situation because they can claim that they transmit the rumor without judging its content. It's 'to each his own' what he or she does with the rumor. The media say they can't be blamed for any consequences of a rumor. Everyone has to judge the rumor's accuracy and validity for himself. This is true to a certain extent. However, the media are responsible for the selection and presentation of news. They well know that how the news is presented tremendously influences the reaction of people. It is their responsibility to judge and evaluate what and how news is presented to the public.

The results of this survey suggest that participants do not necessarily overestimate their ranking concerning the order of hearing a rumor. However, from our results, over 70% of the traders claim that within minutes the entire trader community knows about it. Rumors therefore travel at high speed. A typical statement of an interviewee was, 'All of a sudden there is a rumor and everyone knows about it.'

Believing in rumors depends on the credibility of the source and the plausibility and the desirability of the news. Rumors may be believed because people want to believe them. For most participants the determining factors of believing a rumor are the person they hear the rumor from and the price movement. Some 25% of the respondents mention that they don't care at all if the rumor turns out to be true. The logic behind this answer is simple in that one's personal opinion does not count. The only thing that matters is to anticipate the market's belief.

The determining factors for whether the market believes a rumor can be reduced to one: the price movement. Almost 85% of the respondents say that the price movement is *the* indicator of the market believing the rumor. The price movement therefore reflects the belief of the market as an aggregate of all beliefs.

Astonishingly, many participants not trading on rumors do care in the end if the rumor proves true. Why should these people care? The only reasonable explanation of this is that the market participants feel a certain responsibility or have developed a certain relationship towards it. Even the actors who have traded on rumors would not necessarily have to care, since many such trades are short-term and speculative. If the position is not kept until the verification of the rumor, they would not have to care either.

5.9.3 Investment Strategies on Rumors

It should not be expected that investment strategies on rumors exist to make systematic profits. However, it's worthwhile analyzing the rumor in its early phase in detail. The analysis will help in recognizing the factors driving the emergence process as well as the potential impact of the rumor. This should develop the participant's intuition for judging the market's reaction to the rumor.

Information networks are of value if they are used properly but not if they are simply used as a tool for convincing other people of one's own opinion. Information networks, when used for the exchange of different views and perceptions, can contribute to a more precise and accurate assessment of the situation. The answers of the participants confirm this view and most of them remember the sources that provided them with rumors. Furthermore, most traders spread a rumor to priority people, hoping for mutual action. Many participants believe that it is possible for information networks to know more than other people, at least for a while. This view is not challenged. However, 70% of the traders claim that within minutes the entire trader community knows about the rumor. Since everyone follows the same information services and other media where many of the rumors come from, it is not surprising that it takes only a very short time for everyone to be informed. Following this, the time interval from the establishment of information networks to the instant of everyone knowing the rumor is only a matter of seconds or minutes.

When it comes to systematic price patterns on rumors in financial markets, the participants don't agree on a single opinion. They disagree on whether such patterns do exist, and if so, how they look. Even if price patterns do exist and the price swings to the new anticipated level (as many respondents said), it's still difficult to determine the appearance and the dimension of the swings. This leads to the conclusion that it is very difficult, if not impossible, to anticipate such price swings. Another question is whether the person creating the rumor can profit systematically. While many participants still believe this might be possible, it is argued that the creator faces essentially the same difficulties as other market participants. The creator does not know how the public will react to the initiated news – if it will be ignored or if it will develop into a rumor strongly impacting the price of the asset. Furthermore, if there is a real impact on the market, then anticipating how and how strongly the price will move is very difficult, if not impossible.

One factor to be observed with relatively high accuracy is the market participants' reaction to a rumor after a price movement. They regard the price signal as a sign of belief and jump on the bandwagon; 75% of traders testified that they certainly or possibly will trade on it. This is strong evidence of herd behavior among traders. Herd behavior leads to short-term momentum, excess volatility and long-term reversal that is observed so often in financial markets. Such behavior leads to trends, trends that can be one's friend if anticipated properly. This is exactly the difficulty. It is easy to discover a trend, but is it worthwhile riding it? How does one know its magnitude and its turning point? These questions arising from rumors are absolutely identical to those arising from any event or piece of news and must be tackled on an ongoing basis.

5.9.4   Relating the results to other studies

The results of the survey are almost completely in line with a recent study by Oberlechner and Hocking (2003). They present empirical findings on collective information processing in financial markets. Their results are based on a questionnaire survey of traders and financial journalists from leading banks and financial news providers in the European foreign exchange market. One of the clearest results is that foreign exchange traders rate wire services as the most important market information sources. This result is not surprising and is fully in line with the results of the survey. Second, the traders rate the news item characteristic 'being available to me before others' as most important and 'will influence market participants' as second most important. These results confirm the results of the survey completely, in which the traders are desperate to gather information before others and are worried that others might know something they don't. Additionally, whether the information will influence market participants can directly be linked to rumors, since the traders have to ask themselves the same question when rumors evolve. The authors perform a principal component analysis of important news items characteristics with Varimax rotation. The analysis results in four factors with eigenvalues greater than 1, together accounting for 55.1% of the variance. These four main factors are:[6]

1. *Confirmation*, explaining 17.3% of the total variance.
2. *Accuracy and market influence*, explaining another 13.3% of the total variance.
3. *Timing* of news explains a further 12.3% of the total variance.
4. *Surprise* explains another 12.2%.

In the context of the survey these results do not surprise at all. All factors can directly be applied to the results and interpretations of the rumor survey: *confirmation* as the confirmation of one's own opinion of a rumor, *accuracy and market influence* as evaluating the validity of the rumor and the potential of moving the market, *timing* as the stage when the rumor was heard and *surprise* as the degree of a rumor not being anticipated by the market or oneself.

Concerning the role and information sources of financial journalists, the study suggests an important aspect of the dynamics of information processing in financial markets. Both financial wire journalists and foreign exchange traders mutually value each other as the most important information source. As the authors note: 'Consequently, information of the news services often consists of trading participants' perceptions and interpretations of the market, which are fed back to the traders in the market. As a result, a highly circular cycle of collective information processing in the market emerges.'[7] This circular cycle corresponds to Soros's[8] theory of reflexivity, in that supply and demand are not independent givens, but that the 'participants' expectations about events are shaped by their own expectations'. Models based on higher-order beliefs are often referred to Keynes's metaphor of the market as a beauty contest, as mentioned in the survey in Section 5.5.1, 'Why rumors are believed'.[9] In addition, modern technology and the almost instantaneous availability of market news have not reduced the ambiguity of the news, but probably the contrary, or as one trader in their study mentioned: 'The more news you get, the more you are uncertain of what you do.'[10] While the updating of individuals' beliefs upon receiving new information has been heavily researched in the finance literature, little attention has so far been brought to how the information is interpreted in a sophisticated manner.[11]

The findings lead the authors to the conclusion 'that financial markets may be less about the actuality of economic facts than about how information is perceived and interpreted by market participants'.[12] The results of our survey suggest exactly the same.

6

Rumor Experiments

Rumors generally represent complexities of public feeling that cannot readily be made articulate at a more thoughtful level.

PETER LIENHARDT

As discussed at the beginning of Chapter 5, the theory presented up until now does not have, or only scarcely has, answers to many open questions concerning rumors in financial markets. That's why the survey was conducted with the objective of finding out from practitioners how rumors evolve, spread and are traded on. This objective was clearly achieved. Now that more is known about how practitioners behave when rumors evolve, the question goes back to how theory can deal with this kind of behavior. Do theoretical explanations exist that are in line with the results of the survey received? What kind of theoretical approach would be suitable to capture the observed behavior of real market participants? For future scientific research it is important that theory is not performed in an ivory tower with no application to practice, but serves as an input factor and inspiration for future best practices. The next stage in this work is therefore to take a step backwards and think about research methodologies to try and replicate the observations from the survey. If the results are not replicable, then obviously something is wrong with the theory, since it is not able to explain the real observed behavior. If the results confirm the behavior observed, then the underlying theory and assumptions can be applied to make predictions about what the behavior would look like under other circumstances. This chapter therefore has the objective of applying a suitable theoretical method to replicate at least a certain part of the survey's results and to draw conclusions on why we observe what we observe, and, secondly, with the underlying assumptions, what kind of future behavior we would predict with the assumptions, given other kinds of market conditions? This chapter is therefore again more devoted to theory, of course always with the objective of this chapter as a guide. At the end of each section the results of the experiments are linked to real market examples so that a connection between theory and practice can be built.

6.1 WHY USE EXPERIMENTS AS A RESEARCH METHODOLOGY?

Rumor research has been approached from many different directions. Although a considerable amount of research has been performed, as seen in the first four chapters, important facts and characteristics are still not known. Therefore the survey served to gain additional knowledge of facts and observations. What kind of research would now be suitable to explain why we observe what we observe in financial markets? Initially empirical studies or field studies were considered but were rejected for the following reasons:

- only poor data is available on rumors in financial markets;
- in a field study in fact a lot of data could be gathered, however, it runs the risk of a biased selection, evaluation and interpretation.

To clarify the difficulties concerning the several biases in a field study, reference is made to the one conducted by Schneider (2003) in the German stock market from January 6 to January 17, 2003. During that time, he observed the behavior of traders in regard to evolving rumors. The time period *ex post* turned out to be too short, since it was a rather quiet market period without many rumors. In addition, as the author emphasizes, the traders were probably influenced by his presence and did not react in their usual manner. Schneider consequently aborted his field study and concentrated on performing structured interviews to gain qualitative insights into the market participants' behavior.

Concerning the existing empirical studies on rumors in financial markets, they all have the disadvantage of neglecting their incredibly rapid spreading (compare also in this regard the empirical studies discussed in Chapter 3). Exactly this fact is one of the insights gained from the survey of Chapter 5. With this new insight, the results of the empirical studies should not now be surprising, that all of them observe a significant abnormal return prior to the publication date. For a sophisticated empirical analysis, real-time instead of daily data (such as newspaper headlines) would be necessary in order to make meaningful statements. However, this data is hardly available. In addition, even if the data were available, it would be incredibly difficult to filter out all the noisy information that influences prices as well.

Experiments, rather than field and empirical studies, were considered as a reasonable and sensible research methodology for the following reasons:

- In experiments one can observe real decision-makers in a controlled, clearly structured environment and one can identify the relevant influencing factors of behavior.
- The data collected allow for the verification of economic models (hypothesis testing) and the discovery of causal reasons for economic behavior (theory building).
- In an experiment one can control factors that may influence behavior. Controlling these factors allows for a basic replication of the experiment, applying statistical methods to differentiate systematic from random effects. Furthermore the controllability allows for the isolation of the influencing factors derived from underlying models and contributes to a reduction of complexity. Exactly these conditions cannot be fulfilled with field studies.

The following research questions analyzed in the different experiments are a direct follow-up action to the survey's results and insights. The first stage of experiments (Section 6.4) deals with the question of how market participants react when they are faced with more uncertain news, such as rumors, and how prices and price volatilities evolve in such a context. This question is approached via the theoretical concept of ambiguity. The second stage of experiments (Section 6.5) analyzes the frequently heard statement in the survey that, depending on the plausibility of the content and the source's credibility, they act differently on rumors. Stage three of the experiments (Section 6.6) builds on the results of the survey, where around 70% of the participants stated that they considered action on rumor when the price had already moved. With the experimental approach it is explicitly identifiable whether market participants act as a cluster or if the behavior observed can be linked to herd behavior. The fourth stage (Section 6.7) refers to the statements that personal networks play a very important role when rumors evolve. The hypothesis is tested, whether personal networks add value and whether communication strategies exist to enhance profits.

6.2 Methodological pre-considerations

In economics, experiments do not have the history and tradition as a research methodology that they do in other scientific fields, such as psychology and the natural sciences. During recent decades, several pioneer researchers in experimental economics, such as Ernst Fehr, Charles Plott, Reinhard Selten and Vernon Smith, have contributed in various ways to establishing experiments in economics as an additional cornerstone among the different research methodologies. The various research efforts gained broad publicity in 2002, when the Nobel Prize in Economics was awarded to Vernon Smith and Daniel Kahneman, as it acknowledged economic experiments as a valid, accepted methodology, as well as the influence of psychological factors in economic research.

6.2.1   Internal versus External Validity

Economic experiments are performed as abstract, theoretical decision problems and also as realistic decisions in an economic context. The quality of experiments can be judged using the criteria of reliability (internal validity), or representativeness (external validity). Internal validity can be ensured by an accurate experimental design and therewith replicability. External validity has to be evaluated upon the consistency of the experiment with the real economic context. Since the experimental situation unfolds a reality of its own, the external validation has to comply with the comparability of the two realistic situations. A higher degree of reality or external reality has first of all the advantage of gaining detailed information about human behavior. Consistent with this view is the opinion that one of the basic requirements of behaviorally oriented theories is to explain in what way the decision-maker reduces the complexity of the perceived situation. Furthermore, it is not the task of the researcher to reduce the complexity of the situation presented, but he should explain how the decision-maker simplifies the situation in order to reach a decision with simple rules. The other view of experimental scientists is to plead for the simplest presentation of the decision problem and to focus on basic relationships with few variables, in order to detect causal connections. Economic experiments usually focus on a high internal validity, while psychological experiments put more emphasis on external validity.

The difficulties of internal and external validity cannot be solved separately from each other; they stand in mutual dependence. The postulate of controllability calls for a simplification of the decision problem. On the other hand the experiment should not be too abstract, since otherwise the transferability of the results will suffer. Consequently there exists a trade-off between closeness to reality and therewith higher external validity and controllability (internal validity). Whether the focus is on internal or external validity also depends on the research topic. While fairness experiments, for example, are well suited to focus on high internal validity, finance experiments often require a minimum amount of context within the experimental design in order to observe meaningful participant behavior.

Experiments with high internal validity have been chosen to start with and step by step additional context and complexity are added to the experimental design, which leads to higher external validity. A modular bottom-up approach is followed, so that the single influencing factors for determining differences in the participants' behavior are observable.

6.2.2 Selection of Participants

Another important question is the selection of participants for the experiments. When conducting experiments at a university, students are typically chosen as subjects. This approach has been criticized, with some justification.[1] The argument is that students are a narrow and special segment of the total population. The set of economic behaviors that is applicable to people at large may not coincide with the set that is applicable to this narrowly defined population. An evaluation of students being representative can only be judged upon each individual case. Concerning studies of human behavior in financial markets, economics students especially can be regarded as representative of 'sophisticated private investors'. Furthermore there have been several asset market experiments comparing student behavior with that of experts. The findings of these experiments are that both groups exhibit behavioral anomalies at least to a similar degree.[2] The choice fell on engaging students with a solid mathematical background. A solid mathematical background was required so as to be sure that all participants could understand the mathematical situation presented in the experiment.

6.2.3 Payment of Participants

One other question to be considered is how the participants are paid. The general consensus is that the participants should be paid relative to their performance and receive a reward that is adequate given the duration of the experiment. Nevertheless there are valid theoretical and empirical arguments against this view. One possible argument lies in the performance-related payment of subjects: this kind of payment structure might prevent the development of behavioral patterns leading to the gain of insights beyond traditional imaginations.[3] On the other hand, several studies did not find significant behavioral differences concerning payment effects.[4] Many times no significant behavioral difference could be found dependent on the performance-related payment. Ultimately, for each experiment the following question has to be evaluated: is the stated problem interesting enough so that the participants are intrinsically motivated to think and decide for themselves, or is it necessary to set financial incentives in order to generate extrinsic motivation and prevent arbitrary behavioral patterns? The experiments were considered to be interesting enough for the participants to be intrinsically motivated, nevertheless a performance-related incentive was implemented. Since in all the experiments the participants could experience losses, they received a base payment in the beginning, compensating them for their time opportunity costs. They could gamble away their base payment, walking out of the experiment without any payment.

6.3 REVIEW OF PREVIOUS RUMOR EXPERIMENTS

6.3.1 The Psychological Experiments of DiFonzo and Bordia

DiFonzo and Bordia (1997, 2002) conducted rumor experiments in the context of financial markets. In particular, they ask how rumors affect predictions and trading behavior. In their first paper, participants engaged in a computer simulation investment game in which news summaries were presented to the participants trading a stock. The price changes of the stock were obtained by transforming the actual price change data of the stock (in their specific case that of Goodyear) over a randomly selected 60-day period to deviations from the mean and then multiplying each by a factor of 7.[5] The resultant series was then rescaled to start and end at a price of 35 USD. The participants were assigned 245 USD in cash and 245 USD in the form of seven shares of Goodyear stock valued at 35 USD per share at the beginning of the experiment. The simulation took place over a 60-day period, while each day in the simulation lasted for 20 seconds. The participants could only trade Goodyear stock and perform one transaction during each trading day. They could purchase as many shares as their cash holdings allowed, sell the number of shares they currently possessed, or do neither.

Within the experiment there were four groups. The first group received no news, the second group received news in the form of information, the third group received published rumors and the fourth group received unpublished rumors. Altogether the subjects within groups two to four were presented with eight different Goodyear-relevant news summaries during eight different simulation days. The news appeared on the screen during the trading day. It did not vary in content, though where the news came from varied. Group two was told that the news stemmed from the front page of the *Wall Street Journal*. Published rumors were said to have been published in the *Wall Street Journal's* 'Heard on the Street' (HOSC) column. Unpublished rumors were presented as being from 'your brother-in-law Harry'. The subjects were told that Harry had given you news before, and sometimes it had turned out to be correct and sometimes it had turned out to be incorrect. In an independent manipulation check, another set of subjects was asked to rate the three sources mentioned (the front page of the *Wall Street Journal*, the HOSC column of the *Wall Street Journal* and 'your brother-in-law Harry') of stock-related information for credibility, reliability, and believability on a 0–100 scale. Not surprisingly, the front page of the *Wall Street Journal* was viewed as by far the most credible, reliable and believable source, followed by the HOSC column and 'your-brother-in-law Harry'.

DiFonzo and Bordia analyze the results upon the daily mean shares held by the subjects for the four groups in comparison to the simulated price process. The change of mean shares held from one trading day to the next was viewed as a prediction of the future price movement for the next trading day. In a nutshell, subjects not exposed to news tended to form highly regressive predictions and tracked strongly. Against this, subjects exposed to news, published rumors and unpublished rumors interfered with this process.

The authors link the results obtained from making predictions to events within causal scenarios.[6] When people make predictions, they weight causal information more heavily than non-causal information with equal predictive validity (causality heuristic).[7] Based on insights into stating predictions following events in sequences,[8] the authors propose a similar line of reasoning when making predictions after evolving rumors. DiFonzo and Bordia state that their results 'are consistent with the notion that the causality heuristic underlies rumor-based stock market trading'.[9] No matter if a rumor has been considered as an unreliable, non-credible and untrustworthy information source, the causality information embedded in the rumor dominated the rationale for trading accordingly. The authors conclude that 'rumors do not have to be believed or trusted in order to powerfully affect trading, they simply have to make sense'.[10]

This is a strong statement. Personally, from the set-up of the experimental design I would not have dared to expose myself as much as DiFonzo and Bordia did. One particular concern is the process of how price changes are generated and the participants' interactions in the stock market. Section 6.3.2 discusses in more detail the differences between DiFonzo and Bordia's psychological experiments and the methodology of experimental economics.

In their second paper DiFonzo and Bordia (2002) state the hypothesis that though 'stock market rumors may in fact be non-predictive of tomorrow's price changes, these same rumors will still be viewed as predictive'.[11] Additionally, 'non-predictive rumors will be viewed as predictive and will lead to reductions in tracking; these effects should also be obtained for news. More generally, the strength of stable-cause attributions should predict the degree of anti-regressive trading behavior.'[12]

To test their hypotheses, they played two computer investment games. They again used the same Goodyear stock price data as in their first study. The covariance between the rumor's type (positive is good, negative is bad) and next-day price changes (positive or negative) was zero, though it varied between rumors and the same-day price changes. The percentage of times a set of rumors agreed with that day's price change was varied (five conditions with percentages from 0% to 100%). In comparison to the first paper, there was no difference in the kind of messages (no news, news, published rumors, unpublished rumors) communicated to the participants. In the second part of the paper, they manipulated the participants' stability of cause attribution via a training tutorial in simulated trading experience. The message source was varied as well as either news, published rumors or unpublished rumors. In the stable-cause set of conditions, participants were taught to attribute price changes to stable causes, such as good or bad news, and that prices were therefore somewhat predictable in response to recent events. In the unstable-cause condition, participants were taught to attribute price changes to unstable causes, such as that prices follow a random walk and price changes were therefore not predictable.

From the results of their study, the authors see their hypothesis confirmed that investors receiving unstable-cause training predicted prices more regressively than those receiving no training and those receiving stable-cause training. When the price changes were objectively unpredictable, then stable-cause and no training tended to obscure the unpredictability most among participants with no empirical experience (i.e. the no-news condition). The unstable-cause training enhanced their ability to perceive unpredictability.

DiFonzo and Bordia state that their study is in line with the well-known representative bias, where people tend to extrapolate trends from small series in which in fact there is no trend. 'Brokers earnestly believe that rumors are associated with one or two-day price trends . . . .'[13] The authors find some evidence 'that even if market prices were absolutely unpredictable, perceptions of association would persist'.[14]

This conclusion seems in my opinion more reasonable than the one from their first paper. The representative bias is a well-known stable effect that occurs in many situations and takes on several different forms.[15] The idea that rumors initiate short-term price momentum does not seem to be particularly counter-intuitive and leads to the perception of trends where in fact there are none.

6.3.2 An Economic Approach towards Rumor Experiments and their Structuring in this Book

While DiFonzo and Bordia's research has the characteristic form of psychology experiments, their design and approach are, at least from an economic point of view, not completely satisfying. To make the point more clear, let us discuss briefly how the methodology of experimental economics differs from experimental psychology.[16] First, the incentive structure for the participants is typically an important difference. Economic theories describe and predict what kind of decisions individuals will make in the presence of monetary payoffs.

In addition, economic experimentalists strongly favor incentive structures not as a flat fee, but as an amount contingent on their decisions. Psychologists are more casual about defining their subjects' incentives in the experimental task. The second domain of difference concerns the use of context within the experiments. Economic experiments are primarily context-free or at least context-neutral, while psychology experiments use a lot of context. Why is this a critical issue? Most importantly, context can add systematic biases or demand effects. Systematic biases and changes in the participants' behavior will significantly change the conclusions reached. Therefore economists try to avoid context as much as possible in their experiments. A third methodological difference is the use of deception in experiments. The rule that the researcher may not deceive his participants is one of the strictest in experimental economics. The validity of an economic experiment relies on the link between behavior and payoffs. If that relation is weakened, then the experiment becomes an inferior test of the economic theory addressed. For the same reason, if participants are deceived about that relation, the validity of their decisions is called into doubt as well. In contrast to these strict rules, psychology experiments often deceive participants about the purpose of the experiment, the payoffs to be earned and existence or non-existence of counterparts.

From these comments the experiments of DiFonzo and Bordia lack in particular two aspects from an economic experimentalist point of view. First, they use a lot of context in their experiments, exposing themselves to systematic participants' behavioral biases. Second, the way the stock market and the price changes are set up seem disturbing. Rather than implementing a particular auction type and letting the participants trade in a self-established financial market, the price impact of the participant's actions remains unknown. As a consequence, it is not possible to give precise statements of what the price impact and price differences of the various message treatments are.

All experiments performed for this work are set up in a financial market's context and are structured as follows: in the experiments of the first stage, the goal is to test one of the basic characteristics of a rumor, its ambiguity, in nature. There is an extensive literature on ambiguity, and in particular ambiguity aversion, deriving from the initial experiments by Ellsberg.[17] Therefore the experimental results can be well compared to the existing literature. The second stage experiments are framing experiments. The psychological insights are reexamined, as to whether the rumor content's plausibility as well as the credibility of the rumor's source are determining factors for believing the rumor. Within the third stage of experiments the hypothesis of whether the ratio of precisely to not precisely spread news can be a determining factor for the occurrence of herd behavior is tested. The fourth stage focuses on communication between participants and what purpose it fulfills.

6.4 First stage experiments: Ambiguity aversion in a financial market

In the first stage of the rumor experiments, the question is answered how market participants react when they are faced with more uncertain news, such as rumors, and how prices and price volatilities evolve in such a context. This question is approached via the theoretical concept of ambiguity. In comparison to information where the assumption of truth is automatically implied, a rumor is not known to be true or false in advance and a probability cannot easily be assigned. In the experiment, subjects trade an asset with an unknown value. The value of the asset is drawn from one of two distributions that are overlapping. Subjects do not know which distribution the value of the traded asset is drawn from. In one treatment subjects do not know the probabilities with which the value is drawn from the distributions; in the other treatment the probabilities are known. Details of the experimental design can be found in Section 6.4.2.1, 'Experimental game and procedures' after the literature review.

6.4.1 A Brief Overview of Ambiguity Aversion

6.4.1.1 Subjective expected utility and the Ellsberg paradox

For the last 50 years expected utility (EU) based on the work of von Neumann and Morgenstern (1947) and subjective expected utility (SEU) based on the axioms of Savage (1954) have been the leading theories of choice in economics and psychology.

The concept of expected utility is based on the normative concept of making rational decisions. When formulating a normative concept on decision-making, the difference between making a 'good' decision and a lucky decision has to become transparent. A 'good' decision is 'an action we take that is logically consistent with alternatives we perceive, the information we have, and the preference we feel'.[18] In contrast thereto, a lucky decision simply has a good outcome. The relationship between making decisions and the feelings perceived is established through a utility function.

Making a logical, consistent decision implies that the individual possesses a preference relation and chooses the best alternative according to this preference relation. A preference relation, to be denoted by $\succ$, allows for a comparison between a pair of alternative outcomes $x, y \in X$, where $X \subset R^s$ is the set of possible outcomes, x_s is the outcome in a state $s \in S$ out of the set of possible states S.

Rational decision-making is based on two basic assumptions about preference relations: *completeness* and *transitivity*. The assumption that a preference relation is *complete* states that the individual has a well-defined preference between any two alternatives, i.e. for all $x, y \in X$ we have either $x \succcurlyeq y$ or $y \succcurlyeq x$ (or both). *Transitivity* states that for all $x, y, z \in X$, if $x \succcurlyeq y$ and $y \succcurlyeq z$, then $x \succcurlyeq z$. This assumption implies that the individual does not make choices in which his preferences are recursive. As an example of transitivity, if the individual prefers an espresso over coffee and feels that coffee is at least as good as tea, then he should also prefer an espresso over tea.

A utility function $u(x)$ assigns a numerical value to each element in X, ranking the elements of X in accordance with the individual preferences. A utility function represents the preference relation $\succcurlyeq$, if for all $x, y \in X$ $x \succcurlyeq y$ if and only if $u(x) \geq u(y)$. A sufficient condition for the existence of a utility function that represents $\succcurlyeq$ is the *continuity* of $\succcurlyeq$, i.e. small changes in x lead to small changes in the utility of x.

An additional axiom has to be fulfilled in order to represent an individual's preferences by a utility function in the form of expected utility. The preference relation $\succcurlyeq$ satisfies the *sure-thing axiom*, if for any subset of states $I \subset S$, where I is called an event and S is the set of possible states, whenever $(x_1, \ldots, x_s) \in R^s_+$ and $(x'_1, \ldots, x'_s) \in R^s_+$ differ only in the entries corresponding to I (so that $x'_s = x_s$ for $s \notin I$), the preference ordering between $(x_1, \ldots, x_s)$ and $(x'_1, \ldots, x'_s)$ is independent of the particular (common) payoffs for states not in I. Suppose that $(x_1, \ldots, x_s)$, $(x'_1, \ldots, x'_s)$, $(\overline{x}_1, \ldots, \overline{x}_s)$, and $(\overline{x}'_1, \ldots, \overline{x}'_s)$ are such that for all $s \notin I$: $x_s = x'_s$ and $\overline{x}_s = \overline{x}'_s$. For all $s \in I$: $x_s = \overline{x}_s$ and $x'_s = \overline{x}'_s$. Then $(\overline{x}_1, \ldots, \overline{x}_s) \succcurlyeq (\overline{x}'_1, \ldots, \overline{x}'_s)$ if and only if $(x_1, \ldots, x_s) \succcurlyeq (x'_1, \ldots, x'_s)$. The axiom states that if two random variables cannot be distinguished in the complement of I, then the ordering among them can depend only on the values they take on I. Or, to put it in other words, states conditional on an event should not depend on what the payoffs would have been in states that have not occurred.

When preferences satisfy the four axioms stated, then there exists a numerical utility and probabilities that represent actions by their subjective expected utility:

$$SEU(x) = \sum_{s \in S} p_s u(x_s)$$

There has been a long tradition of questioning whether these rules describe the individuals' behavior adequately. Keynes (1936) made a distinction between the *implications* of evidence and the *weight* of evidence. The *implication* of evidence referred to the probability judgment that evidence implies, while the *weight* of evidence referred to the confidence of the estimated probability. Keynes raised the question of whether a single probability measure could capture both dimensions of evidence.

Knight (1921) made a distinction between the notions of *risk* and *uncertainty*. With risk, he associated known probabilities, with uncertainty, unknown probabilities. He suggested that economic returns should only be earned upon bearing projects under uncertainty, but not under risk.

A far more direct challenge to the SEU was brought up by Ellsberg (1961) and the paradox that carries his name, based on the results observed in an experiment conducted in 1961. He described the situation as follows: Subjects are presented with an urn containing 90 balls. Of the 90 balls, 30 are red, the rest are either yellow or black. However, the proportion of the yellow to black balls is not known. The subjects have to bet on which color ball will be drawn.

The payoff matrix for the different lotteries is shown in Table 6.1. When subjects have to state a preference between lotteries A or B, it is very common that they choose A. Lottery A gives a precise 1/3 chance of winning USD 100, whereas in lottery B the subject does not know the likelihood of a black ball.

The second choice subjects are faced with is the one between lotteries A' and B'. Most subjects prefer lottery B' over A'. B' offers a precise 2/3 chance of winning USD 100, whereas with A' the subject knows only a chance of 1/3 of a red ball for certain.

When subjects prefer A over B and B' over A', they violate the sure-thing axiom. This is the case because when the yellow outcome is ignored, the two lotteries A and B as well as A' and B' are absolutely identical. The explanation for the preference reversal is that people prefer definite information over indefinite information. If the urn contains more yellow than black balls, then lottery A' is more attractive than lottery B'. However, people tend to prefer the 'devil they know' in lottery B' where they can win USD 100 with a certain probability of 2/3.

Ellsberg also presented a two-color balls problem using two urns, where one urn contains 50 red and 50 black balls and the other contains 100 balls in an unknown combination of red and black balls (Figure 6.1). The subjects have to bet on which color ball will be drawn.

Table 6.1 Payoff matrix of the Ellsberg three-color balls problem

		red	yellow	black
	A	USD 100	0	0
Lotteries	B	0	0	USD 100
	A'	USD 100	USD 100	0
	B'	0	USD 100	USD 100

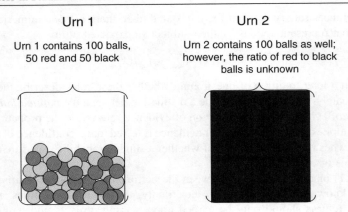

Figure 6.1   Graphical illustration of the two-color Ellsberg problem

Table 6.2   Payoff matrix of the Ellsberg two-color balls problem

Urn 1	Number of balls	
	50 red	50 black
C	USD 100	0
D	0	USD 100

Urn 2	Number of balls	
	100	
	red	black
C′	USD 100	0
D′	0	USD 100

The payoff matrix is shown in Table 6.2. When people are asked to bet on a red ball, they prefer it to be drawn from urn 1 and play lottery C rather from urn 2 and play lottery C′. When people are asked to bet on a black ball, they again prefer it to be drawn from urn 1 and play lottery D rather than from urn 2 and play lottery D′. However, most people are indifferent concerning the two colors when betting on only one of the two urns. As Ellsberg shows,[19] this pattern violates SEU.

6.4.1.2   Conceptual matters of ambiguity[20]

1. A simple but ineffective way to get rid of the difficulty of ambiguity is to state that no ambiguous events exist. To all events one can assign subjective probabilities, so there exists no such thing as an unknown probability. Therefore the term 'ambiguity' is meaningless. This view has been expressed by de Finetti (1977), among others. This may be reasonable concerning *normative* propositions; however, it does not help to explain the extensive *descriptive* evidence of ambiguity aversion.

2. A second strategy for dealing with ambiguity about probabilities $p(s_i)$ is to regard it as a second-order probability (SOP) distribution of its possible values. This is then denoted by $\Theta(p(s_i))$.[21] Relating it to the two-color Ellsberg paradox problem, then $p(black\_ball)$ might be uniformly distributed between 0 and 1, rather than setting $p(black\_ball)$ just at 0.5. In this case ambiguity should not matter, since EU and SEU are linear functions of probabilities and therefore only the expected value of an SOP should matter.

   While the SOP view is intuitive and popular,[22] it also has some drawbacks. It seems not to be able to capture the two-color problem of Ellsberg completely. This is the case because individuals prefer to bet on known SOPs rather than on ambiguous urns. An additional drawback is the fact that SOP will only lead to the same choices with known probabilities if compound lotteries are reduced to equivalent single-stage bets. But Camerer and Ho (1991) find that exactly this reduction principle is often violated in experiments. As a result, approaches based on SOP do not describe the observations well. From a practical standpoint, replacing subjective probabilities by SOPs seems not very promising either. If an individual has difficulty in expressing a first-order probability, then how can he express precise second-order distributions or even third-order distributions over second-order distributions?

3. The third strategy is more psychologically influenced. The goal is to define ambiguity, capturing its psychological essence. Frisch and Baron (1988) have elaborated the following definition based on the original definition of Ellsberg:

   > Ambiguity is uncertainty about probability, created by missing information that is relevant and could be known.

   The authors state that not knowing important information leads to people being reluctant and scared. The authors argue that one explanation for ambiguity aversion is that people apply a heuristic to simply 'avoid betting when you lack information others might have'[23] to situations in which their fears are as a matter of fact unfounded.

4. Other definitions of ambiguity focus primarily on missing information, such as source credibility and expert disagreement[24] or weight of evidence.[25]

6.4.1.3   Degrees of ambiguity[26]

Since the notion of ambiguity and degrees of uncertainty are not treated uniquely, they should be distinguished precisely. We make the following assumption: the corresponding utilities of the different actions consequences $C = \{c(s_1), c(s_2), \ldots, c(s_n)\}$, $u(c(s_i))$, are known. Then the probabilities of the actions are $p(s_i)$.

   When an individual knows that a state will occur with *certainty*, then $(p(s_i) = 1\ for\ some\ i)$ (refer to Figure 6.2(a)).

   When an individual does not know which state will occur, but knows the probabilities of each state precisely, then this situation is referred to as *risk* or *unambiguous probability* (refer to Figure 6.2(b)).

   When an individual does know which states can occur but does not know their probability distribution, then the state probabilities are called *ambiguous*. Two kinds of ambiguity definitions have to be distinguished. The first refers to second-order probability beliefs (refer to Figure 6.2(c)). Then the probability distributions in the set of conceivable distributions can themselves be assigned probabilities. In the second definition, the distributions cannot be assigned probabilities (refer to Figure 6.2(d)). Then ambiguity is expressed by a set of probability distributions.

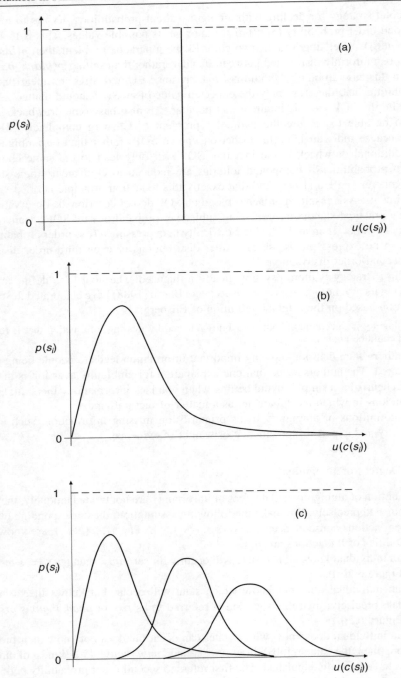

Figure 6.2 Distributions under certainty, risk and ambiguity.[27] (a) Certainty, (b) risk, (c) ambiguity
(second-order probability) and (d) ambiguity (a set of probability distributions)
Source: C. Camerer and M. Weber: Recent developments in modeling preferences: uncertainty and ambiguity,
Journal of Risk and Uncertainty, **5**: 325–370 (1992). With kind permission of Springer Science and Business Media.

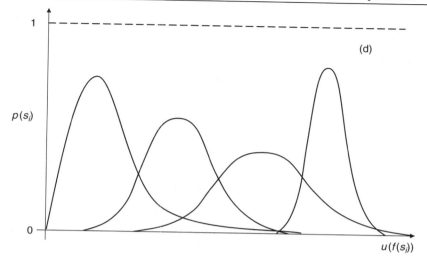

Figure 6.2 (Continued)

There is often confusion about ambiguity regarding probabilities and ambiguity regarding outcomes. If individuals are averse to ambiguity regarding outcomes, but the outcome probabilities are known (Figure 6.2(b)), then the individuals are *risk averse*, which is consistent with EU. But if individuals are ambiguity averse regarding probabilities of outcomes, then they are *ambiguity averse*, which is inconsistent with SEU. The two forms of ambiguity are therefore fundamentally different from each other.

6.4.1.4 Empirical studies of the Ellsberg paradox

Camerer and Weber[28] find that there exist roughly three kinds of empirical work on ambiguity. The first strand analyzes Ellsberg's original experiments and replications thereof, changing various parameters. The second strand deals with the psychological foundation and causes of ambiguity aversion. These two strands have established facts and insights leading to a wide range of definitions, models or studies in an applied setting (the third strand).

Table 6.3 summarizes the questions analyzed about ambiguity effects that have been developed by various studies. These studies are all part of the first strand of empirical work.

The second strand of empirical work explores the psychological foundations of ambiguity aversion. The following studies are particularly worth mentioning.

Curley et al. (1986) test several plausible hypotheses about the source of ambiguity aversion using variants of the two-color Ellsberg problem. They find that even when subjects are allowed to be indifferent between two choices, many of them are still ambiguity averse, indicating a strict preference for avoiding ambiguity. As a second result, they do not find any correlation between the individual's risk and ambiguity aversion attitudes. Third, subjects are not more ambiguity averse when the content of the urn is revealed after the choice has been made. Fourth, subjects are significantly more ambiguity averse when the experiment takes place and the urn's content is revealed *ex post* in front of other subjects.

Heath and Tversky (1991) suggest in their study that competence, such as knowledge, skill and comprehension, is the determining factor for the gap between probability beliefs

Table 6.3 Questions analyzed about ambiguity effects.[29] (Reproduced, with permission, from Camerer and Weber (1992))

Questions analyzed	Studies	Comments
1. Replication of Ellsberg	Becker and Brownson (1964), table 2 Slovic and Tversky (1974) Einhorn and Hogarth (1986), table 1 Curley and Yates (1989)	
2. Strict aversion to ambiguity	Cohen et al. (1985) Curley et al. (1986), table 2 Einhorn and Hogarth (1986), table 1 Curley and Yates (1989)	Test for allowing indifference
3. Aversion to partial ambiguity	Chipman (1960) Gigliotti and Sopher (1996)	Subjects get samples from ambiguous urns
4. Immunity to persuasion	MacCrimmon (1968) Slovic and Tversky (1974) Curley et al. (1986), table 4	Ambiguity aversion persists after exposure to written arguments
5. Aversion to SOP	Yates and Zukowski (1976)	
6. Aversion to increasing range of probability	Becker and Brownson (1964) Yates and Zukowski (1976) Larson (1980) Curley and Yates (1985)	
7. Ambiguity preference at low probabilities (gains) and high probabilities (losses)	Curley and Yates (1985) Einhorn and Hogarth (1986) Kahn and Sarin (1988) Curley and Yates (1989) Hogarth and Einhorn (1990)	
8. Extension to natural events	MacCrimmon (1968) Goldsmith and Sahlins (1983) Einhorn and Hogarth (1985, 1986) Heath and Tversky (1991) Keppe and Weber (1991) Taylor (1994)	
9. Less ambiguity aversion for losses than for gains	Cohen et al. (1985) Einhorn and Hogarth (1986), table 1 Kahn and Sarin (1988) (no difference) Hogarth and Einhorn (1990), table 4	
10. Independence of risk attitude	Cohen et al. (1985) Curley et al. (1986), table 1 Hogarth and Einhorn (1990), p. 797 Lauriola and Levin (2001) Chen et al. (2003)	Low correlations could be due to measurement error

and true decision weights. Subjects had to give probability estimations for natural events, such as temperatures in Tokyo. Then they had to choose between betting on the event or on a chance device constructed to have the same subjective probability as the estimated event. If subjects are ambiguity averse, then they should prefer betting on the device with the matched probability, since betting on the event is inherently ambiguous. They find that the subjects are not uniformly ambiguity averse. The subjects prefer to bet on events they know a lot about (e.g. those subjects knowing a lot about football), holding beliefs constant. Keppe and Weber (1995) get the same results as Heath and Tversky when using certainty and probability equivalents.

Fox and Tversky (1995) extend the competence hypothesis to the so-called comparative ignorance hypothesis (CIH). The CIH is derived from the same general framework as Tversky and Kahneman's Cumulative Prospect Theory (CPT).[30] The hypothesis states that ambiguity aversion is driven primarily by a comparison between events or a comparison between individuals, and it is greatly reduced or eliminated in the absence of such a comparison. As an example, subjects in California had to price a bet on the temperature in San Francisco/Istanbul for the next week. When the subjects were asked to price only one bet (either San Francisco or Istanbul temperature) the price differences were marginal. However, when the subjects were asked to price bets for San Francisco (familiar) as well as Istanbul (unfamiliar) temperature, there were significant price differences observed.

Tversky and Fox (1995) develop Tversky and Kahneman's CPT of choice under ambiguity further by generalizing the weighting function and introducing the principle of bounded sub-additivity. Bounded sub-additivity refers to a pattern in which increasing a fixed prize from probability 0 to 0.1 or from 0.9 to 1 has a greater impact on the perceived decision weight than increasing the probability in the middle of the probability distribution. The (upper and lower) sub-additivity of the decision weights are referred to as *source sensitivity*. In comparison thereto, *source preference* refers to the observation that not only the degree of uncertainty of one particular source determines the choices, but also from which source the uncertainty stems (e.g. San Francisco temperature vs. Istanbul temperature from the Fox and Tversky study). Tversky and Fox emphasize that it is important to distinguish the two different sources. *Source preference* and *source sensitivity* are logically independent of each other, and people sometimes prefer one source of uncertainty over a second source, even though they are less sensitive to the former than the latter. For instance, subjects believing that they are competent in football preferred to bet on football game outcomes rather than on chance, although they exhibited greater sub-additivity (i.e. less sensitivity) for football bets than for chance bets.

Fox and Tversky (1995) argue that ambiguity aversion is characterized by *source prefer-ence* rather than *source sensitivity*. The authors find strong results supporting their hypothesis. Chow and Sarin (2001) performed a replication study of Fox and Tversky, adding in comparative as well as non-comparative situations, as suggested by Heath and Tversky. They find the results to be consistent with those of Fox and Tversky, although the results obtained are more fragile. In addition Chow and Sarin conclude that the complete disappearance of ambiguity aversion in non-comparative conditions may not be as robust as Fox and Tversky have supposed. Fox and Weber (2002) extend Fox and Tversky's CIH and emphasize that comparative ignorance refers to the state of mind of the decision-maker. They find that ambiguity aversion is greatly influenced by features of the context in which a decision is made. Four novel manipulations of decision context are identified that do not rely on the comparative–non-comparative elicitation paradigm producing context effects that cannot be reconciled with prevailing economic models of ambiguity aversion. The authors demonstrate comparative ignorance effects (1) within an entirely comparative context, (2) in a context that shifts from non-comparative to comparative, (3) within an entirely non-comparative context, and (4) in a strategic (interactive) context. Their results provide converging support for the CIH. Dolan and Jones (2004) experimentally test the existence of the CIH when it is tested on events with a range of different likelihoods. Their results do not lend support to the theory, although the relationship between risk and ambiguity does appear to correspond with other theories and previous empirical work.

The third strand of research has focused on studying ambiguity aversion in various applied settings. Most notably, ambiguity aversion has been studied in experimental markets, such as insurance and financial markets. These studies are extensively reviewed in the discussion of the results obtained.

6.4.1.5 Ambiguity models

Models of ambiguity can be grouped into four classes:[31]

1. Models that account for ambiguity leading to modifications in the utilities of outcomes.[32]
2. Models that assume a single SOP distribution with mean $E(p)$ but relax the axiom of compound lottery reduction and weight SOPs nonlinearly.[33]
3. Models accepting sets of probabilities, but that do not assume a unique distribution of probability over elements of the set (in opposition to the SOP approach).[34]
4. Models that avoid unique SOPs or sets of probabilities entirely. Some models assume the expected probability $E(p)$ to be known or at least measurable.[35] In other models, where $E(p)$ is unknown or not measurable, non-additive probabilities are used to express ambiguity aversion.[36]

Two classes of models (numbers 3 and 4 above) have created a number of subsequent research papers to be discussed.

Models based on sets of probabilities
The first models based on sets of probabilities stem from Hodges and Lehmann (1952) and Ellsberg (1961). The two studies suggest that people make choices using a weighted average of a gamble's expected utility (averaged over possible distributions) and its minimum expected utility over those distributions. Gardenfors and Sahlin (1982) propose a rule where people choose according to the minimum expected utility over all probability distributions satisfying a threshold level of risk in probability judgment.

In a seminal contribution, Gilboa and Schmeidler (1989) present an axiomatic framework where preferences are represented by the minimum of all the expected utilities of a lottery over its possible probability distributions. The crucial axioms of the Gilboa–Schmeidler max-min representation are 'uncertainty aversion' and 'certainty independence'.

Let L be the space of lotteries and a lottery $l = (p_1, \ldots, p_N)$ with $p_n \geq 0$ for all n and $\sum_n p_n = 1$ where p_n is interpreted as the objective probability of outcome n occurring. Let l_1, l_2, l_3 be lotteries and elements of L. Then the 'uncertainty aversion' axiom states that for all $l_1, l_2 \in L$ and $0 \leq p \leq 1$, $l_1 \sim l_2$ implies that $pl_1 + (1-p)l_2 \succcurlyeq l_1$. Verbally, combining lotteries l_1 and l_2 with objective probabilities p can only be an improvement to l_1. The max-min representation is consistent with uncertainty aversion, since the minimum expected utility for $pl_1 + (1-p)l_2$ cannot be worse than the minima of l_1 and l_2 taken separately.

Certainty independence is an independence axiom restricted to mixtures of actions with sure outcomes. The action with the sure outcome is denoted by h. Then $l_1 \succcurlyeq l_2$ if and only if $pl_1 + (1-p)l_3 \succcurlyeq pl_1 + (1-p)l_3$ for $0 \leq p \leq 1$. On an intuitive basis, the axiom states that the sure outcome l_3 has the same expected utility for *any* distribution of probabilities. This implies that combining the sure outcome l_3 with l_1 and l_2 does not affect the determination of the distributions minimizing the expected utility for l_1 and l_2. Furthermore, the minimum expected utilities for l_1 and l_2 will be ranked in the same way as the minimum expected utilities for $pl_1 + (1-p)l_3$ and $pl_2 + (1-p)l_3$. The standard independence axiom is stronger than the certainty independence axiom, as it allows l_3 being any lottery in L rather than restricting it to actions with sure outcomes.

Gilboa and Schmeidler's paper induced many further studies with their axiomatic setting to models highlighting a few specific empirical predictions of ambiguity aversion. As an example, Dow and Werlang (1992) show how ambiguity aversion can naturally generate limited equity market participation effects in an investor's optimal portfolio. This result even holds in the absence of transaction costs or other market frictions. Several authors have applied the static max-min expected utility setting of ambiguity aversion into a discrete time setting. Epstein and Wang (1994) study some asset pricing implications thereof. Epstein and Schneider (2003) provide a discrete-time axiomatic intertemporal setting of ambiguity aversion. They show that a dynamically consistent conditional version of Gilboa and Schmeidler's (1989) preferences can be represented by means of a recursive max-min expected utility criterion over a set of multiple distributions. They also refer to it as Recursive Multiple Priors Utility (RMPU), since the prevalent intertemporal utility is also recursive. Chen and Epstein (2002) extend the RMPU setting to continuous time. Hansen et al. (1999) have proposed an additional, though non-axiomatic setting of ambiguity aversion based on an alternative form of the max-min utility preferences. Their setting is based on an extension of robust control theory to an economic context. Anderson et al. (2003) extend the latter approach into continuous time. Trojani and Vanini (2004) study empirical predictions of ambiguity aversion for settings based on robust control optimization, where one of their settings allows for RMPU interpretation.

Models with non-additive probabilities
Non-additive probability distributions based on axiomatic subjective expected utility have been proposed by Schmeidler (1989). His approach is an extension of Anscombe and Aumann's (1963) framework using both objective and subjective probabilities. Choquet (1953) showed that when probabilities are non-additive, then expected utilities must be calculated in a rather unorthodox way. The application to utility theory was first introduced by Schmeidler (1989). An axiomatic approach with non-additive probabilities in a Savage framework using only subjective probabilities in an infinite state space was introduced by Gilboa (1987). Other approaches based on non-additive probabilities followed, as for example the models from Wakker (1984, 1989a, 1989b) and Sarin and Wakker (1990), and discuss them in the context of belief theories.[37] Further extensions of ambiguity aversion in a Choquet expected utility setting have been applied to financial markets,[38] risk sharing[39] and other areas such as incentive contracts and game theory.[40]

The models based on decision weights or non-additive probabilities have been criticized by Fox and Tversky[41] as well as by Fox and Weber,[42] since they only can accommodate for *source sensitivity*, but not in a satisfactory manner for *source preference*. This is because these models do not distinguish between comparative and non-comparative evaluation. Fox and Tversky suggest modeling the comparative ignorance effect using a contingent weighting approach.[43]

6.4.2 Experimental design

In this first stage of experiments the impact of ambiguity is studied in a financial market setting. Altogether three different designs are implemented. The first design is an auctioneer design, where two bidders compete against a minimum price set by the auctioneer. The second design is set up as a batch auction, in which market participants set their prices and quantities of their bids and asking prices before a predefined deadline and transactions are executed at once for all at the same price. Within the third design the experiment is set up as a continuous double auction as applied in real financial markets.

6.4.2.1 Experimental game and procedures

The experimental procedure for the design with an auctioneer is as follows (for detailed instructions, please refer to Appendix I.1):

$t = 0$: Every participant is randomly assigned as either an auctioneer or a bidder. Roles of the participants are fixed for the entire session.

$t = 0$: The bidders have to bid for an asset, the auctioneer has to set a minimum auction price. Participants are assigned randomly to a group of three in each period, consisting of two bidders and one auctioneer.

- The value of the asset is determined in each period from one of two distributions:

  — The first distribution is uniform, with values between 70 and 80 (distribution with high values).
  — The second distribution is uniform, with values between 1 and 80 (distribution with low values).
  — In each period the value of the asset is determined randomly. However, in the non-ambiguous experiment, the participants know that the asset's value is drawn with 70% from the first distribution (high values), and with 30% from the second distribution (low values). In the ambiguous experiment the probabilities of drawing from the first and second distribution are not known.

$t = 2$: The auctioneer sets a minimum auction price for the asset. If neither of the two bidders bids at least the minimum auction price, the asset does not get auctioned and the auctioneer has a *payoff of zero*. If the asset is auctioned, then the auctioneer receives the *higher bid price as a payoff.*

$t = 3$: The bidders are informed about the minimum auction price.

$t = 4$: The bidders independently give their bids for the asset. The bids are collected and the asset is allocated according to the rules of the auction.

- Rules of auction for the bidders (in each period):

  — If your bid is less than the minimum auction price, you don't get the asset and *your payoff is zero*.
  — If your bid is higher or at least the same as the minimum auction price and

    — if your bid is higher than the other bid, then you receive the asset and pay your bid: *your payoff = the value of the asset − your bid*.
    — if your bid is lower than the other bid, then you don't receive the asset: *your payoff is zero*.

$t = 5$: The auctioneer and the bidders are informed about their payoff.

This process corresponds to one period. The session consists of 30 periods.

To make sure that the participants have fully understood the decision process and the payment structure of the game, each participant has to read a detailed set of instructions before the session is started. After the participants have read the instructions, they have to correctly answer a set of control questions. There were no practice periods. The participants were paid for the decisions from the first period on.

Before the actual experiment started, the participants played the known two-urn Ellsberg game in a gain–loss treatment. In this way it is possible to determine the ratio of ambiguity to non-ambiguity averse subjects within the experimental group (for detailed instructions please refer to Appendix I.1).

The subjects have to choose between a lottery A or B.

- In lottery A, a fair coin is thrown

  — If heads appears, then the payment is drawn randomly and uniformly between numbers 14 and 16.
  — If tails appears, then the payment is drawn randomly and uniformly between numbers 0 and 16.

- In lottery B, a ball is drawn from an urn with red and blue balls. However, the ratio of blue and red balls is not known.

  — If a blue ball is drawn, then your payment will be drawn randomly and uniformly between numbers 14 and 16.
  — If a red ball is drawn, then your payment will be drawn randomly and uniformly between numbers 0 and 16.

Which lottery is chosen? The payoff in both lotteries is the drawn number minus 11.5 multiplied by 1 CHF per point. So if 5 is drawn, then the subject loses CHF 6.50, if 13 is drawn, the subject wins CHF 1.50 correspondingly.

6.4.2.2 Treatments

In order to study the effects of ambiguity aversion in a rumor context within a financial market setting, three treatments were implemented. The first treatment is an auctioneer set-up as described in the experimental game and procedures above. The second treatment is a batch auction, whereas the third treatment is performed as a continuous double auction. Within the third treatment, two additional variables, notably the absolute numbers as well as the underlying distributions, were modified. The reason for the implementation of these modifications is to detect whether changes in absolute numbers and probabilities of the underlying distributions alone can impact the degree of the participant's ambiguity aversion.

Experiments 1 and 2 are the experiments performed with an auctioneer, experiments 3 and 4 as a batch auction. Experiments 5 to 12 are conducted as continuous double auctions. Within the continuous double auction treatment, two variables are modified for controlling reasons. In experiments 9 to 12 other absolute numbers were used than were used in experiments 1 to 8. In addition, the probability of drawing underlying distribution was modified in experiments 7, 8, 11 and 12 in comparison to the original continuous double auction treatment.

The instructions for the batch auction and continuous double auction treatment differ from the auctioneer treatment as follows:

- *Batch auction:* The participants are all assigned as a trader to buy and sell the asset during all periods. At the beginning of each period, the participants receive an endowment of 10 shares and 1,000 cash points. In addition they are asked to state bid and asking offers for the asset. The participants are in each period allowed to state several bid and asking offers (quantities and prices). After the participants have stated their bid and asking offers and they have been collected, the price is determined at which the largest number of assets can be traded. The asset is then traded at that price in the particular period. This process is repeated for every period. For detailed instructions, please refer to Appendix I.2.
- *Continuous double auction:* The participants are all assigned as a trader to buy and sell the asset during all periods. As in the batch auction, the participants receive at the beginning of each period an endowment of 10 shares and 1,000 cash points. They are allowed to buy and sell the asset simultaneously and continuously during the trading period. The trading period lasts for 90 seconds. For detailed instructions, please refer to Appendix I.2.

6.4.2.3   Subjects and sessions

All experimental participants were volunteers. They were all participating for the first time in such an experiment, and each participant could only participate in one session. All participants were students of the University of Zurich or the Swiss Federal Institute of Technology (ETH).

In total, 12 experimental sessions were conducted, in each case two sessions for the first two treatments and eight for the third treatment. The computerized experiment was programmed and conducted with experimental software z-Tree.[44] A session lasted approximately 120 minutes and subjects earned on average CHF 48 (approximately USD 38.5, October 2004).

6.4.3   Results of the First Stage Experiments

First, the typical result of the individual two-color Ellsberg experiment is received. As can be seen from Figure 6.3, from the total of 632 subjects asked, 385 or 61% chose lottery A or the throw of a fair coin. Only 247 or 39% chose lottery B or to draw a ball from the urn with unknown probabilities.

As in many experiments, the proportion of ambiguity-averse subjects is higher than the non-ambiguity-averse subjects. However, the ratio is not even two to one. This indicates that

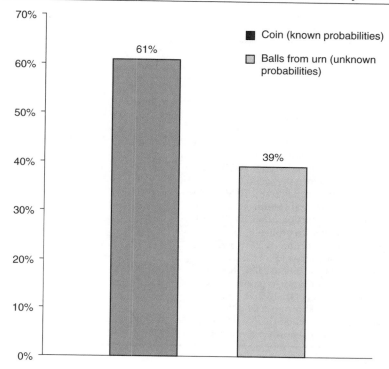

70%

60% — 61%

Coin (known probabilities)

Balls from urn (unknown probabilities)

50%

40% — 39%

30%

20%

10%

0%

Figure 6.3 Lottery choices of the two-urn Ellsberg game
Source: C. Camerer and M. Weber: Recent developments in modeling preferences; uncertainty and ambiguity. *Journal of Risk and Uncertainty*, **5**: 325–370 (1992). With kind permission of Springer Science and Business Media.

the general assumption of ambiguity-averse subjects might be too strong. Indeed, it is an area of special interest to observe and analyze the consequences of the subjects' interaction with heterogeneous attitudes towards ambiguity.

For all treatments within the first stage of experiments, the corresponding testable hypothesis is the following:

Ambiguous news is priced as non-ambiguous news.

$$H_0 : \mu_1 - \mu_2 = 0$$

where μ_1 is the price of ambiguous news and μ_2 is the price of non-ambiguous news.

$$H_A : \mu_1 - \mu_2 \neq 0$$

The hypothesis is tested as follows. The two experimental designs are compared; they only differ by the (un)known probabilities of the value distribution. The average bids or traded prices (depending on the auction set-up) are compared to the expected value when the probabilities are known. Second, they are compared to the expected value with Bayesian updating when the probabilities are not known. This comparison leads to a premium measure, which is calculated as follows:

$$\text{Premium} = (\text{Expected value} / \text{Traded price}) - 1$$

Table 6.4 Average premium, variance thereof and number of observations of the first stage experiments

No.	Treatment	Average premium (%)	Variance of premium (%)	No. of observations
1	Auctioneer with known probabilities	31.50	19.79	226
2	Auctioneer with unknown probabilities	30.50	29.73	219
3	Batch auction with known probabilities	−2.90	0.10	687
4	Batch auction with unknown probabilities	−1.70	0.50	885
5	Continuous double auction (0/80 70/80) with 30%/70% and known probabilities	0.84	0.18	1,730
6	Continuous double auction (0/80 70/80) with 30%/70% and unknown probabilities	2.86	0.77	1,586
7	Continuous double auction (0/80 70/80) with 50%/50% and known probabilities	1.04	0.35	2,251
8	Continuous double auction (0/80 70/80) with 50%/50% and unknown probabilities	3.42	1.00	3,392
9	Continuous double auction (0/200 160/200) with 30%/70% and known probabilities	−1.57	0.27	2,084
10	Continuous double auction (0/200 160/200) with 30%/70% and unknown probabilities	1.32	0.50	1,341
11	Continuous double auction (0/200 160/200) with 50%/50% and known probabilities	−3.39	1.17	3,039
12	Continuous double auction (0/200 160/200) with 50%/50% and unknown probabilities	−3.08	1.87	2,130

The distributions of premiums are compared with each other. If the ambiguous news is priced as non-ambiguous news, then the average premiums should not differ from each other systematically.

The results of the first stage experiments are presented in Table 6.4.

Comments:

- *Comparison of the different auction types:* The average premium in the auctioneer setting is far higher than for the other auction settings (batch auction and continuous double auction). The explanation for this effect could be the following. The participants only stand in competition with one other participant for buying a share. This has led many participants to state bids below the expected value. In the batch auction and continuous auction setting, the participants are in competition with all other participants to buy and sell shares. It seems reasonable to assume that the increasing competition leads to bids and asking prices closer to the expected value.
- *Comparison of the average premiums:* The average premiums of the experimental settings with unknown probabilities are slightly higher than with known probabilities (between 0.3% and 2.9%; see Table 6.5), with the exception of the auctioneer setting. For the experiments with an auctioneer, the average premium is slightly lower with unknown probabilities. A one-sided Kolmogorov–Smirnoff test is performed to test for significance differences in the premiums. For the auctioneer treatment, the hypothesis of higher average premiums cannot be rejected at a 10% level (χ^2 values with two degrees of freedom $=1.04$). For all other treatments, however, the average premiums are significantly higher for the experiments with unknown probabilities (χ^2 values with two degrees of freedom > 14).

Table 6.5   Comparison of the average premiums and premium variances

No.	Treatment	Difference of average premiums (unknown probabilities – known probabilities) (%)	Factor of premium variances (unknown to known probabilities)
1/2	Auctioneer	−1.0	1.5
3/4	Batch auction	+1.2	5.0
5/6	Continuous double auction (0/80 70/80) with 30%/70%	+2.0	4.3
7/8	Continuous double auction (0/80 70/80) with 50%/50%	+2.4	2.6
9/10	Continuous double auction (0/200 160/200) with 30%/70%	+2.9	1.9
11/12	Continuous double auction (0/200 160/200) with 50%/50%	+0.3	1.6

This implies that hypothesis 1: *Ambiguous news is priced as non-ambiguous news*

$$H_0 : \mu_1 - \mu_2 = 0$$

can be rejected at a 0.1% level for the batch auction and continuous double auction experiments. But for the auctioneer treatment, the hypothesis cannot be rejected at a 10% level.

• *Comparison of the premium variances:* What stands out in Tables 6.4 and 6.5 is that the premium variances of the sessions with unknown probabilities are a lot higher than for the corresponding experiments with known probabilities. In fact, the variances are in all cases at least 50% higher.

It is to be noted that, for the auctioneer setting, the absolute level of premium variances is far higher than for the other settings. It seems reasonable to assume that this observation is also due to the lower competition in comparison with the other auction settings.

A two-sided Kolmogorov–Smirnoff test is performed to test for significance differences in the premium variances. For the auctioneer treatment, the hypothesis of different premium variances cannot be rejected at a 10% level (D value = 0.048). For all other treatments, however, the average premiums are significantly different for the experiments with unknown probabilities (D values > 0.2).

Additional comment: A striking feature in the continuous double auction settings is the amount of trading. An experiment lasted for 30 periods of 90 seconds each. Looking at sessions 8 and 11, there were over 3,000 trades, which corresponds to over one trade per second. This incredible amount of trading is an additional indicator for very heterogeneous attitudes towards risk and ambiguity.

6.4.4   Discussion

The results obtained fit well into the existing literature. The relationship between ambiguity aversion and asset pricing characteristics has been studied by several authors.

The study closest to the experiments is the one by Bossaerts et al. (2004). Their experimental analysis is carried out in the context of simultaneously traded state securities, some of which pay in states for which probabilities are unknown (the ambiguous states) and others pay in states for which probabilities are known (the risky states). The authors point out that, in the discussion about the Ellsberg paradox and ambiguity aversion, 'it is often overlooked that the data clearly shows that not everybody violates the axioms of expected utility . . . '.[45] Therefore not all individuals should be considered ambiguity-averse and there exists heterogeneity with respect to attitudes towards ambiguity. The authors ask the following question, given such heterogeneity, what are the outcomes in a market setting where securities are traded whose payoffs have varying levels of ambiguity?

Bossaerts et al. argue that heterogeneity in ambiguity aversion increases the range and variance of equilibrium state price probability ratios. When markets are complete, these ratios refer to the ratio of equilibrium state prices over state probabilities and will be ranked inversely to the aggregate wealth across states.[46] For most price configurations highly ambiguity-averse agents prefer to hold ambiguous securities in equal quantities. They leave the less ambiguity-averse and the ambiguity-neutral to absorb the entire imbalance in relative supplies of ambiguous securities. The imbalance to be accommodated is far greater than if the ambiguity-averse subjects had taken their share, as they would have in the absence of ambiguity (in which all agents remain at least exposed to risk). The less ambiguity-averse individuals will ask for a higher compensation to absorb the supply imbalance in ambiguous securities only if compensated appropriately. This leads to the increase in the spread, with regards to range and variance, of the state price probability ratios.

Second, if ambiguous securities are in high supply, the more ambiguity-tolerant agents may demand so much compensation for holding the ambiguous securities that the simple ranking relationship between state price probability ratios and aggregate wealth is upset. When ambiguous states exist, then the state price probability ratios of some of the ambiguous states may rise above those of pure-risk states, even when aggregate wealth in the latter states is lower.

There have been other experimental studies on the effect of non-standard preferences on choices in competitive markets. Sarin and Weber (1993) perform sealed-bid as well as double-oral auctions for lotteries. They find that individual bids and market prices for lotteries with ambiguous probabilities are consistently lower than for equivalent lotteries with well-defined probabilities. The authors try to find a possible explanation for that effect. For the sealed-bid auction setting they suspect that 'subjects do not directly interact with each other, and the announced market price at the end of each period does not convey sufficient information on individual bid prices. Thus, the market force is not strong enough to induce rationality in such situations.'[47] However, the same result is found for the double-oral auction setting, which allows for a more active interaction among participants. The authors therefore conclude that ambiguity aversion does not disappear in market settings.

Bossaerts et al. point out that the recent literature has tried to explain the equity premium puzzle by applying a representative and ambiguity-averse agent with simple state-independent utility.[48] The authors strongly emphasize that their result of ambiguity heterogeneity, even in relatively small groups, induces pricing effects that cannot be modeled simply as if there is an ambiguity-averse investor with state-independent preferences. The results of the individual two-color Ellsberg experiment as well as the observation of very different trading strategies among the subjects allow me to agree with Bossaerts et al.'s standpoint completely. The importance of heterogeneous beliefs and expectations on optimal trading strategies and equilibrium asset pricing is also explicitly mentioned in Ziegler.[49] Furthermore Mandelbrot states that 'once you drop the assumption of homogeneity, new and complicated things can happen in your mathematical models of your market'.[50]

Although Epstein and Schneider (2004) model a representative ambiguity-averse agent model, they provide new insights on asset pricing implications from the valuation and updating of ambiguous information. In their discrete-time framework, ambiguous information is incorporated into a choice-theoretical framework and studied in a financial market. In their model, Φ denotes a parameter that the agent wants to learn to update beliefs upon the incoming ambiguous information. The authors make the assumption that an information signal g is related to the parameter Φ by a family of probability:

$$g = \Phi + \varepsilon, \qquad \varepsilon \sim N(0, \rho_g^2), \qquad \rho_g^2 \in \left[\underline{\rho}_g^2, \overline{\rho}_g^2 \right]$$

The authors capture the quality of the ambiguous information by the range of precisions, denoted by $[1/\overline{\rho}_g^2, 1/\underline{\rho}_g^2]$. Bayesian models are the special case of single probability, $\underline{\rho}_g^2 = \overline{\rho}_g^2$, and measure the quality of information of the signal g by the precision $1/\rho_g^2$. The quality of ambiguous information has two dimensions: the overall location of the interval determines how quickly an agent expects uncertainty to be resolved, while its width measures the (lack of) confidence in the reliability of the signal. The latter dimension is unique to the case of ambiguity.

The authors model preferences as recursive multiple-priors utility (RMPU). Epstein and Schneider (2003) provide an axiomatization for this class of utility functions. The axioms describe behavior consistent with an ambiguity-averse agent who acts as if he maximizes, in every period, expected utility under a worst-case belief that is chosen from a set of conditional probabilities. The modeling of preferences as RMPU has two key effects on behavior:[51]

1. *After* a signal has arrived, the agent responds asymmetrically. Bad news affects conditional choices more than good news. If an ambiguous signal conveys good (bad) news, the worst case is that the signal is unreliable (very reliable).
2. *Before* a signal arrives, agents who anticipate the arrival of the low-quality information will discount their consumption plans for which this information may be relevant.

Epstein and Schneider compare information quality across situations by measuring the information content of a signal *relative* to the volatility of the parameter. When ρ_g^2 is fixed, then the coefficient $\gamma(\rho_g^2)$ provides such a measure. It determines the fraction of prior variance in Φ that is resolved by the signal. With ambiguous signals, $\underline{\gamma} = \gamma(\overline{\rho}_g^2)$ and $\overline{\gamma} = \gamma(\underline{\rho}_g^2)$ provide lower and upper bounds on the (relative) information content. In the Bayesian case $\overline{\gamma}$ is equal to $\underline{\gamma}$. Therefore the agents know precisely how much information the signal contains. In the ambiguous case, $\overline{\gamma} - \underline{\gamma}$ is positive and not equal to zero. The greater $\overline{\gamma} - \underline{\gamma}$ is, the less confident the agents feel about the information content. This dimension of information quality is new with ambiguous signals.

The authors embed a three-period model of news release into an infinite-horizon asset price model. The level of dividends of the asset is given by a mean-reverting process $d_t = \kappa \overline{d} + (1 - \kappa) d_{t-1} + \mu_t$, where d_t is the level of dividends at time t, $\kappa \in (0, 1)$ measures the speed with which the dividends adjust back to their mean $\overline{d}$, and μ_t is a shock at time t. In every period, agents observe an ambiguous signal about the shock of the next period's dividend $g_t = \mu_{t+1} + \varepsilon_t^g$ where the variance of ε_t^g is $\rho_{g,t}^2 \in [\underline{\rho}_g^2, \overline{\rho}_g^2]$. For econometric reasons, Epstein and Schneider assume that there is a true variance of noise $\rho_g^{*2} \in [\underline{\rho}_g^2, \overline{\rho}_g^2]$ and that $\gamma^* = \gamma(\overline{\rho}_g^{*2})$ is defined as a measure of the true information content of the news arriving in a typical trading period.

Various asset price properties are derived under the conditions formulated above, such as the equity premium, idiosyncratic risk, excess volatility and negative skewness. In particular, the variance of the stock price in their model is:

$$\mathrm{var}(q_t) = \rho_\mu^2 \left(\frac{1-\kappa}{r+\kappa} \right)^2 \left(\frac{1}{\kappa(2-\kappa)} + \frac{1}{2\gamma^*} \left(\overline{\gamma}^2 + \underline{\gamma}^2 - \frac{1}{\pi} (\overline{\gamma} - \underline{\gamma})^2 \right) \right)$$

where q_t is the stock price, r is the risk-free interest rate and π is the probability measure concerning the anticipation of future ambiguous news. Price volatility is proportional to the volatility of the shock μ, so in the case where $\overline{\gamma} = \underline{\gamma} = 0$, the asset's price volatility is equal to that of the present value of dividends. In the Bayesian case where $\overline{\gamma} = \underline{\gamma} = \gamma^*$ for a given κ, price volatility is increasing in information quality and is bounded above. In particular when κ is small, changes in information quality only have small effects on price volatility in comparison to the volatility of the present value of the dividends. With ambiguous signals, the volatility of prices is increasing both in $\overline{\gamma}$ and $\underline{\gamma}$. In addition, as the authors note, the possibility of ambiguous news removes the upper bound on price volatility imposed by the Bayesian model. They therefore conclude that 'ambiguous signals can thus contribute to excess volatility of prices'.[52]

Concerning the volatility of returns, changes in information quality due to the ambiguity of signals affect volatility of prices and returns in the same way, contrary to the Bayesian case.[53]

Epstein and Schneider conclude that the additional structure of ambiguity in signals (i) clarifies the anticipation of ambiguous news to be sufficient for the ambiguity premium and (ii) creates a direct link between the size of the ambiguity premium and the measured volatility of fundamentals.[54] From these insights, the equity premium should be higher and the traded prices lower for shares with ambiguous fundamentals. In particular, as the authors note, 'the premium changes to different degrees depending on the way in which information quality is increased'.[55] The lower the information quality is, the higher is the demanded premium.

Relating their formal model to the experiments, two aspects are noteworthy. The first aspect concerns the traded prices and the level of ambiguity aversion in the traded prices. For the participants, the information quality is generally high in the first stage experiments. The reason for this is that the distributions are just slightly overlapping. It is therefore fairly easy for participants to judge from which distribution the value of the asset's share stems. If the two distributions were not overlapping, then a perfect Bayesian updating would be possible. Therefore the results are well in line with Epstein and Schneider's model, as the participants show a slight aversion towards ambiguity as can be seen in the traded prices.

The second aspect to be discussed is the volatility of the traded prices. In Epstein and Schneider's model, price volatility is increasing in $\overline{\gamma}$ and $\underline{\gamma}$. As the authors note, the price and return volatility depends on how much the worst-case conditional expectation of fundamentals fluctuates. If the range of precision perceived by ambiguity-averse agents is large, they will attach more weight to the ambiguous signal than when agreeing on the same, true precision. Therefore information with a large range of perceived precision can cause large price fluctuations. This aspect can be linked to the first stage experiments. When the probabilities of the distributions of the share's value are known, the precision is the same for all participants and it is clear-cut. In the experimental set-up with unknown probabilities, however, it is not unlikely that a participant will perceive the precision of the information signal not uniquely. This would therefore lead to a range of perceived precision which could be one of the causes for the strong increase in the observed price volatility.

6.4.5   Conclusion

In the first stage experiments the impact of one particular aspect of rumors has been studied, namely their ambiguity in nature, in a financial markets setting. First, on average slight though significant ambiguity aversion is found. Second, and probably the greater effect of the two, significantly higher price volatilities are observed when subjects trade given ambiguous information.

The experiments conducted differ from the other two experimental studies mentioned above in the following respect: Bossaerts et al. conduct continuous double-auction experiments where subjects trade assets simultaneously, some of which pay in states with known and some in states with unknown probabilities. Sarin and Weber conduct sealed-bid as well as double-oral auctions. In their experiment, subjects trade two types of assets, some for which probabilities of states are known, and some for which probabilities are not known. They let the subjects trade the assets independently as well as simultaneously; however, all subjects trade both types of assets. In this experiment, subjects trade only one type of asset in a continuous double auction.

While Sarin and Weber focus on the resulting market price effects and find that ambiguity aversion does not disappear, Bossaerts et al. provide additional insights into the subjects' heterogeneity towards ambiguity aversion and the range of state price probability ratios. The results of the experiments lead to the same conclusions as Bossaerts et al. concerning the subjects' heterogeneity as well as the strong increase of the asset price's volatility. Concerning the market pricing effect of ambiguity, a direct comparison with the two other experiments is not possible. The reason for this lies in the special construction of the two overlapping distributions constructed to reflect a potential rumor.

Relating the experimental insights to the theoretical models of ambiguity aversion and the empirical observations after rumor evolvement, the following points seem worth noting. When rumors evolve,

- the information signal is typically very ambiguous, and
- agents have heterogeneous attitudes towards ambiguity.

Rumors are exemplary for being ambiguous in nature and for having poor information quality. This feature leaves room for different perceptions and interpretations of the signal's precision. When the range of the signal's precision perceived by an ambiguity-averse agent is large, then this kind of ambiguous information can cause large price fluctuations and excess volatility. In addition, the assumption does not seem so strict that many market participants are overconfident in estimating the rumor's validity (compare also the results of the survey in Chapter 5). Various papers have shown that overconfidence is one of the sources of over- and under-reaction to information signals and excess volatility of asset prices.[56] When agents are overconfident, their perceived precision of an information signal is higher than the 'true' precision. Therefore the agents' response is more aggressive than under rational expectations and leads to excessive volatility. The concepts of overconfident and ambiguity-averse agents are not incompatible, but rather complementary. While overconfidence is an assumption about the relationship between the true and subjectively perceived precision of signals, ambiguity aversion is an assumption about subjective preferences only. It is therefore possible to describe overconfident and at the same time ambiguity-averse agents. Concerning a rumor to be an ambiguous information signal, it seems reasonable to assume that among the participants there is a large range of perceptions of how precise the rumor actually is. The model of Epstein and Schneider has shown that this range of perceived precision can cause large asset price fluctuations.

As a conclusion, there are well-founded theoretical arguments for the empirically observed phenomena. When market participants have heterogeneous attitudes towards ambiguity, they perceive and interpret ambiguous information differently and are overconfident about the estimating rumor's validity, each of the three factors can separately and independently increase the asset price's volatility. It should therefore not come as a surprise to see high asset price fluctuations after a rumor appears on financial markets.

As an implication for the real world, it definitely pays off for a company to make crystal-clear statements when communicating to the public and the financial analysts in particular. Otherwise, all of a sudden, misunderstandings provoke unwanted rumors. As an example, John Coomber, CEO of Swiss Re, stated in an interview in June of 2003 that Swiss Re had to further increase their provision for depreciation on their financial assets. Although this was just a repetition of the announcement of the year-end figures for 2002, the financial community interpreted it differently. This started rumors on a possible earnings warning and the stock price fell up to 10%, before Swiss Re reiterated that the statement in the interview contained no new information. The stock price recovered, but not to quite the same price level as before.

6.5 SECOND STAGE EXPERIMENTS: VARYING RUMOR MESSAGES

In the second stage rumor experiments, psychological arguments for believing a rumor are investigated. The hypothesis is tested whether the credibility of the source and the plausibility of the rumor's content have an impact on the traded prices. This was an often-mentioned statement in the survey, that depending on the plausibility of the content and the sources' credibility people act differently on rumors. In order to test the hypothesis, text messages are spread that vary in the content of the text's message.

6.5.1 A Brief Discussion of the Existing Literature

Psychology research has determined primarily three reasons why rumors are believed:

1. The *source*, meaning the person or institution communicating the rumor to us:[57] Attention is paid only to those messages people want to listen to, and they scrutinize the source to decide what to think of the message.[58] Several factors are responsible for trusting a source:[59] the impression of its know-how, reliability, unselfishness, dynamic and personality.

   In financial markets the degree of the source's credibility is greater from personally transmitted rumors than from those transmitted by media. The media usually refer to sources such as 'industry sources, insiders and other credible people'. It is somewhat difficult to estimate the source's credibility from that kind of specification. A rumor heard from an industry research analyst is certainly more credible than one from your neighbor who occasionally trades as a hobby in financial markets. Personally communicated rumors can take either of two forms.[60] First, the person communicating wants to persuade the other person and identifies himself with the rumor. The informant therefore does not have a neutral attitude towards it. The other form is more informal where the person mentions having picked up the rumor from hearsay. Then it is not referred to an expert or an original source and there is no desire to achieve a well-considered approval.

2. The *plausibility* of the rumor's content: It is necessary that the content of the rumor is at least plausible.[61] No matter how high the credibility of the source, the message requires a certain plausibility to affect one's opinion. As an example, if there were a rumor that Novartis, a pharmaceutical company, and UBS, a large bank, would merge, no one would believe it because it is simply not plausible.

3. The *desire* to believe: In some cases the rumor is a message people *want* to believe, so that the traditional measures of objectivity and credibility are overridden.[62]

    The rumor of McDonald's adding earthworms to their hamburgers in the early 1980s in the U.S. is an example of this kind. Although it seems absolutely incredible, it was widely believed at the time. The rumor was desired by those people who were worried about the eating habits of the American people. Not by accident the term 'junk food' was created at the time. When rumors are desired, they bring something to the surface that has been hidden below and has never had the chance to be expressed. The rumor can then be used as a valve for psychological relief.

Economic experiments have typically not focused on the question of how the presentation of information content of messages determines asset prices. From a conceptual view, one of the experimental studies closest to the second stage is that of Ackert et al. (2004). The authors investigate whether providing participants with information about a firm's home base is sufficient to change investment behavior, i.e. whether it predisposes participants to invest more in domestic securities. In addition they study whether familiarity, specifically the revelation of the firm's name, underlies the home-bias effect, controlling for the information available to participants. Several experiments have been conducted in the U.S. and Canada investigating agents' portfolio allocation decisions, controlling for the availability of information. They find that providing information about a firm's home base without disclosing its specific identity is not sufficient to change the agents' portfolio allocation decisions. Rather, in order to change the agents' portfolio allocation, they need to know the firm's name *and* home base. Additional evidence indicates that participants have a greater perceived familiarity with local and domestic securities and, in turn, invest more in such securities. The authors conclude that familiarity is therefore a key determinant of portfolio allocation decisions and one of the sources of the home bias effect. The explicit presentation of the firm's name therefore does make a difference.

Relating these insights to the second stage rumor experiments, the question is asked whether the explicit mentioning of the plausibility of the rumor's content as well as the credibility of the rumor's source have an impact on the traded prices. The third argument (desire to believe) is difficult if not impossible to test in such a context, since it is not possible to tell the participants how much they *want* to believe a rumor. However, it is possible to communicate the credibility of the source as well as the plausibility of the rumor's content.

In comparison to Ackert et al.'s study, the experiments would not be classified as testing explicitly familiarity, only testing what kind of informational content is able to impact traded prices.

6.5.2   Experimental Design

6.5.2.1   Experimental game and procedure

The experimental procedure follows the same structure as that of the first stage experiments in the continuous double-auction treatment, with the following modifications (for the detailed instructions, please refer to Appendix II.1):

- You will be endowed each period with 10 shares of company X and 2500 'cash' points. In each period you are given the possibility to submit bid and asking prices for buying and selling shares. At the end of the period the positions will be closed. For every period you will be endowed with the same amount of shares and 'cash' points. Your gains and losses will be counted for each period and summed up in the end.
- You are requested to give asking prices and bids for the shares you hold or would like to purchase. Type your bids and asking prices into the corresponding fields on your screen. Remember that you can only give as many bids for shares as you have cash for. Second, you are allowed to ask for up to the 10 shares you have (no short selling allowed).

    In each of the 12 periods the value of the share of company X will be between 0 and 200. In addition during each period you will receive on your screen further news about the value of the share. All messages are communicated to you via newsticker.

    Attention! The news that you will receive during each period can be, but does not have to be, truthful. If, though, within the messages probability measures are specified, then these are always correct.

    At the end of each period you are informed about the value of the share.

The sequence of the spread messages, as in Appendix II.1, is random. In addition, the time within each period when the message is spread is random as well. It is, though, always spread within the first 30 seconds of each period. The participants receive the messages all at the same time. They do not know anything concerning the probabilities of the underlying distributions, from which the value of the share is drawn. The actual distribution probabilities are available in Appendix II.1.

The messages differentiate from each other as follows:

1. *Positive vs. negative rumor:* In the first message it is stated that company X is in merger talks and the value of the share will be at least 160. In the second message it is stated that company X will release a profit warning and the value of the share will be at the most 40.
2. *Plausible vs. non-plausible content of the rumor:* In addition to the positive or negative statement, the participants receive an estimation of the rumor's content plausibility. In the first message it is stated that in their opinion the rumor's content appears to be plausible. In the second message it is stated that in their opinion the rumor's content appears to be not plausible.
3. *Credible vs. non-credible source of the rumor:* In addition to the positive or negative statement, the participants receive an estimation of the rumor's source credibility. In the first message it is stated that in their opinion the rumor's source appears to be credible.

In the second message it is stated that in their opinion the rumor's source appears to be not credible.

In addition to the messages spread, two neutral messages are spread as a controlling function. The first neutral message does not contain any addition to the positive or negative rumor. The second neutral message contains the additional sentence that the probability of the rumor becoming true is estimated at 50% (see also Appendix II.1).

6.5.2.2 Subjects and sessions

Concerning the subjects, the same rules apply for the second as for the first stage experiments. In total five experimental sessions were conducted. The computerized experiment was programmed and conducted with experimental software z-Tree.[63] A session lasted approximately 90 minutes and subjects earned on average CHF 42 (approximately USD 33.6, October 2004).

6.5.3 Results of the Second Stage Experiments

For the second stage experiments, the corresponding testable hypothesis is the following:

Hypothesis 1: *There is no difference in the traded prices upon the presentation of the different messages.*

$$H_0 : \mu_1 - \mu_2 = 0, \qquad H_A : \mu_1 - \mu_2 \neq 0$$

where μ_1 represents the average traded price after rumors presented with a credible source / plausible content, and μ_2 represents the average traded price after rumors presented with a non-credible source/non-plausible content.

The hypothesis is tested as follows. The average traded prices in the two periods after the rumor has been spread are compared with each other. The two periods are compared with each other in which the respective messages differ only in the credibility/non-credibility and plausibility/non-plausibility of the rumor. This is done for the positive (at least 160) as well as for the negative (at the most 40) rumors. The message number in Table 6.6 corresponds to the number of the message stated in Appendix II.1. Message numbers 1, 2, 7 and 8 are control messages.

The results show that average traded prices are higher after positive than after negative rumors. This result should not be surprising. The H_0 hypotheses are tested with a one-sided Wilcoxon–Mann–Whitney test, using the average traded prices of each of the five sessions (see Table 6.7).

When rumors with plausible content are spread, the average traded price is significantly higher at a 5% level than when non-plausible rumors are spread. This holds for positive as well as for negative rumors. In the latter case the traded prices are significantly lower. When rumors with credible sources are spread, the average traded prices are not significantly higher at a 5% level (though at a 10% level) than when rumors with non-credible sources are spread. This holds for positive as well as for negative rumors.

Therefore the hypothesis H_0 can be rejected for the plausible / non-plausible content rumor, though it cannot be rejected for the credible / non-credible source of the rumor.

Table 6.6 Average traded prices after the rumor has been spread with the corresponding message

	Message number	Message spread	Average traded prices over the five sessions after the rumor has been spread
Positive rumor	1	160	128.1
	2	160 with 50% true	143.8
	3	160 and plausible content	140.9
	4	160 and non-plausible content	124.3
	5	160 and credible source	137.8
	6	160 and non-credible source	122.5
Negative rumor	7	40	101.9
	8	40 with 50% true	103.9
	9	40 and plausible content	89.1
	10	40 and non-plausible content	111.6
	11	40 and credible source	95.3
	12	40 and non-credible source	111.2

Table 6.7 p-Values of the Wilcoxon–Mann–Whitney test for the traded prices of the second stage experiments

Message spread	p-Values of the Wilcoxon–Mann–Whitney test
160 plausible vs. 160 non-plausible content	0.028
160 credible vs. 160 non-credible source	0.075
160 with 50% true vs. 160 plausible content	0.421
160 with 50% true vs. 160 non-plausible content	0.004
160 with 50% true vs. 160 credible source	0.155
160 with 50% true vs. 160 non-credible source	0.016
40 plausible vs. 40 non-plausible content	0.016
40 credible vs. 40 non-credible source	0.075
40 with 50% true vs. 40 plausible content	0.048
40 with 50% true vs. 40 non-plausible content	0.210
40 with 50% true vs. 40 credible source	0.210
40 with 50% true vs. 40 non-credible source	0.210

How can this difference between the two hypotheses be interpreted? As with the study by Ackert et al., it is important to state what kind of additional information content is presented with the asset traded. In Ackert et al.'s case, the name of the firm creates a familiarity for the participants that is not available when mentioning the asset's home base alone. This additional, familiar content is the determining factor for allocating more capital to the home-based asset. In my opinion, the critical issue for their study, and this one, is that through the additional information content participants are able to establish a connection to the asset traded. In Ackert et al.'s study, it is the name of the firm; in these experiments it is either the plausibility of the rumor's content or the credibility of the rumor's source. Ackert et al. state in their conclusions that 'participants need to know firms' names, presumably to establish a connection or association with particular firms'. In the case of the rumor's plausibility, it is fairly easy to establish such a connection, since the participants know something about the asset (profit warning or in merger talks). In comparison thereto, participants are not able to build a connection to the source, since they do not know anything more about it. This missing possibility of creating a connection to the source could be a potential reason for the different results.

The overall picture of the results looks very consistent for the case of spreading positive rumors (value of at least 160), while for the negative rumors it is a bit more ambiguous. The traded prices for spreading positive rumors with 50% are also significantly higher in comparison with non-credible and non-plausible rumors (*p*-values 0.004 and 0.016). However, when comparing them with credible and plausible rumors there are no significance differences (*p*-values 0.421 and 0.155). With negative rumors, the results are not clear-cut. Within the exception of 50% true vs. plausible content (*p*-value = 0.048), no significant price differences could be observed. It is not to be ruled out that the participants had more difficulty assessing and interpreting negative rumors in comparison with the positive rumors.

An additional insight is how much stronger the price impact is with positive rumors than for negative rumors, measuring it from the mean value of the distribution. Indeed, using a Wilcoxon–Mann–Whitney test, for all sessions and messages spread the price impact for positive rumors is significantly higher than for negative rumors (all *p*-values = 0.004). Two explanations for this effect seem reasonable: First, the participants are biased by being long in the stock, since they receive in the beginning a basic amount of cash and stocks to trade with. Second, the market participants are not allowed to short-sell. The short-selling restriction limits the possibility of positioning the participants short of stock. Which of the two explanations is the more suitable for discussion? Possibly it is a combination of the two factors accentuating the effect in such a pronounced manner.

One of the striking features concerning the first stage experiments has been the higher price volatility observed when the probabilities, from which distribution the value is drawn, are not known. The volatility of traded prices in the second stage experiments is shown in Table 6.8. The results are interesting and somewhat surprising, though not clear-cut. Again using the Wilcoxon–Mann–Whitney test (see Table 6.9), there seems to be a significant difference in the traded prices' volatility, depending on the rumor messages spread.

Table 6.8 Standard deviation of the traded prices after the rumor has been spread with the corresponding message

	Message number	Message spread	Average traded price volatilities over the five sessions after the rumor has been spread (standard deviation)
Positive rumor	1	160	10.97
	2	160 with 50% true	7.22
	3	160 and plausible content	10.78
	4	160 and non-plausible content	8.00
	5	160 and credible source	10.48
	6	160 and non-credible source	7.05
Negative rumor	7	40	14.59
	8	40 with 50% true	8.71
	9	40 and plausible content	16.07
	10	40 and non-plausible content	9.77
	11	40 and credible source	17.20
	12	40 and non-credible source	8.38

Table 6.9 *p*-Values of the Wilcoxon–Mann–Whitney test for the traded prices' standard deviation in the second stage experiments

Message spread	*p*-Values of the Wilcoxon–Mann–Whitney test
160 plausible vs. 160 non-plausible content	0.075
160 credible vs. 160 non-credible source	0.048
160 with 50% true vs. 160 plausible content	0.048
160 with 50% true vs. 160 non-plausible content	0.421
160 with 50% true vs. 160 credible source	0.004
160 with 50% true vs. 160 non-credible source	0.421
40 plausible vs. 40 non-plausible content	0.075
40 credible vs. 40 non-credible source	0.048
40 with 50% true vs. 40 plausible content	0.075
40 with 50% true vs. 40 non-plausible content	0.274
40 with 50% true vs. 40 credible source	0.048
40 with 50% true vs. 40 non-credible source	0.579

Interestingly enough, for both positive and negative rumors, the significance of the volatility's difference is much lower for 50% true vs. non-plausible and 50% true vs. non-credible rumors in comparison to the other messages. For some volatility differences, the significance for some messages is strong (both credible vs. non-credible source and 50% true vs. credible source), for some it is weak (plausible vs. non-plausible content and 50% true vs. plausible content). But it appears that concerning traded prices and volatility three types of rumor messages can be differentiated:

1. The rumor is going to be true with 50% (positive and negative): There is a strong price impact, though the volatility of the traded prices stays low.
2. Rumors with credible sources and plausible contents (positive and negative): There is a strong price impact and the volatility of the traded prices is high.
3. Rumors with non-credible sources and non-plausible contents (positive and negative): There is no strong price impact, and the volatility of the traded prices is low.

The second stage experiments fit well into the results of the first stage experiments. A direct comparison, though, is only possible with experiments no. 11 and no. 12 of the first stage. Comparing experiment no. 11 of the first stage and spreading of message no. 2 of the second stage, in both experiments the average traded price is slightly above the expected value. The average premiums to the expected value are −3.4% and −2.7% correspondingly. In addition, in both cases the price volatility is comparably low. One difference to be mentioned between the two experiments of the first and second stage is that in the first stage the participants were explicitly informed about the two distributions, while in the second stage they were only informed that the value of the share would be at least 160. In addition, they received the message during the period and not at the beginning of it. Whether these two minor differences actually had an influence on the trading behavior is difficult to estimate.

As a final comment, concerning the traded volume in the second stage experiments the exact same phenomenon is observed as in the first stage experiments. The amount of trading is very high, sometimes at a rate of one trade per second. This again is a strong indicator of the great heterogeneity not only of attitudes towards ambiguous situations, but also towards the perception and interpretation of the messages spread.

6.5.4   Conclusion

The way information content is presented can have an impact on the traded prices. The add-on of the plausibility of the rumor's content leads to significantly different traded prices: higher prices for positive rumors and lower prices for negative rumors. The same effect does not hold for the credibility of the source, at least not on a 5% significance level. A possible interpretation thereof is that the market participants have to be able to build a connection to the traded asset to influence asset prices. This argumentation is consistent with the conclusions of Ackert et al., in which they suggest that participants presumably need to establish a connection or association with particular firms in order to change their investment behavior. These experiments do not test for familiarity as in Ackert et al., only for additional informational content affecting traded asset prices.

When the probability of 50% is known, then the traded price moves without much volatility even a little beyond the expected price. When the rumor's content is plausible or the source is credible, there is also a strong price movement, with much larger volatility, however, than in the case when the rumor is known to be true with 50%. In comparison thereto with non-plausible content of rumors and non-credible sources, the price movement is smaller and the volatility is lower.

Concerning the test of psychological insights, they can be confirmed to a strong degree. Significantly different prices with plausible rumors are observed. With the credibility of the source, there is too little context and the participants are not able to learn its credibility. Therefore the results should not surprise us too much: the significance of different prices is only obtained at a 10% level.

The results of the survey can therefore be fully confirmed. It seems also intuitively very comprehensible that when rumors evolve with a credible source or at least have been communicated via a credible medium, the rumor is more believed by the market and the price will move accordingly. Concerning the plausibility of the content, this seems almost to be a precondition in the marketplace. If the rumor's content is too implausible, the market will simply ignore it. A good example in this regard is the German bank Commerzbank. There were literally hundreds of rumors about which bank it would merge with. Nothing happened. While at first the stock price reacted to the new rumors, the subsequent rumors had less and less of an impact on the stock price, especially because more and more implausible merger candidates were named. Meanwhile it seemed, and this is what the executive board of Commerzbank had always been pointing out, that they indeed would not merge with anyone, and that the market seemed slowly to be accepting this.

6.6   THIRD STAGE EXPERIMENTS: TESTING HERD BEHAVIOR

In the third stage of rumor experiments, the question to be answered focuses on the phenomenon of herd behavior. From the results of the survey (see Section 5.7.4), the presumption of herd behavior after rumor evolvement seems not too bold. Around 70% of the participants stated that they would consider action on rumor when the price had already moved. In addition, market participants are often said to be influenced by others, whether it is rational or not. The irrational convergence in actions and beliefs is then referred to as 'herd instinct' or a contagious response driven by emotions in stressful situations.

The third stage experiments closely follow the model of Avery and Zemsky (1998). The goal is to verify one of their model predictions in an experimental setting. Their model is discussed in detail in the next section. Details on the experimental design can be found in Section 6.6.2.1. 'Experimental game and procedure'.

6.6.1 A Brief Overview of Herd Behavior in Financial Markets

6.6.1.1 Basic structuring of herd behavior

People are influenced by others taking action in almost all activities, in particular in financial markets. This influence is often referred to as herd behavior. It has become for many people a synonym for acting irrationally. Indeed, there have been many examples underscoring such behavior, such as the stock price bubble of technology stocks in the late 1990s. When market prices move to levels that are not justifiable by fundamental news, then many practitioners and the media find proof of irrational herd behavior.

The academic literature has put a lot of effort into the theoretical and empirical investigation of the influence of irrational investors on asset prices.[64] However, academic research also suggests that these apparent irrational phenomena can also arise naturally in settings with rational investors. Since this might appear confusing, it seems necessary to distinguish the different forms of herd behavior.[65]

Originally, a herd referred to a physical group of animals. Economists have extended its original meaning to a convergent behavior based on social influence. Convergent behavior does not include mere random formations with the illusory appearance of systematic groupings nor cluster behavior wherein people act in a similar way from parallel independent influences of a common external factor. Convergent behavior is hereby understood as taking the same actions as a result of interactions with other individuals. Social influence can affect different areas of our being, e.g. our thoughts, feelings and actions. Many forms of how this influence is exerted can be imagined: by communication and talking with each other, by the observation of actions and the consequences of those actions. The learning process initiated by the influence experienced may be rational or, partly rational, or it may not improve the affected person's decision-making at all. Social influence may lead to convergent behavior or may cause exactly the opposite: divergent behavior. Herd behavior is always considered convergent behavior, though not every convergent behavior is herd behavior. In particular, clustering, where people act in a convergent manner due to a simultaneous and independent influence of an external factor, is usually not regarded as herd behavior. Therefore, one of the unique characteristics of herd behavior is the social influence and interaction between individuals.[66]

Wärneryd distinguishes four different kinds of social influences concerning financial affairs:[67]

1. Small group influence: direct contact from person to person, e.g. a client and a professional advisor.
2. Direct observation and interpretation of other people's behavior.
3. Reports of behavior in news media: news and comments on stock-price changes, trading and transactions, reports on investor behavior.
4. Bandwagon effects: compelling people to conform to an attitude, opinion or action by a large group of people or population segment.

People may seem to be acting independently when making investment decisions on financial markets, but usually they are not. In situations with great uncertainty, people feel the need for advice and support from others. Investment decisions are decisions with great uncertainty, and these are the situations where social influence is largest, when other people are assumed to possess knowledge useful for finding the best decision. According to Festinger (1954), people have a number of reasons why such influences occur. For instance, people have an innate tendency to compare themselves with others. In particular when there are no objective and non-social objects for comparison, then people evaluate their own attitude and capability against those of others.

To relate the statements above more concretely to practice, when portfolio managers are honored when losing 27% in comparison to their benchmark of losing 30% and are punished when gaining 27% in comparison to their benchmark of gaining 30%, they are forced to adjust to the majority as a matter of existence. When market participants decide to invest their capital in financial markets, their actions are, with the information they have and in coordination with other market participants, thought to be advantageous. Such behavior can be considered to be rational, although it does not fulfill the classical economic assumptions of rational behavior. The actions are subjective to achieve their own defined goals. In addition it is assumed that investors are price takers. This is not a critical assumption. At least for large capitalized, liquid stocks, it does not seem possible for a single market participant to steer and control the traded price over a longer period of time.

As already specified in Section 3.2.5, the price is the unintended result of the sum of all intended actions. This is obviously what interests the market participants most. They are therefore forced to adjust their positions to the unintended result. This can happen, for example, based on the development of their portfolio relative to a benchmark or due to new news, such as rumors. These kinds of adjustments lead to an act on the high wire between authenticity and conformity, which causes stress. Stress can be reduced by the integration of groups. Belonging to a group reduces stress, since the members of the group are in the same way affected by future events. However, to be a member of a group requires that the group has an accepted structure of opinion. The positive influence, the reduction of stress, however, has its price: it requires conformity. If you don't act in the same manner as the group, then you cannot feel associated to the group. In stock markets, significant price movements only occur when there are strong groups. It requires many market participants sharing similar opinions leading to widely consistent expectations to move highly capitalized stock markets significantly. However, there does not have be any unity among the group on the methodology of how these expectations are formed. When groups with different methodologies come up with the same expectations and form a coalition, then this will lead to party composition. Parties' composition follow structures and developments as mass psychological movements.[68]

The statements above provide a direct link to the social influence called the 'bandwagon effect'.[69] The fact that many people act in the same manner puts pressure on the others to act in the same way. The more people start to sell a stock and the price starts to fall, the more pressure builds on those keeping the stock. They will not sell the stock for a price so low until other participants are willing to take the risk of not jumping on the bandwagon. This effect has also been regarded as plausible for actors in financial markets.

> Bandwagon effects are plausible for several reasons, for example the homogeneity of the information signals received by the investment community; the similarity in interpretation of news items because of mental frames that are socially and professionally shared; incentive systems that encourage money managers to mimic each other's trades; and notions of prudence and fiduciary duty that depend on external validation.[70]

Hirshleifer and Teoh (2003) have provided guidance on various forms of social influence leading to different degrees of convergent behavior that can be hierarchically structured. Figure 6.4 shows a hierarchical structure of convergent behavior.[71] Letter A refers to a degree of behavior from social influence that can lead to either convergent or dispersing behavior. The degree of convergent behavior gets stronger and stronger until letter D. In letter D the social influence of the interaction is so strong that the individual's action follows that of the other in any case, no matter what information the individual possesses himself.

- *A: Convergence/dispersing:* The observation of others' behavior (communication, actions, or consequences thereof) influences the behavior in such a manner that it may lead to convergent as well as dispersing behavior.
- *B: Observational influence:* The observation of the others' behavior influences the behavior in an imperfect rational way.
- *C: Rational observational learning:* The observation of the others' behavior leads to a rational Bayesian inference.
- *D: Information cascades:* The observation of the others' behavior is so informative that the private signal is neglected and the individual's action follows, in any case, the other, irrespective of the individual's own existing information.

Herd behavior is classified as convergent behavior of type A. It is important to point out the difference between herd behavior and an information cascade, since in the literature the terms are often used interchangeably. Smith and Sorensen[72] emphasize that an information cascade occurs when an infinite sequence of individuals ignore their private information

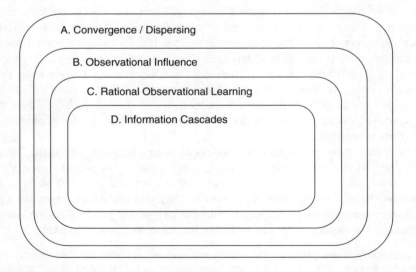

Figure 6.4 Hierarchical structure of convergent behavior.[73]
Source: D. Hirshleifer and S.H. Teoh: Herd behaviour and cascading in capital markets: a review and synthesis, *European Financial Management* **9**(1): 25–66 (2003). Reproduced by permission of Blackwell Publishing.

when making a decision. In comparison, herd behavior occurs when an infinite sequence of individuals makes an identical decision, though not necessarily ignoring their private information. As a consequence, as can be seen in Figure 6.4, an information cascade implies a herd but a herd is not necessarily the result of an information cascade. As Celen and Kariv (2004) note, there is practical importance attached to the distinction between the two. While in a cascade the behavior is purely imitative and does not reveal any information, in a herd the behavior will become more and more like imitation, though the actions may still be informative. In addition, 'in a herd the group settles on a single pattern of behavior and, at the same time, the behavior is fragile in the sense that a strong signal may cause behavior to shift suddenly and dramatically'.[74] On the other hand, an information cascade is stable, meaning no outside signal can change the pattern of the group.

An example of the distinction between herd behavior and an information cascade: I possess shares in Microsoft in my portfolio and have received private information that I should buy more shares of Microsoft. A good friend of mine tells me that has just recently bought shares in Microsoft. If I know the friend well and know that he is competent and has done well in the past when making decisions on financial markets, I could interpret this as a signal for buying more Microsoft shares. I will therefore incorporate his decision into the private information I already possess. If this additional information influences my decision to buy shares in Microsoft, this behavior would be classified as convergent behavior. If the additional information that my friend has recently bought Microsoft influences my decision so that I will actually sell Microsoft shares, this behavior would be classified as dispersing behavior. Both kinds of behavior would be classified in category A of Figure 6.4. If I have heard that not a friend of mine but, instead, Warren Buffett has bought shares in Microsoft, I might ignore everything I know about Microsoft and buy their shares simply because Warren Buffett has bought them. If this is the case, this kind of behavior would be classified as an information cascade as in category D of Figure 6.4. The influence of the signal is so strong that, no matter what I think and what private information I possess, I will follow it in any case.

6.6.1.2   Rational versus irrational herd behavior

While there is an extensive literature in psychology and zoology on imitation and observational learning, the formal literature strand of economically rational observational learning (item C) and in particular information cascades (item D) is comparatively new.[75] The second major literature strand has incorporated non-perfect rational agents into a context of observational learning or information cascades.[76] There have been two approaches in particular:

- Applying mechanistic or imperfect rational decision-makers using rules of thumb or heuristics.
- Applying assumptions of imperfect rational behavior drawn from experimental psychology.

The question of rational behavior in such a context is tricky. In many cases, the behavioral assumptions used from experimental psychology have not been explicitly tested for the situation modeled. Therefore, when behavioral assumptions are incorporated, they should be verified in advance.

In the end the question of rational vs. irrational investors being socially influenced becomes almost philosophical. Several researchers suggest that there is evidence for emotional contagion in manias and fads.[77] However, on the other hand, other researchers find no reason for irrational behavior, even in historically famous bubbles such as the Dutch Tulip Bubble.[78] Actually, there exist rational models of bubbles and crashes not involving any herding or information cascades at all.[79]

6.6.1.3   Models of herd behavior and information cascades in financial markets

In a perfect market[80] no systematic risk-adjusted security excess returns are possible. In addition there is no excess price volatility relative to the value of the news arrival. In such a market, no herd behavior or information cascades are able to evolve. This is the case because in perfect markets there is no social influence. Therefore no models based upon perfect markets can explain the existence of herd behavior and information cascades. To be able to explain the return patterns evolving from herd behavior, it is compulsory to introduce some kind of market imperfections.[81]

In the basic market models of herd behavior and information cascades,[82] the price therein is exogenous, meaning that the supply is perfectly elastic. For trading currencies with fixed exchange rates this might be a reasonable set-up, though for classical stock markets this assumption clearly does not hold. Avery and Zemsky (1998) were the first to relax this assumption. Their model is reviewed in detail, because the third stage experiments are based on one of their particular model specifications. Suppose that after every trade the price of the traded asset reveals the information possessed by the action taken. With competitive market-makers, the new stock price will always reflect its expected value conditional on the available public information. This implies that a speculator basing his actions upon all public information (including the past) will be neutral between buying and selling. A speculator is meant to be a market participant who is not interested in the asset's value itself but simply wants to generate capital from trading with it. Furthermore, when an informed investor trades, he will automatically reveal his private information. Therefore an information cascade never starts. Every subsequent investor will follow his own private information. The price adjusts exactly in a manner that is based on the publicly available information and the speculators stay neutral between buying and selling. As a consequence, in such a setting herd behavior is not able to evolve when prices reflect public information. The stock market is informationally efficient, there is no mispricing and prices reflect fundamentals. Therefore, another dimension of uncertainty has to be introduced.

Assume that a claim on a random variable ϕ can take on values in the set $\{0, \frac{1}{2}, 1\}$. The 'normal' state is defined by $\phi = \frac{1}{2}$. If a shock occurs, then ϕ is equal either to 1 or to 0. An informed investor knows perfectly whether a shock occurs, i.e. $\phi = \frac{1}{2}$ or $\phi \in \{0, 1\}$, but he does not know what kind of shock there will be. If a shock occurs and $\phi \in \{0, 1\}$, then each informed investor receives a signal about ϕ. The signal has two possible precisions: with probability p it is of precision m, and with probability $(1 - p)$ it is of precision m', where $1 \geq m > m' > \frac{1}{2}$. The precision measures m and m' are defined as the precision when receiving a signal about ϕ. While a value for $m = 1$ indicates that investors are perfectly informed, a value for m close to $\frac{1}{2}$ indicates that the signal received is very noisy. Each investor knows the precision of the signal m or m'; however, he does not know the value of p. The value of p defines the *precision* of the economy, i.e. the proportion of market participants with a high precision, though it is not known in the market, not even by market-makers. The value of p is set randomly at the same time as ϕ in the set of two values $\{p_L, p_H\}$ with $0 < p_L < p_H$. The unknown composition of the market complicates learning for market participants. In a poorly informed market a sequence of buy orders is natural due to herd behavior. In a well-informed market, a sequence of buy orders is also natural because the market participants have the same (very informative) signal. When the composition of the market is unknown, then it can be difficult to know whether a sequence of buy orders reveals a large amount of information about the value of the asset (because the market is well informed), or almost none at all (due to a poorly informed market and the herd behavior of informed traders).

The aggregate state of the economy is defined by the realization of the two random variables ϕ and p, which are independent of each other. Avery and Zemsky provide a numerical example in which they show that a price bubble and subsequent crash can evolve from rational herd behavior.[83] Consequentially, as Bikhchandani and Sharma note, an 'informationally inefficient herd may occur and can lead to price bubbles and mispricing when the accuracy (or lack thereof) of the information with market participants is not common knowledge. Traders may mimic the behavior of an initial group of investors in the erroneous belief that this group knows something.'[84]

There have been several other attempts to model the incomplete information revelation (some authors refer to this as information blockage). Gervais (1996) finds information blockage when there is uncertainty about the precision of the investors' information. Cipriani and Guarino (2001) find that with investors having non-speculative motives for trading, information cascades can evolve. Lee (1998) models quasi-cascades due to temporary information blockages which then can lead to so-called information avalanches. Beaudry and Gonzales (2000) apply a simultaneous trading approach, in which information cascades are due to costly information acquisition. Kuran and Sunstein (1999) develop the notion of availability cascades. If information concerning a security is more 'available' to investors, then this can be applied to familiarity effects[85] and local[86] as well as home bias effects.[87]

6.6.1.4 Empirical evidence of herd behavior in financial markets

It is not an easy task to test empirically for herd behavior in financial markets. As Bikhchandani and Sharma note, in order to examine herd behavior, 'one needs to find a group of participants that trade actively and act similarly'.[88] This is the case when the group is sufficiently homogeneous; one is able to observe the trades of the other group members and its size relative to the market is not too large. True herd behavior may be inefficient and can lead to excess volatility and even systemic risks. One of the difficulties is to measure and empirically to distinguish 'true' herd behavior from clustering or spurious herd behavior.

The empirical studies performed so far have typically not tried to directly test a certain herd behavior model, but rather use statistical measures in order to detect it.[89] It has to be noticed that the statistical measures applied by the various studies have not been able to create a direct link from theoretical considerations to empirical specifications. In addition, it is empirically very difficult to distinguish between true and spurious herd behavior. Several authors have proposed different measures of herd behavior.[90] Lakonishok et al. (1992) find little evidence of herd behavior in pension funds at a stock level. Grinblatt et al. (1995) find that mutual funds have the tendency to buy past winner stocks. Concerning herd behavior and momentum investing, the average level is not very large, though statistically significant. The authors note that the cross-sectional dispersion across the different mutual fund styles is large. The highest degree of herd behavior is found among aggressive growth, growth and income mutual funds. Wermers (1999) uses a data superset of Grinblatt et al. and finds that during the period 1975–1994 herd behavior among mutual funds is low on a stock level, though much higher among small stocks and growth-oriented mutual funds. Kodres and

Pritsker (1997) report that on a daily basis there is herd behavior by large futures markets institutional traders. However, the authors admit that to these findings there are serious measurement challenges.

How should herd behavior be measured? This question has been discussed extensively by several researchers. One important challenge is to distinguish simple clustering from herd behavior. Lakonishok et al. (1992) provide a first measure that is based on trades conducted by a subset of market participants and is defined as follows:

$$H(i, t) = |B(i, t)/[B(i, t) + S(i, t)] - p(t)| - AF(i, t)$$

where:

- $H(i, t)$ is the measure for herd behavior in stock i for quarter t.
- $B(i, t)$ is the number of money managers who increase their holdings (net buyers) in the stock i for quarter t.
- $S(i, t)$ is the number of money managers who decrease their holdings (net sellers) in the stock i for quarter t.
- $p(t)$ is the excepted proportion of money managers buying in quarter t relative to the number active.
- $AF(i, t) = E\{|B(i, t)/[B(i, t) + S(i, t)] - p(t)|\}$ is an adjustment factor. It accounts for the fact that under the null hypothesis of no herd behavior, i.e. when the probability of any money manager being a net buyer of any stock is $p(i)$, the absolute value of $[B(i, t)/B(i, t) + S(i, t)] - p(t)$ is greater than zero. $AF(i, t)$ is therefore the expected value of $|[B(i, t)/B(i, t) + S(i, t)] - p(t)|$ under the null hypothesis of no herd behavior.

Lakonishok et al. define and measure herd behavior as the average tendency of a group of money managers to buy (sell) particular stocks at the same time, relative to what could be expected if the managers were trading for themselves. The subset of market participants consists of 769 tax-exempt equity funds managed by 341 different money managers whose major fund sponsors are corporate pension plans. This selection process is performed in order to create a sufficiently homogeneous group. While the authors call their measure a herd behavior measure, it in fact measures the correlation in trading patterns for a particular group of fund managers to buy and sell the same stocks. As Bikchandani and Sharma[91] note, the measure has two drawbacks. First, it measures the number of investors on each side of the market without taking the volume traded into account. Second, it is not possible to identify intertemporal trading patterns. Those drawbacks have been two of the reasons for Wermers (1999) to develop a new measure he calls portfolio change measure (PCM). While it overcomes the first drawback mentioned above, it itself has some other drawbacks.[92] Another measure of herd behavior is proposed by Christie and Huang (1995). They analyze whether returns of individual stocks cluster more tightly around the market return during large changes. The authors analyze daily returns of U.S. equities and find relatively higher dispersion around the market return at times of large price movements. They interpret this result as evidence against herd behavior. However, as mentioned by Richards (1999), the test of herd behavior by Christie and Huang is too specific and only relates to the asset-specific component in returns. When asset prices of a complete industry or country move in the same direction, the measure does not allow for that.

6.6.1.5   Experimental evidence of herd behavior in financial markets

With all the difficulties that exist, several researchers have performed experiments to rule out the possibility of an omitted influence. Starting with Anderson and Holt (1997), a growing literature has found evidence for the development of information cascades in the laboratory.[93] Another literature strand working with experimental asset markets has focused on information aggregation. It has been shown that in complex environments information blockages start to form, so that the information aggregation is not perfect.[94] Research directly combining experimental asset markets and herd behavior has been performed by Cipriani and Guarino (2004) as well as Drehmann et al. (2004). Those two studies aim to test the model of Avery and Zemsky, in that the presence of a flexible price prevents herd behavior. The focus of the third stage experiments is a bit different. Instead of testing Avery and Zemsky's model as a whole, one particular aspect is accounted for. According to their model, the higher the ratio of less informed market participants, the more herd behavior should be observed. This hypothesis is tested in the third stage experiments. Another important difference to the model stated is the fact that market makers are forgone. There exists one group of precisely informed and one of less precisely informed market participants trading with each other, but not with a market maker. Those two groups make the market themselves.

6.6.2   Experimental Design

6.6.2.1   Experimental game and procedure

The experimental procedure follows the same structure as the second stage experiments, with the following modifications (for the detailed instructions, please refer to Appendix III.1):

- You will be endowed each period with 10 shares of company X and 2500 'cash' points. In each period you are given the opportunity to submit bids and asking prices for buying and selling shares. At the end of the period the positions will be closed. For every period you will be endowed with the same amount of shares and 'cash' points. Your gains and losses will be counted for each period and summed up in the end.
- In each of the 12 periods the value of the share of company X will be between 0 and 200. In addition you will receive during each period on your screen further news about the value of the share.

    Attention! There are two different groups of participants. One group will receive during each period more precise news than the other concerning the value of the share. But it is not known what the ratio of the corresponding groups is. Please note that the news you will receive during each period can be, but does not have to be, truthful. If though within the messages probability measures are specified, then these are always correct. All messages are communicated to you via newsticker.

    In addition it is possible that after each period you might change from one group to the other. This is not communicated to you either. At the end of each period you are informed about the value of the share.

The first group receives the messages as in the second stage experiment. This is the group receiving the less precise news. The second group receives the same messages, though explicitly mentioning the probability of the rumor becoming true. An exemplary message spread to the second group is: 'Rumor! Company X is in merger talks with company Y. With a probability of 70% the share of company X will be worth at least 160.'

The details concerning the messages spread can be found in Appendix III.1. As in the second stage experiments, a control message is spread to the first group stating the probability of the rumor becoming true. The sequence of the spread messages, as in Appendix III.1, is random. In addition, the time within each period when the message is spread is random as well. It is, though, always spread within the first 30 seconds of each period. The participants receive the messages all at the same time. The group receiving the less precise news does not know anything concerning the probabilities of the underlying distributions from which the value of the share is drawn. The actual distribution probabilities are available in Appendix II.1.

6.6.2.2 Treatments

Two treatments were set in order to test for the ratio of precisely to less precisely informed market participants being a determining factor of herd behavior. In the first treatment the ratio of precisely informed traders is set to 25%, in the second treatment it is set to 75%. The two treatments are then compared with each other concerning the observation of herd behavior.

6.6.2.3 Subjects and sessions

Concerning the subjects, the same rules apply for the third as for the first and second stage experiments. For each treatment five sessions were conducted. The computerized experiment was programmed and conducted with experimental software z-Tree.[95] A session lasted approximately 90 minutes and subjects earned on average CHF 42 (approximately USD 33.6, October 2004).

6.6.3 Results of the Third Stage Experiments

6.6.3.1 Ratio of precisely informed market participants and herd behavior

For the third stage experiments, the corresponding testable hypothesis is the following:

Hypothesis 1: *The ratio of precisely to less precisely informed market participants does not have an influence on their herding behavior.*

$$H_0 : \mu_1 - \mu_2 = 0, \qquad H_A : \mu_1 - \mu_2 \neq 0$$

where μ_1 represents the measure of herd behavior with a low ratio of precisely informed market participants, and μ_2 represents the measure of herd behavior with a high ratio of precisely informed market participants.

The hypothesis is tested as follows. The herd behavior of market participants after the rumor has been spread for two periods is compared. In the two periods compared to each other, only the ratio of precisely informed market participants varies.

Being aware of the difficulties in measuring herd behavior, a herd behavior index is constructed to attempt to overcome the typical drawbacks of other measures. The measure is constructed as follows:

$$HBI = \frac{\Delta P * V}{\Delta T} * R$$

where:

- *HBI* is the herd behavior index.
- ΔP is the maximal price movement in the corresponding direction (depending on positive or negative rumor) from the mean of the original distribution after rumor development.
- V is the number of trades from the time of rumor development to the point in time of the maximal price movement.
- ΔT is the length of time from the rumor development to the maximum price movement.
- R is the ratio of precisely informed market participants to the ratio of their buys/sells during ΔT (depending on positive or negative rumor).

Example: At time 78 a positive rumor is spread. The ratio of precisely informed market participants is 25%. The maximum traded price of the asset is 174 at time 46. From time 78 to 46, 29 trades are observed. Of those 29 trades, 8 were executed buy orders from the precisely informed market participants.

Then the HBI for the example is:

$$HBI = \frac{(174 - 100) * 29}{(78 - 46)} * \frac{0.25}{(8/29)} = 60.775$$

The HBI measure has the following plausible properties:

- The height of the price movement is a positive influence factor for herd behavior. When $\Delta P = 0$, there is no herd behavior.
- The traded volume is also a positive influence factor for herd behavior. When $V = 0$, there is no herd behavior.
- The length of time is a negative influencing factor for herd behavior. When the price movement (ΔP) takes place over a long period of time ($\lim \Delta T = \infty$), then it is hardly considered to stem from herd behavior. Rather when a price movement takes place in a very short period of time, then it is said that market participants are trading with the herd.
- If only the three factors above were considered, then the constructed index would only identify clustering behavior, since all market participants act according to their individual signal received. Therefore the actions of the two different groups have to be distinguished. The higher the ratio of less precisely informed market participants is, the more they will neglect their own received signal and mimic the other market participants' actions in the erroneous belief that they know something. If as a result the price movement stems only from buyers/sellers (depending on positive/negative rumor) with less precise information, then they have reacted to a much greater extent on the previous price movement than on their own information signal. So when the ratio of buyers/sellers (again depending on positive/negative rumor) with low precise information is high in comparison to their actual fraction in the market, then this is an indication of herd behavior. If, though, all buyers/sellers are market participants who have received high precision information, then they don't act as a herd but rather individually according to their precise information received.

The H_0 hypothesis of the third stage experiments, that there is no difference in the herd behavior measure, is tested with a one-sided Wilcoxon–Mann–Whitney test using the HBI values of each of the five sessions for both treatments (see Table 6.10) (for the HBI values of the treatment with 75% precisely informed market participants see Table 6.11).

The results are intriguing. The hypothesis H_0 cannot be rejected (see Table 6.12) for all

Table 6.10 Expected values, average traded prices, price volatilities and HBI values with 25% ratio of precisely informed market participants

Message spread	Expected value of the share	Average measures over the five sessions after the rumor has been spread		
		Prices	Price volatilities (standard deviation)	HBI values
160	140	141.8	18.90	
160 with 50% true	140	144.5	12.05	
160 and plausible content	156	145.9	17.72	88.4
160 and non-plausible content	124	129.5	12.87	38.4
160 and credible source	156	145.9	14.22	145.6
160 and non-credible source	124	124.9	15.19	61.5
40	60	101.1	20.29	
40 with 50% true	60	76.1	16.40	
40 and plausible content	44	63.1	25.42	107.9
40 and non-plausible content	76	96.4	16.85	20.0
40 and credible source	44	58.2	23.11	85.4
40 and non-credible source	76	96.7	15.65	25.6

Table 6.11 Expected values, average traded prices, price volatilities and HBI values with 75% ratio of precisely informed market participants

Message spread	Expected value of the share	Average measures over the five sessions after the rumor has been spread		
		Prices	Price volatilities (standard deviation)	HBI values
160	140	136.8	21.04	
160 with 50% true	140	137.5	16.70	
160 and plausible content	156	145.0	16.61	49.0
160 and non-plausible content	124	126.4	11.65	29.2
160 and credible source	156	143.3	17.18	44.4
160 and non-credible source	124	124.9	11.94	30.8
40	60	105.1	24.64	
40 with 50% true	60	79.6	20.15	
40 and plausible content	44	68.5	17.55	45.2
40 and non-plausible content	76	92.1	16.54	33.3
40 and credible source	44	70.3	19.07	38.2
40 and non-credible source	76	88.7	15.19	18.1

Table 6.12 p-Values of the Wilcoxon–Mann–Whitney test for the average traded prices, HBI values and price volatilities of the two treatments (25% vs. 75% precisely informed)

Message spread	p-Values of the Wilcoxon–Mann–Whitney test		
	Prices	Price volatilities (standard deviation)	HBI values
160 with 50% true	0.210	0.111	
160 and plausible content	0.210	0.421	0.028
160 and non-plausible content	0.274	0.345	0.155
160 and credible source	0.210	0.075	0.004
160 and non-credible source	0.155	0.155	0.111
40 with 50% true	0.274	0.075	
40 and plausible content	0.210	0.155	0.004
40 and non-plausible content	0.075	0.421	0.075
40 and credible source	0.111	0.075	0.008
40 and non-credible source	0.155	0.155	0.075

messages with the exception of those (positive and negative rumors) with a plausible content and a credible source. These are the messages in which the price movement is the strongest. So in other words, if there is a strong price movement, then there are significant differences in herd behavior depending on the ratio of precisely informed market participants. But if there is no, or little, price movement, there are no significant differences in herd behavior. This result also seems intuitively comprehensible. With regard to the predictions of Avery and Zemsky's model, they can be confirmed. A higher ratio of less precisely informed market participants leads to higher herd behavior.

Two things have to be pointed out in particular. First, the messages '160 with 50% true' and '40 with 50% true' are special cases in that all participants have received the same message, but they believe that others must have received less precise news. Measuring herd behavior in such a setting is not very reasonable, since all market participants receive the same precision of news. Though what is interesting to compare is the price volatility of such a setting to the price volatility of the second stage experiment. This effect is discussed later on when generally comparing average traded prices and price volatilities to the second stage experiments. Second, the argument that the difference in herd behavior is caused by different average traded prices or price volatilities in the same messages of the two treatments, can be declined. Table 6.12 shows that using the one-sided Wilcoxon–Mann–Whitney test, no significant differences in average traded prices or price volatilities of the same messages occur. Therefore neither the average traded prices nor the price volatilities are able to explain the significant differences in the HBI values for the corresponding messages.

6.6.3.2 Comparison with the results of the second stage experiments

Comparing the results of the third stage to those of the second stage, the effects are clear for the average traded prices, though less clear concerning the price volatility. Table 6.13 shows the p-values of the one-sided Wilcoxon–Mann–Whitney test for the average traded prices and price volatilities thereof. For both treatments of the third stage experiments, the p-values of the average traded price after positive rumors (at least a value of 160) are 0.075

Table 6.13 *p*-Values of the Wilcoxon–Mann–Whitney Test for the average traded prices and price volatilities comparing the second stage with the third stage experiments

Message spread	P-Values of the Wilcoxon–Mann–Whitney Test	
	Prices	Price volatilities (standard deviation)
25% precisely informed market participants		
160 with 50% true	0.421	0.048
160 and plausible content	0.274	0.075
160 and non-plausible content	0.421	0.111
160 and credible source	0.111	0.048
160 and non-credible source	0.500	0.016
40 with 50% true	0.008	0.048
40 and plausible content	0.004	0.111
40 and non-plausible content	0.028	0.004
40 and credible source	0.004	0.075
40 and non-credible source	0.075	0.048
75% precisely informed market participants		
160 with 50% true	0.111	0.004
160 and plausible content	0.155	0.016
160 and non-plausible content	0.345	0.155
160 and credible source	0.075	0.008
160 and non-credible source	0.210	0.075
40 with 50% true	0.008	0.016
40 and plausible content	0.028	0.274
40 and non-plausible content	0.004	0.008
40 and credible source	0.016	0.155
40 and non-credible source	0.004	0.028

and above. In contradiction thereof, all *p*-values of the average traded price after negative rumors (at most a value of 40) are significant at a 5% level, though with one exception. The exception is the message '40 and non-credible source' with 25% precisely informed market participants. In that case the *p*-value is 0.075. The average traded price after negative rumors is therefore significantly lower than in the second stage experiment and closer to its expected value. Consequently, the introduction of information precision asymmetries with negative rumors has led to a reduction of the demanded risk premium, while for positive rumors no significant impact is observable.

On the other hand, concerning price volatility, the picture is not as clear. Introducing information precision asymmetries in general seems to increase volatility, though not in a consistent manner. While these results are difficult to interpret and explanations for this effect are not easy to find, at least one thing seems comforting: comparing the messages of the second stage experiments with a stated probability to those of the third stage, in all cases a significant increase in price volatility is observed (*p*-values 0.048 or lower). This result is to be expected and is not surprising. However, exactly what effects cause the ambiguous reaction in the price volatilities observed for the other messages remains unclear.

6.6.4   Discussion and Conclusion

The two studies in which experiments are performed to test Avery and Zemsky's model of herd behavior in financial markets both come to the same conclusion.[96] The model predicts that in a financial market with sequential trading and privately informed traders, no herd behavior should be observed. This is due to the fact that all trading decisions are immediately incorporated in the market price reflecting all public information. And, as the model predicts, both experimental studies find no significant evidence for herd behavior. However, again as both studies note, market participants frequently do not follow their private information but act as contrarians. Drehmann et al.[97] define contrarian behavior as trading against your own received signal and against the market. As the authors note, such contrarian behavior can only be (*ex post*) rational if the trader is convinced that prior trades irrationally drove the price to an extreme. The authors provide an error model allowing for the possibility of market participants challenging and mistrusting the other market participants' rationality of decisions. They reach the conclusion that 'one could even argue that the observed contrarian behavior, which we find sometimes to be profitable, has a stabilizing effect as it implies that agents tend to differentiate their investments from those of their predecessors'.[98]

The observation and insights of the studies can be concurred with from the third stage experiments. What is observed in the experiments is that when traded prices have exceeded the asset's expected value, market participants step in to drive the price towards the asset's expected value. This kind of behavior should not be considered as contrarian but, rather, for risk-neutral agents, as rational decisions stabilizing the market.

The main focus, though, of the third stage experiments has been on testing a particular potential influencing factor of herd behavior, namely the ratio of information precision asymmetry. In Avery and Zemsky's model this corresponds to the well- and less well-informed market participants. Indeed, the results lead to the conclusion that, when introducing a new herd behavior index, the ratio of high to low precision informed market participants is a significant influencing factor for herd behavior. The difference in the measure is explainable neither by different average traded prices nor by differences in price volatilities. The predictions of Avery and Zemsky's model can therefore be agreed upon.

Can these results and conclusions be applied to real world events? Indeed, here is just one of the countless examples it would be possible to quote. On Friday, March 17, 2006, the *Wall Street Journal* reported that U.S. insurance company St. Paul Travelers was interested in Zurich Financial Services, another large Swiss insurance company. This was news out of the blue, and market comments were in general quite skeptical concerning a potential merger due to high regulatory hurdles and the general strategic outlook of the potentially merged company. Nevertheless the stocks of Zurich Financial Services soared on during the day almost 11% and closed the day 5% up, although no further news was published. As one trader mentioned later: 'Everyone was thinking: Did I miss something, does someone know more than I do? If it's the *Wall Street Journal* that has published it, there has got to be something to it, although they explicitly mentioned that the talks were in an early stage and the deal could still fail. These worries and the general implausibility or at least improbability of the rumor itself did not matter, everyone was excited and wanted to be part of it. Well, as we know now, there was absolutely nothing to it. But it was a good story.' When analyzing the story, everyone was reacting to the price movement in the illusory belief that others knew more than they did, although that was not the case. It was sufficient that a piece of vague information was received, an initial price movement happened and off it went. What was unusual in this case was the following reaction by St. Paul Travelers. On

Monday they announced a press release stating that while its policy is 'to avoid any comment on, or response to, market rumors or speculation, the factual and definitive manner in which these reports were made, both nationally and internationally, has prompted the company to provide this clarification'. The clarity with which St. Paul Travelers reacted to the rumor was surprising. The typical reaction of most corporations involved is 'we don't comment on rumors' – this with good reason: if the public expects that the corporations react to every possible rumor available, this would create an immense amount of effort. In addition, if all of a sudden the corporation were not to comment on a rumor, then this would then be a clear signal that the rumor was be going to be true. This is, of course, something everyone wants to avoid. However, in the case of St. Paul Travelers, the clear denial of the rumor was a success, because the rumor did not reappear and plain and simply died.

6.7   FOURTH STAGE EXPERIMENTS: COMMUNICATION

One of the major insights of the survey conducted has been that communication and personal networks are an important feature for market participants to form asset return expectations after rumor development. The hypothesis tested is whether personal networks add value and whether communication strategies exist to enhance profits. The fourth stage experiments, therefore, have the task of exploring when and what participants communicate with each other, how participants create personal networks, and whether it pays to communicate.

6.7.1   A Brief Overview

The research area of communication economics has mostly focused on the creation, role and value of economic networks stemming from communication between individuals. The importance of economic networks for social and economic outcomes has been emphasized for many different functions.[99] Typically the literature structures the topic of economic networks into four categories: coordination networks, cooperation networks, buyer–seller networks and network formation. But it has to be pointed out that researchers from other social sciences, such as sociology, started investigating the role of networks much earlier than economists.[100]

Personal relationships among market participants are important for the effectiveness of communication in financial markets. These relationships can be of a more formal nature, including a written contract, or more informal such as friendships. Brown[101] provides an overview of the existing empirical and experimental evidence of market-related relationship contracts. Market-related informal personal relationships have been analyzed by ethnographical and sociological studies. Brügger,[102] for example, describes the world of foreign currency traders and their way of communicating with each other. Rumor communication belongs to their daily life. Brügger states that personal networks are viewed as important for traders in order to receive valuable information from other traders, such as rumors. Knorr Cetina and Brügger (2002) emphasize that the exchange of news and rumors tends to flow through interpersonal and inter-organizational relationships that are based on rules of trust, exclusivity, and loyalty. In such cases it does not matter if the other person works for a competitor or not. Certain relationships among traders are purely informative with no business relations. Then, however, it is important that both parties provide the other one with valuable information so that a certain balance is assured. The relationship is therefore reciprocal.

6.7.2 Experimental Design

The fourth stage experiments performed are more difficult to compare with the theoretical approaches of communication economics. The first specific characteristic of the experimental set-up is that the payoff is only indirectly influenced by communication. Communication itself and the creation of a personal relationship with another market participant do not automatically lead to better decisions and therefore to a higher payoff. Secondly, communication does not cost anything. This feature is an important distinction to those set-ups where communication is costly.

In the first communication experiments designed, the market participants could trade and communicate simultaneously. The experiments with this design had to be aborted after the first few sessions. The reason for the abortion was that many participants stated that they were overwhelmed by the hectic atmosphere, the moving prices, potential news arriving through the newsticker and having at the same time to be able to communicate. One of the results was that participants hardly communicated with each other at all, and they only started to communicate when the largest price movement was already over. While this kind of behavior was also very interesting to observe and is worth mentioning, the design clearly showed that the experimental set-up had reached the limit of complexity manageable by the participants. As a consequence, trading and communication were separated into different phases during each period. In the trading phase only trading was allowed and in the communication phase only communicating with each other was allowed.

6.7.2.1 Experimental game and procedures

The experimental procedure follows the same structure as the third stage experiments, with the following modifications (for the detailed instructions, please refer to Appendix IV.1).

At the beginning of each period there is a trading phase. This phase lasts until the first message is communicated via newsticker. The trading rules follow the same instructions as in the other experiments. After the first trading phase is over and the first message has been communicated via newsticker, the first communication phase follows. In the communication phase participants have the possibility of contacting other market participants and communicating with each other. The communication can serve, for example, to find out what other market participants know, to receive insights on their trading strategy or to convince them of one's own strategy. They can communicate on their trading screen via e-mail, however, with predefined messages. The communication thread can therefore be controlled for. It is possible to communicate with a maximum two other participants at the same time. When a communication line is hung up, it is possible to open a new one. The participants are identifiable via their participant number seen on their screen. It is therefore possible to build up a relationship over several periods with other market participants. At the same time there exists a reputation risk, since each participant is identifiable and keeps his number throughout the entire experiment.

The initial messages to be communicated are predefined and can be divided into inquiring and convincing messages. They follow a dependent tree structure with five levels. Altogether over 150 messages have been implemented. The first two levels of messages can be found in Appendix IV.2.

The first communication phase lasts for 45 seconds. During this time it is not possible to trade. Nor is it possible to state new sell and buy orders. The offers to sell and the offers to buy that have been stated before the communication phase starts, however, stay in place. After the first communication phase is over another trading phase follows. The trading phase lasts for 45 seconds as well. During this time it is not possible to communicate with each other. The communication status already existent before the trading phase starts, however, stays in place. After the second trading phase another communication phase follows. This communication phase lasts for 30 seconds. After the second communication phase is over another trading phase follows until the complete time of one period (3 minutes) has elapsed.

Two limitations of the experimental design have to be mentioned at this point. First, since the experiment lasts for only 12 periods, it is not, or is only possible to a limited extent to build up longer-term relationships. The limitation is not that there exists no reputation risk for the individual market participants, since they are identifiable via their participant numbers. However, it comes up for discussion how large the reputation risk actually is. This links to the second point to be mentioned in the experiment, the participant's 'anonymity'. In comparison to the study by Brügger, the person the messages are exchanged with stays 'anonymous' in the sense that there is no possibility of building a personal relationship with the other person in the experiment, and it is only a business relationship over the phone. Because of the 'anonymity', participants could be tempted to try and convince other participants to follow their own strategy more often than they would in reality.

6.7.2.2   Treatments

In comparison to the first three stages only one treatment was implemented in the communication experiments. The ratio of precisely informed traders is set to 50% for all treatments conducted.

6.7.2.3   Subjects and sessions

Concerning the subjects, the same rules apply as for all other experiments. Altogether five sessions were run. The computerized experiment was programmed and conducted with experimental software z-Tree.[103] A session lasted approximately 90 minutes and subjects earned on average CHF 46 (approximately 39 USD, April 2005).

6.7.3   Results of the Fourth Stage Experiments

It has to be noted that the comparison of the fourth stage experimental results with the other experimental stage results is not possible offhand. The need for the special design of the experimental set-up, with the separation of the communication and trading phase, leads to behavioral effects that cannot simply be transferred to the other experiments. While it makes sense to compare the average traded prices and price volatility, it does not make too much sense to calculate and compare herd behavior index (HBI) values as in the third stage experiments. Tables 6.14 and 6.15 present the average traded prices and corresponding price volatilities over the five sessions after the rumor has been spread. They are in line with the results from the third stage experiments. As a matter of fact, the p-values of the Wilcoxon–Mann–Whitney test for average traded prices and price volatilities are all > 0.05 in comparison with both treatments of the third stage experiments. This is an indication that the fourth stage experiment was as well understood as the other experiments.

Table 6.14 Average traded prices after the rumor has been spread with the corresponding message of the communication experiment

	Message number	Expected value of the share	Message spread	Average traded prices over the five sessions after the rumor has been spread
Positive rumor	1	140	160	140.8
	2	140	160 with 50% true	141.5
	3	156	160 and plausible content	144.1
	4	124	160 and non-plausible content	126.9
	5	156	160 and credible source	143.5
	6	124	160 and non-credible source	127.5
Negative rumor	7	60	40	101.7
	8	60	40 with 50% true	91.3
	9	44	40 and plausible content	69.7
	10	76	40 and non-plausible content	102.8
	11	44	40 and credible source	75.1
	12	76	40 and non-credible source	101.9

Table 6.15 Standard deviation of the traded prices after the rumor has been spread with the corresponding message of the communication experiment

	Message number	Expected value of the share	Message spread	Average price volatilities over the five sessions after the rumor has been spread
Positive rumor	1	140	160	19.69
	2	140	160 with 50% true	15.89
	3	156	160 and plausible content	16.89
	4	124	160 and non-plausible content	13.19
	5	156	160 and credible source	18.52
	6	124	160 and non-credible source	16.12
Negative rumor	7	60	40	25.97
	8	60	40 with 50% true	22.16
	9	44	40 and plausible content	25.09
	10	76	40 and non-plausible content	17.64
	11	44	40 and credible source	21.44
	12	76	40 and non-credible source	17.40

While there are no obvious reasons why the average traded prices should be different from the first, second and third stage experiments, it could be supposed that price volatilities are lower. On the basis that the participants are able to communicate with each other, the exchange of news could lead to more homogeneous expectations of the asset's value. This supposition is declined. Price volatilities with communication are just as high as when no communication is possible.

Concerning the communication between the participants, during the five sessions altogether 831 messages were initiated and 1,945 messages sent. This corresponds to an average number of messages exchanged per communication thread of 2.34. On average the 89 participants received or sent 1.82 messages per period or 21.85 messages per session. Of the total of 831 messages initiated, 673 or 81% were inquiring messages and 158 or 19% were convincing messages. It has to be noticed here that the participants had an equal amount of convincing and inquiring messages to choose from in the beginning, so there is no selection bias included in the ratio of messages initiated. Of all convincing messages sent, 84 or 53% of them were answered whereas 74 or 47% of them were aborted. For the inquiring messages, the corresponding numbers are 476 or 71% that were answered, and 197 or 29% that were aborted. An interesting detail to be noticed is that 52% of all answers to convincing messages were inquiring messages again, such as questions as, 'Are you sure?'. The ratio of convincing to inquiring messages sent is somewhat comforting since it shows that the limited reputation risk did not lead to extensive use of sending convincing messages.

The amount of communication did not depend on whether the participants received precise or less precise information. Out of the 831 messages initiated, 416 or 50.1% originated from participants receiving precise information and 415 or 49.9% from participants receiving less precise information. In addition the kind of messages communicated also did not depend of the precision of the news received. Out of the 158 convincing messages sent, 76 or 48% stemmed from precisely informed participants and 82 or 52% from less precisely informed participants. Concerning the inquiring messages the figures are similar. Some 340 or 50.5% of the inquiring messages sent were from participants receiving precise news, 337 or 49.5% from participants receiving less precise news.

Perhaps the most interesting question to be answered is whether it pays to communicate with other market participants and if there exists something like a best communication strategy. It is first noteworthy to analyze whether there exist systematic differences in profits resulting from receiving precise or less precise news. Figure 6.5 shows the distribution of profits per period, differentiating between receiving precise or less precise news over the five experimental sessions run.

The average per period profit for market participants receiving precise news is 8.66, and for the market participants receiving less precise news is -8.86. A two-sided Kolmogorov–Smirnov test shows that the two distributions do not systematically differ at a 5% level (p-value $= 0.75$) from each other concerning average per period profit and the shape of the distribution.

Therefore, receiving precise or less precise news is not a determining factor for the profit in that particular period. Figure 6.6 provides insights to the question whether it pays to communicate, no matter whether receiving precise or less precise news.

The average per period profit for market participants when they communicate with others is 14.4, and for the market participants that do not communicate in that period -8.7. A two-sided Kolmogorov–Smirnov test shows that the two distributions do systematically differ at

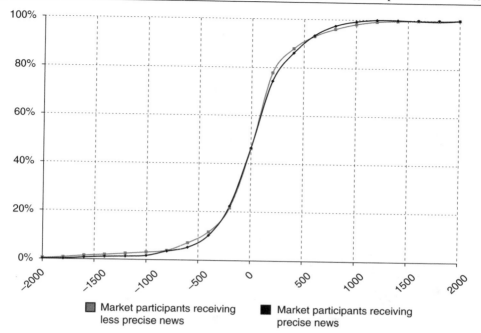

Figure 6.5 Cumulative distribution function of the per period profits of market participants receiving precise and less precise news

a 5% level (p-value $= 0.000073$) from each other concerning average per period profit and the shape of the distribution. Therefore, communication seems to pay, though only slightly.

This could lead to the conclusion that the more communication there is, the higher the overall profits are. Figure 6.7 analyzes whether the number of messages communicated is a determining factor for the overall profits of the different market participants.

Figure 6.7 shows the total profits over an entire session of one market participant in relation to the number of different messages sent. No matter whether the number of messages sent are taken in total or split up between convincing and inquiring messages, the results remain the same. There is no significant relationship between the different measures. No linear regression was inserted into the figure. Table 6.16 provides statistical measures on the linear regressions. The results are not more significant when splitting up the messages distinguishing between those sent from precisely and less precisely informed participants. The R-squares are still low and the T-values are all in the non-significant range. Therefore the communication of the different messages is not the sole determining factor for the overall profits.

While the communication of the various types of messages cannot explain the overall profits of the market participants, they could possibly help to explain the profits of the particular period they are sent in. Figures 6.8–6.10 present the cumulative distribution functions of the per period profits for convincing and inquiring messages sent by participants receiving precise and less precise news. Table 6.17 summarizes the types of messages sent together with the precision of the news received and the corresponding average per period profits. Since a single period as well as the entire experiment is a zero sum game, the averages of the different profit distributions are tested for significant differences to zero.

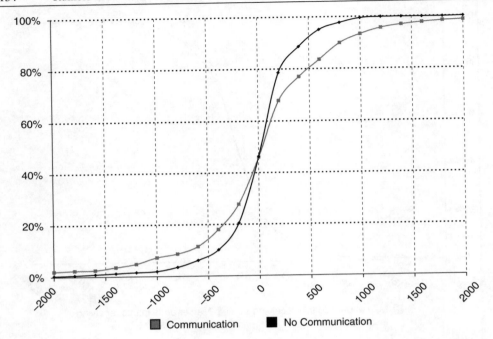

Figure 6.6 Cumulative distribution function of the per period profit when market participants communicate vs. do not communicate with each other

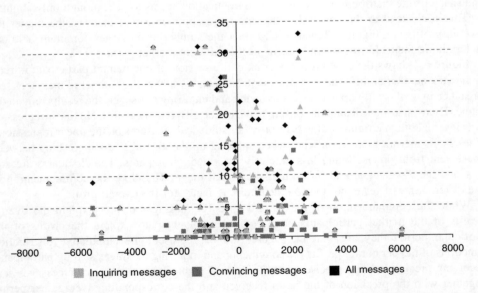

Figure 6.7 Total profits per market participant in relation to the number of different messages sent

Table 6.16 Linear regression statistics of the different types of messages sent to the total profits

Types of messages sent	Equation of the linear regression	R-square	T-value
All messages	$y = 5\text{E-}05x + 9.3371$	0.0002	0.11
All convincing messages	$y = 0.0002x + 1.7753$	0.015	1.15
All inquiring messages	$y = -0.0002x + 7.5618$	0.0017	−0.38
Convincing messages from precisely informed participants	$y = -0.0001x + 2.4121$	0.0057	−0.41
Convincing messages from less precisely informed participants	$y = 4\text{E-}05x + 2.7053$	0.0005	0.12
Inquiring messages from precisely informed participants	$y = -7\text{E-}05x + 4.8603$	0.001	−0.27
Inquiring messages from less precisely informed participants	$y = -0.0003x + 4.9408$	0.026	−1.32

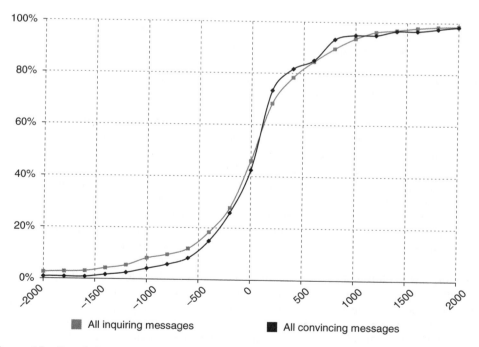

Figure 6.8 Cumulative distribution function of the per-period profit for all inquiring and all convincing messages

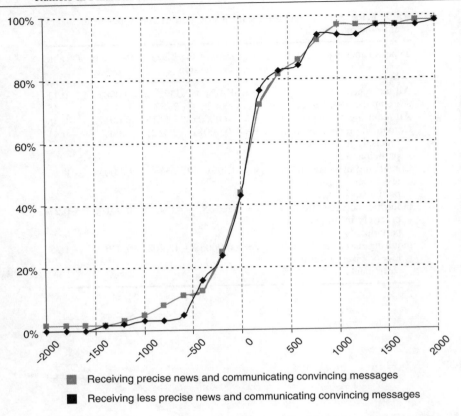

Figure 6.9 Cumulative distribution function of the per-period profit for convincing messages sent by participants receiving precise and less precise news

As can be seen from Table 6.17, there exist significant differences in the average profit per period for different types of messages sent. Five of the six message types are also significantly different from zero, three of them positively and two of them negatively. The results show that it is important to distinguish between the precision of news received, since the results vary greatly, depending thereon. In fact, the results were surprising. It seems especially surprising that the communication strategy to send a convincing message when having received less precise news turned out to be the highly profitable (on average a profit over 77 per period). This communication strategy could be called a 'bluffing strategy'. After all, the participant has received less precise news and tries to convince another participant to buy or sell the asset. If the participant is asked on what grounds he builds his arguments, he inevitably has to bluff and give the impression that he actually knows something more. The two other communication strategies which gave per-period profits that were significant by different from zero were the two strategies sending inquiring messages. When participants send inquiring messages after having received precise information, they are unsure how to deal with the risky situation presented to them. They need confirmation of their perception and interpretation of the news signal received. That is the reason this communication strategy is called 'confirmation strategy'. Obviously this communication strategy does lead to better decisions, since the average per period payoff of 46.63 is significantly above zero. In the

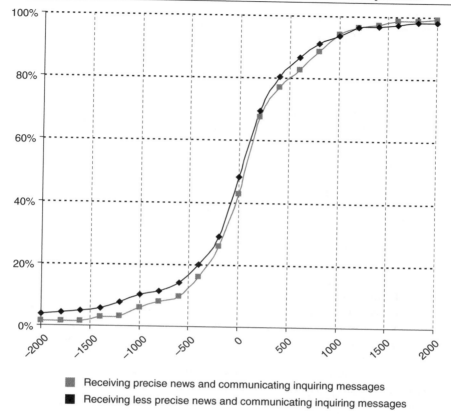

■ Receiving precise news and communicating inquiring messages
■ Receiving less precise news and communicating inquiring messages

Figure 6.10 Cumulative distribution function of the per-period profit for inquiring messages sent by participants receiving precise and less precise news

opposite case, when participants receive less precise news and send inquiring messages, the market participants want to know more about the asset's true value. This communication strategy is therefore called the 'want to know more' strategy. However, the actions based on this communication strategy seem not to be very successful, since the average per period profit of −65.65 is negative and highly significant. The limited knowledge of those participants about the signal's true precision seems to be exploited by the other participants.

6.7.4   Discussion and Conclusion

The fourth stage experiments have provided insights into the communication behavior and strategies of market participants when faced with a rumor about an asset's value. As a first result, the receipt of less precise or precise news did not determine the participants per period profit. Second, a single communication strategy was not able to explain the overall profits of the participants. Third, for single periods, however, significant per-period profits were achievable by the 'bluffing' as well as the 'confirmation' communication strategy, while the 'want to know more' communication strategy produced significant negative profits per period.

Table 6.17 Average per-period profits and the types of messages communicated

Types of messages sent	Average profit per period
All inquiring messages (sample size 419 data points)	−9.04**
All convincing messages (sample size 114 data points)	26.60**
Receiving precise news and sending convincing messages (sample size 57 data points)	−23.71
Receiving non-precise news and sending convincing messages (sample size 57 data points)	77.05***
Receiving precise news and sending inquiring messages (sample size 211 data points)	46.63***
Receiving non-precise news and sending inquiring messages (sample size 208 data points)	−65.65***

*Significant at a 10% level; **significant at a 5% level; ***significant at a 1% level.

As interesting as all these results are, one should be aware of the limited explanatory power they have. First, if the profits from a certain communication strategy were systematically positive or negative over a longer time period, this should have been apparent in the results presented in Figure 6.7 and Table 6.16. However, none of the different communication strategies come even close to explaining parts of the overall profits. This is an indication that such a strategy may work for a single period; however, it is doubtful whether they produce systematic profits over a longer period of time. As an additional limitation of the experimental set-up in comparison to reality, the subjects start to communicate with other participants they do not know and slowly build up a relationship over several periods. However, in reality the relationship typically exists beforehand and market participants communicate only with those people whom they know and trust to a certain degree. Furthermore, the experimental set-up contains informational asymmetries between the two groups of participants receiving precise and less precise news. But, as the survey in Chapter 5 showed, when rumors evolve in financial markets the asymmetry between market participants is more on the rumor's perception and interpretation and not on its informational content or the point in time when it is received.

One of the strongest results of the communication threads analyzed is the desire and need to reduce uncertainty about the asset's value. That is one of the reasons why four times as many inquiring messages as convincing messages are initiated. A second strong indication for the interpretation above is that the answer rate to inquiring messages is higher, namely 71%, in comparison to only 53% of convincing messages. On top of that, about half of the answers to convincing messages are inquiring messages again. These results are obtained in an environment where the reputation risk is comparatively small. The participants are in fact identifiable via their participation number; however, they are otherwise anonymous. In addition, the length of 12 periods per experiment is too short to create trustful longer-term personal relationships. Still many participants explicitly mentioned in the questionnaire distributed at the end of the experiment that if they once had received a convincing message and it turned out that the sender was wrong, they consequently ignored future messages they received from the same participant.

This line of argumentation fits well into the results of the survey, as in Chapter 5 and the sociological studies presented in the introduction of this chapter. Market participants close to the market, such as traders, keep track of the people who have provided them with rumors.

In addition, traders particularly show strong signs of reciprocal behavior in that they spread rumors to priority people and hope they will do the same, staying on top of the news flow. The survey pointed out that traders regard this feature as one of the most important when dealing with rumors in financial markets. The exchange of news and rumors then flows through interpersonal and inter-organizational relationships that are based on rules of trust, exclusivity, and loyalty.[104] In such a case it is important that both parties provide the other with valuable information so that a certain balance is assured. The relationship is therefore reciprocal.

There is in fact a growing literature, such as Fehr and Gächter (2000), that shows that individuals have a strong desire for reciprocal behavior. The individuals may have preferences about the type of social interaction the decision and outcome thereof is based on. Indeed, almost all utility theories fail to take into account that individuals may have preferences in this regard. Falk and Fischbacher (2000) present a formal theory of reciprocity. Their theory takes into account that interacting individuals evaluate not only the consequences of another individual's action but also the intention underlying it.

7

Conclusions and Outlook

Though we only listen to the rumor
and know by all means nothing.

HOMER, Greek poet, around eighth century BC

Rumors are perceived as something mysterious, almost magical. They fascinate, overwhelm, entrap and stir up people's minds. Rumors are the oldest mass medium in the world and their nature is still difficult to grasp. What is so special about rumors? Why do people get so excited, anxious and nervous? Why do companies release press bulletins saying, 'We don't comment on rumors?' Rumors are in no case mysterious or irrational but follow mechanisms that can be analyzed. This study has attempted to provide new insights into a topic that scientific research has largely neglected, that of rumors in financial markets. Financial markets are a special case where rumors evolve, since every action there is based on information. Knowing more than other market participants can lead to real money profits. But even if the rumor turns out not to be true, there can be severe financial consequences. Rumors were utilized in the early days of financial markets with such efficiency and effectiveness that books have been written warning against the effects of rumors.

Financial markets are a fruitful ground for rumors. They are seen as a substitute for news, which in financial markets is absolutely critical. Therefore, in the absence of news, something is simply invented. In a tense, stressful working atmosphere, all traders operate with highly sensitive antennas. The fear that other people may know something they don't know leads to stress and anxiety. In these situations the traders need confirmation of their views and positions. Gaps in information are often filled with speculative thoughts. The communication of speculative thoughts is a classical form of rumor evolvement. Rumors can only evolve when the content is interesting and relevant. Merger or takeover talks are an example of an event in favor of rumor evolvement. Statements such as, 'We are always interested in reasonable and beneficial acquisitions', or, 'We decline to comment on that issue', open the door to rumors and fantasies.

The starting point for this study was the fact that rumors in the context of financial markets are built on three scientific cornerstones: Finance, Psychology and Sociology. The theoretical approach of Behavioral Finance fulfills these requirements to a high degree. While with this approach many reasonable explanations for behavioral patterns can be found, it has to be mentioned at the same time that the theory is not perfect. For instance, it is in many cases not clear how the insights from psychological experiments can be translated into real financial decision-making.[1] Second, the area with probably the highest potential to improve the theory of how assets are valued and traded is the social process and the influence of how expectations of asset returns are formed and communicated.[2] Much research has focused on information asymmetries in time and content, though less on information processing asymmetries. In particular in financial markets, where market participants are faced with an information overflow, it does not seem justifiable to speak of information asymmetries in time or content, but rather in information processing and interpretation. In addition, whereas in most cases the future state's outcome is not directly influenced by one's own actions, the future asset return expectations have to be adjusted to the outcome. In that sense the individual behavior is socially influenced, in that the expectations of an asset's return are adjusted to the new outcome, which is an expression of the sum of actions of an anonymous, though very much socially influenced, mass of people.

With the different kind of rationality concepts discussed, it became evident that the notion of rationality applied by the traditional economic literature lacks important empirical observation on financial markets to be explained. Only advanced concepts such as procedural rationality allow us to come up with reasonable explanations for market participants being still considered to act rationally when rumors evolve, for the New Economy Bubble actually taking place and for high trading volumes on equity markets.

The survey among practitioners revealed that many people still believe there is something mysterious about rumors in financial markets. It is not by chance that rumors often appear in financial markets. The general environment of financial markets is very beneficial for the development of rumors. While the question of source is always asked first, it is not the most interesting feature from a scientific point of view. The idea of a hidden, strategic operating source survives consistently and permits the public to justify believing a 'false' rumor. The source then can be blamed for everything and the responsibility for its creation can be shrugged off completely. The evaluation of the rumor's source is considered almost impossible, at least by most traders. Non-traders claim to know the source more often, which leads to the conclusion that they are probably highly overconfident concerning their ability to evaluate the rumor's source. Rumors are heard most often through media such as information services, e-mail and television or orally by telephone or face to face on average a few times a week. Since everyone is connected to the same information resources, the rumors spread incredibly fast. Over 70% of the survey participants state that within minutes the entire trader community is informed about it. This statement provides additional support for the argument that in most cases it is not justifiable to speak of information asymmetries in time and content, although asymmetries in information processing and interpretation are justifiable.

Rumors are not spread automatically; people have to talk about them. By talking about a rumor it is hoped that more accurate, validated news will be received. It's important to realize that by contacting others the person inquiring already exposes himself to considering the rumor to be significant. The people approaching others are already biased and look for views supporting their own. If the person did not consider it to be significant, he would not want to talk about it. Rumors can only spread because they are believed in! The media are in a very convenient situation because they can claim that they transmit the rumor without judging its content. It's 'to each his own' what he or she does with the rumor. The media say they can't be blamed for any consequences of a rumor. Everyone has to judge the rumor's accuracy and validity for himself. This is true to a certain extent. However, the media are responsible for the selection and presentation of news. They well know that how the news is presented tremendously influences the reaction of people. It is their responsibility to judge and evaluate what and how news is presented to the public.

Of the survey participants 85% state the price movement upon a rumor to be *the* indicator of whether the market believes it. The price movement therefore reflects the belief of the market as an aggregate of all beliefs. The results of the survey seem to support the view that herd behavior is apparent after rumor development. When the price moves upon a rumor, the market participants view this as a signal and jump on the bandwagon. Some 75% of the traders testified that they will certainly or seriously consider trading upon it. This kind of behavior leads to short-term momentum, excess volatility and long-term reversal of traded prices. As a consequence, trends evolve, leading to questions to be answered, as is the case with any event or piece of news.

It is an often-heard statement that economic theory and economic models in particular are in a crisis, since they are said to be not useful. The opposite is the case. Only by the existence of rigorous economic models has it been possible to derive predictions that can be tested and to evaluate them against the empirical and experimental evidence. They are an essential ingredient for obtaining clear behavioral predictions and for testing empirically observed behavior against them. While intuition is good and needed, and without intuition too often a problem is too difficult to grasp, it alone does not fulfill the requirements for solid statements rejecting or confirming a drawn-up hypothesis. Intuitions are often all too vague and sometimes simply wrong.

The first stage experiments showed that the main effect of creating ambiguity in a financial market setting leads primarily to significantly higher price volatility. In the experimental setting, a small though significant effect of ambiguity aversion could be found. In the context of rumors, three factors seem to be determining for the large increase in price volatility:

1. Heterogeneous market participants: Bossaerts et al. (2004) provide convincing evidence for heterogeneity among market participants, even in relatively small groups, that induces pricing effects that 'cannot be modeled simply as if there is an ambiguity-averse investor with state-independent preferences'. For most price configurations highly ambiguity-averse agents prefer to hold ambiguous securities in equal quantities. They leave the less ambiguity-averse and the ambiguity-neutral to absorb the entire imbalance in relative supplies of ambiguous securities. The imbalance to be accommodated is far greater than if the ambiguity-averse subjects had taken their share, as they would have in the absence of ambiguity (in which all agents remain at least exposed to risk). The less ambiguity-averse individuals will ask for a higher compensation to absorb the supply imbalance in ambiguous securities only if compensated appropriately. This leads to the increase in the spread, with regards to range and variance, of the state price probability ratios. The importance of heterogeneous beliefs and expectations on optimal trading strategies and equilibrium asset pricing is also explicitly mentioned in Ziegler.[3] Furthermore, Mandelbrot states that 'once you drop the assumption of homogeneity, new and complicated things can happen in your mathematical models of your market'.[4] In fact, contributions from the Santa Fe Institute[5] or from DeGrauwe and Grimaldi (2003) show that with just two types of market participants following different strategies, price bubbles and crashes can arise, and that spontaneously.

2. Ambiguous information: Economic research has been very limited on the updating of ambiguous information. The model of Epstein and Schneider (2004) provides valuable insights into asset pricing effects resulting from poor information quality. The additional structure of ambiguity in signals firstly clarifies the anticipation of ambiguous news to be sufficient for the ambiguity premium and secondly creates a direct link between the size of the ambiguity premium and the measured volatility of fundamentals. When the information is very ambiguous, the agent will form a range of perceived precisions rather than agreeing on the unique, true precision of the signal. The larger the range of precision perceived by ambiguity-averse agents is, the larger the price fluctuations caused by the ambiguous information will be. Rumors are exemplary in being ambiguous in nature and in having poor information quality. This feature leaves room for different perceptions and

interpretations of the signal's precision, leading to strong increases in price volatility and resulting in the empirically observed effects as described above.

3. Overconfidence: DeBondt and Thaler (1995) state that overconfidence is probably the most robust result within the research area of psychological decision-making. The results of the survey also indicate that overconfidence is prevalent among market participants when forecasting a rumor's validity. There exist meanwhile a number of research contributions showing that overconfidence is one of the sources leading to over- and under-reaction upon information signals, and in particular contributes to excess volatility of asset prices.[6]

To summarize, there are well-founded theoretical arguments for the empirically observed phenomenon of strong increases in the asset price volatilities when rumors evolve. When market participants have heterogeneous attitudes towards ambiguity, they perceive and interpret ambiguous information differently and are overconfident about estimating a rumor's validity; each of the three factors can separately and independently increase the asset price's volatility. These three concepts are all independent of and do not contradict each other, but are rather complementary. It is easy to describe an ambiguity-averse, yet overconfident agent who perceives and interprets ambiguous information with a range of precisions. Therefore it should not come as a surprise to see high asset price fluctuations after the appearance of a rumor in financial markets.

The second stage experiments strongly supported the psychological insights on rumors, in that the credibility of the source and the plausibility of the rumors' content are determining factors for believing them. The significance of the price reaction is higher for the plausibility of the rumor's content. The possible explanation for this effect lies in the connection the participants have to the message's content. While the participants can relate to the rumor's content and evaluate its plausibility, they do not know more concerning its source and are unable to learn its true credibility over time.

It is often claimed that market participants show signs of herd behavior when rumors evolve in financial markets. The results of the survey seem to support this view. The hypothesis of herd behavior is tested for a particular specification of Avery and Zemsky's (1998) model. Their model predictions can be confirmed that the higher the ratio of less precisely informed market participants, the more they will neglect their own signal and mimic the behavior of other market participants in the erroneous belief that they know something. Herd behavior is in those prevalent cases, where strong price movements, no matter whether upwards or downwards, are observed. In cases where the validity of the rumor is low and no strong price movements are observed, no systematic differences in herd behavior can be found. More important, the differences in herd behavior can be ascribed neither to differences in traded prices nor to differences in the volatility of traded prices. These results are truly valuable, since they demonstrate under what circumstances herd behavior is to be expected from market participants in financial markets. To my knowledge this effect has not been shown so far in the literature, because empirically it is so difficult to distinguish between clustering and herd behavior. The experimental results performed have practical implications for the explanation of market participants' behavior as well. When news is uncertain, no matter whether it is a rumor or not, and market participants are not sure how to interpret the news, then a small price movement can cause a strong price reaction, simply because the market participants have the illusory belief that someone out there has to know more, or at least more precise, information than they do. This kind of behavior can be very short-term and is in fact frequently observable after rumor development. Prices then move very quickly, either up or down, with increasing traded volumes and volatility.

The communication experiments carried out showed that the experimental set-up reached a limit of manageable complexity for the participants. The results indicate that there exist communication strategies to be profitable for a single period. However, no communication strategy is able to explain parts of the overall profits. One of the strongest results of the communication threads analyzed is the participant's desire and need to reduce uncertainty about the asset's value. That is one of the reasons why four times as many inquiring messages as convincing messages are initiated. The exchange of news and rumors then flows through interpersonal and inter-organizational relationships that are based on rules of trust, exclusivity, and loyalty.[7] In such a case it is important that both parties provide the other with valuable information so that a certain balance is assured. The relationship is therefore reciprocal. Market participants are in this regard like social animals in that they value not only the assets they consume and own, but also how they compare against those of other individuals. A growing literature strand, e.g. Fehr and Gächter (2000), show that individuals have a strong desire for reciprocal behavior.[8] Indeed, almost all utility theories fail to take into account that individuals may have preferences about the type of social interaction they engage in. Falk and Fischbacher (2000) present a formal theory of reciprocity. Their theory takes into account that interacting individuals not only evaluate the consequences of another individual's action but also the intention underlying it.

Altogether, much has been learned about why we see what we see when rumors evolve in financial markets. There exist many reasonable theoretical explanations, based on rigorous economic models, for several empirically observed facts: volatility rocketing to the sky; why on apparent unfounded grounds strong price movements are observed; the factors responsible for herd behavior; and, with reservation, when and why personal networks are activated.

While much has been learned, even more questions remain to be answered. Where will the future take us and what kind of research areas seem promising to provide us with an even better understanding of individual as well as aggregate behavior in financial markets? Admittedly, the following list is subjectively colored:

- The rumor experiments carried out showed that we lack knowledge about the exact role of personal networks and communication in financial markets: how they evolve, when they are used with exactly what intention and what is to be expected from them. The question of self-interest vs. cooperative behavior seems especially relevant in such a context. Experimental research studies such as those of Fehr and Fischbacher (2003) provide insights into when and how individuals act altruistically or selfishly in social interactions. In addition Brown et al. (2004) provide evidence on the nature of long-term relationships. They emerge endogenously in the absence of third-party enforcement of contracts, where in the vast majority of trades the parties share the gains. Low effort or bad quality is then penalized by the termination of the relationship. This line of research provides a promising approach for subsequent studies.
- Humans are social beings. The psychological insights of decision-making from Behavioral Finance gained so far typically stay at a cognitive level with no social interaction. However, when people start interacting and making decisions under the influence of those social interactions, it is quite different from when they decide for themselves. Where exactly is the direct link between decision-maker and the social influence when making the decision? On an aggregate price level, many anomalies have been observed, starting from over- and under-reaction on various levels and from different information, market size, seasonalities, etc. While some of these anomalies have disappeared and those inefficiencies have been eliminated, some of them seem to last longer. What is lacking is a more general theory

based on an evolutionary perspective. What are long-term surviving investment strategies? What will evolutionary stable portfolios look like? Can the idea of efficient markets be approached from an evolutionary perspective? This kind of question is being tackled by the research discipline called Evolutionary Economics and Finance. This discipline is clearly gaining ground, as works from, for example, Farmer and Lo (1999), Hens and Schenk-Hoppé (2005), Hirshleifer and Luo (2001), Hodgson (1995), Lo (2004) and Luo (1998) demonstrate.

• The third research path follows a similar route to the second one. The literature seems now to understand how financial decisions are made in a closed, static and unemotional context. However, when rumors are present, emotions such as hope, fear and anxiety are likely to evolve. How do these emotions affect the rationality of decisions? What is the relationship between rationality and emotionality, and what are their effect cognition and neurobiological influences on cognition and decisions under stress, e.g. time pressure? This field remains open for research. First attempts in this direction have been conducted, for example, by Bossaerts (2003) and de Quervain et al. (2004).

Concerning rumors specifically, this work just touches the tip of the iceberg. Still very many things concerning this fascinating and oldest form of mass communication remain open, in particular on financial markets. The field for future research lies wide open. Rumors are nothing to be afraid of, nor are they something that we should worry about. They will always be out there. As long as people communicate with each other, no matter where, when or how, rumors will be a part of it.

Appendices

APPENDIX I

Appendix I.1: Formal Presentation of Preference Relations and Choice Rules

Definition: A choice rule $C(\cdot)$ in a set of subsets $\mathbb{B}$ of $\mathbf{X}$ fulfills the weak axiom of revealed preference (WARP), if the following precondition is fulfilled:

If for a $B \in \mathbb{B}$ with $x, y \in B$ it holds that $x \in C(B)$, then for every $B' \in \mathbb{B}$ with $x, y \in B'$ and $y \in C(B')$ it has to hold that $x \in C(B')$.

Proposition: If choice rule $C(\cdot)$ is rationalizable, then it fulfills WARP.

Proof: Since $C(\cdot)$ is rationalizable, there exists a preference relation $\geq$ with

$$C(B) = \{x \in B | x \geq y \text{ for all } y \in B\} \text{ for all } B \in \mathbb{B}.$$

If now $B \in \mathbb{B}$ is given with $x, y \in B$ and $x \in C(B)$. WARP is fulfilled, if for any other set $B' \in \mathbb{B}$ with $x, y \in B'$ and $y \in C(B')$ it follows that $x \in C(B')$. It has to be shown that $x \geq z$ for all $z \in B'$.

Since $x \in C(B)$ it follows that $x \geq y$. Equally it follows from $y \in C(B')$ that $y \geq z$ for all $z \in B'$. The transitivity of $\geq$ implies though that $x \geq z$ as well for all $z \in B'$, so $x \in C(B')$.

Completeness: Given $x, y \in X$ and $B = \{x, y\} \in \mathbb{B}$. Since $\emptyset \neq C(B) \subseteq B$, has to be $C(B) = \{x\}$ or $C(B) = \{y\}$ or $C(B) = \{x, y\}$. So $x \geq^* y$ or $y \geq^* x$ or both. Thus $\geq^*$ is complete.

Transitivity: Given $x \geq^* y$ and $y \geq^* z$. It has to be shown that $x \geq^* z$. It is sufficient to show that $x \in C(B)$, whereas $B = \{x, y, z\} \in \mathbb{B}$. If $y \in C(B)$, then it follows from WARP that $x \in C(B)$ and done. If $z \in C(B)$, then it follows from WARP that $y \in C(B)$ and you are in the case before and done. If $y \notin C(B)$ and $z \notin C(B)$, then $x \in C(B)$ has to be since $C(B) \neq \emptyset$. Therefore $\geq^*$ is transitive.

Appendix I.2: Formal Presentation of Preference Relations with Utility Functions

Proposition: Every continuous preference relation $\geq$ on $X \subset \mathbb{R}^m$ is being represented by a continuous utility function.

Proof: The proof is only shown for the case that $X \subset \mathbb{R}^m_+$ and that $\geq$ is additionally monotone, i.e. that for $x, y \in X$ from $x_i > y_i$ for all $i = 1, \ldots, m$, it follows that $x > y$. The general case is a lot more complicated.

Given $e = (1, 1, \ldots, 1) \in \mathbb{R}^m_+$ and $x \in X$. From the monotony of $\geq$ it follows that $x \geq 0$ and $\alpha e \geq x$ for $\alpha \geq 0$ large enough. Since $\geq$ in addition is continuous, there exists for all $x \in X$ exactly one $\alpha(x)$ with $\alpha(x)e \approx x$.

$$\mu(x) := \alpha(x) \text{ is defined for all } x \in X$$

and it has to be shown that μ represents the preference relation $\geq$. Then it has to be shown that for $x, y \in X$,

$$x \geq y \Leftrightarrow \mu(x) \geq \mu(y).$$

Given that $\mu(x) \geq \mu(y)$. Then $\alpha(x) \geq \alpha(y)$ and from monotony of $\geq$ it follows that

$$\alpha(x)e \geq \alpha(y)e.$$

Since $x \approx \alpha(x)e$ and $y \approx \alpha(y)e$ it follows though that $x \geq y$ from the transitivity of $\geq$.

To the contrary, given $x \geq y$. Since $x \approx \alpha(x)e$ and $y \approx \alpha(y)e$ it follows again from transitivity that

$$\alpha(x)e \geq \alpha(y)e.$$

Then though it has to be that $\alpha(x) \geq \alpha(y)$, otherwise $\geq$ would not be monotone. Because of the definition of μ it follows that $\mu(x) \geq \mu(y)$.

The proof of continuity of μ is more complex and can be seen in Mas-Colell et al. (1995).

Formal presentation of expected utility

Given Λ the space of all lotteries with monetary payments.

Definition: $V: \Lambda \to \mathbb{R}$ is an expected utility function if a $\mu: \mathbb{R} \to \mathbb{R}$ exists such that for all $x^\backprime \in \Lambda$

$$V(x^\backprime) = E[\mu(x^\backprime)]$$

The function μ is called the von Neumann–Morgenstern or Bernoulli utility function.

Proposition: (Uniqueness of the expected utility function)

Given $V: \Lambda \to \mathbb{R}$ an expected utility function that represents a preference relation $\geq$ on Λ. Then $W: \Lambda \to \mathbb{R}$ another expected utility function, that represents $\geq$ exactly then when constant $a > 0$ and b exist with

$$W(x^\backprime) = aV(x^\backprime) + b \text{ for all } x^\backprime \in \Lambda.$$

For the proof see Mas-Colell et al. (1995).

To show the existence of an expected utility function, three axioms are required that have to fulfill the preference relation $\geq$ on Λ.

Axiom 1: (State independence)

Given $x', y' \in \Lambda$ with distribution functions $F_{x'}$ and $F_{y'}$. Then it holds that

$$F_{x'} = F_{y'} \Rightarrow x' \approx y'.$$

Axiom 2: (Continuity)

Given $x', y', z' \in \Lambda$. Then the sets

$$\{\alpha \in [0, 1] | \alpha x' + (1\text{-}\alpha)y' \geq z'\} \text{ and } \{\alpha \in [0, 1] | z' \geq \alpha z' + (1\text{-}\alpha)y'\}$$

are closed.

Axiom 3: (Independence)

Given $x', y', z' \in \Lambda$ and $\alpha \in [0, 1]$. Then it holds

$$x' \geq y' \Leftrightarrow \alpha x' + (1\text{-}\alpha)z' \geq \alpha y' + (1\text{-}\alpha)z'.$$

Proposition: (Existence of an expected utility function)

Given $\geq$ a preference relation on Λ, that fulfills the axioms 1–3. The there exists an expected utility function V, that represents $\geq$, i.e. there exists a $\mu : \mathbb{R} \to \mathbb{R}$ with

$$x' \geq y' \Leftrightarrow E[\mu(x')] \geq E[\mu(y')] \text{ for } x', y' \in \Lambda.$$

For the proof see Mas-Colell et al. (1995).

APPENDIX II

Appendix II.1: Experimental Instructions for the Rumor Setting with an Auctioneer (Experiments 1 and 2)

Welcome!

Introduction

- You are about to participate in an experiment analyzing human behavioral characteristics when faced with decision-making under uncertainty. Two experiments will take place, an individual experiment and a market experiment. All participants will take part in both experiments. If you follow the instructions carefully and make good decisions you may earn a considerable amount of money. You will be paid in cash at the end of the experiment. The funds for this experiment have been provided by the Swiss National Science Foundation.

- *During the experiment, we ask that you please do not talk to each other. Violating this rule will lead to exclusion from the experiment and non-payment.* If you have a question, please raise your hand and an experimenter will assist you.

1. Individual experiment

Please choose between lottery A and lottery B. The payment for the individual experiment is determined by the lottery you have chosen.

Lottery A: A fair coin is thrown.

— If heads appears, then your payment will be drawn randomly and uniformly between numbers 14 and 16.
— If tails appears, then your payment will be drawn randomly and uniformly between numbers 0 and 16.

Lottery B: One ball is drawn from an urn with red and blue balls. However, the ratio of blue and red balls is not known to you.

— If a blue ball is drawn, then your payment will be drawn randomly and uniformly between numbers 14 and 16.
— If a red ball is drawn, then your payment will be drawn randomly and uniformly between numbers 0 and 16.

Which lottery do you choose?
The payoff in both lotteries is the drawn number -11.5 multiplied by CHF 1 per point.

Example: If 5 is drawn, then you lose CHF 6.50; if 13 is drawn, you win correspondingly CHF 1.50.

2. Market experiment

- You have each drawn a laminated slip, which corresponds to your PC terminal number. If the number on your slip is from PC no. 2 to PC no. 9, you will be a bidder for the entire experiment. If the number on your slip is from PC no. 10 to PC no. 13, you will be an auctioneer for the entire experiment.
- In each of 30 periods, you will be *randomly* matched with two other participants in a group. Each group has an auctioneer and two bidders. You will not know the identities of the other participants in your group. Your payoff each period depends ONLY on the decisions made by you and the other two participants in your group.
- In each of 30 periods, the **value** for all bidders for the object will be randomly drawn from one of two distributions:

  — **High value distribution**: If the bidder's value is drawn from the high value distribution, then

    — it is randomly drawn from the set of integers between 70 and 80, where each integer is equally likely to be drawn.

— **Low value distribution**: If the bidder's value is drawn from the low value distribution, then

— it is randomly drawn from the set of integers between 0 and 80, where each integer is equally likely to be drawn.

— Therefore, if your value is drawn from the high value distribution, it can take on any integer value between 70 and 80. Similarly, if your value is drawn from the low value distribution, it can take on any integer value between 0 and 80.

— In each of 30 periods, each bidder's value will be randomly and independently drawn from the high value distribution with a predetermined chance of $x\%$, and from the low value distribution with $(100 - x)\%$ chance. You will not be told what x is. You will not be told which distribution your value is drawn from, either. The other bidders' values are drawn from the same distribution as your own.

Auctioneers are also not informed of the value of x.

Comment: In experiment 2, the '$x\%$' was replaced by 70% and '$(100-x)\%$' by 30%.

• Each period consists of the following stages:

— Each auctioneer will set a minimum selling price, which can be any integer between 0 and 80, inclusive.

— Bidders are informed of the minimum selling prices of their auctioneers. Then each bidder will simultaneously and independently submit a bid, which can be any integer between 1 and 80, inclusive. If you do not want to buy, you can submit any positive integer below the minimum selling price.

— The bids are collected in each group and the object is allocated according to the rules of the auction explained in the next section.

— Bidders will get the following feedback on their screen: the value, your bid, the minimum selling price, the winning bid, whether you got the object, and your payoff.

— Auctioneers will get the following feedback: whether you sold the object, your minimum selling price, the bids, and your payoff.

• The process continues.

Rules of the Auction and Payoffs

• **Bidders**: In each period,

— if your bid is less than the minimum selling price, you don't get the object:
Your Payoff = 0.

— if your bid is greater than or equal to the minimum selling price, and:

— if your bid is greater than the other bid, you get the object and pay your bid:
Your Payoff = Your Value − Your Bid;

— if your bid is less than the other bid, you don't get the object:
Your Payoff = 0.

— if your bid is equal to the other bid, the computer will break the tie by flipping a fair coin. In this case,

— with 50% chance you get the object and pay your bid:
Your Payoff = Your Value − Your Bid;
— with 50% chance you don't get the object:
Your Payoff = 0.

- **Auctioneers**: In each period, you will receive two bids from your group.

  — If both bids are less than your minimum selling price, the object is not sold, and:
  Your Payoff = 0;
  — If at least one bid is greater than or equal to your minimum selling price, you sell the object to the higher bidder and
  Your Payoff = the Higher Bid.

For example, if the minimum selling price is 1, bidder A bids 25, and bidder B bids 55: Since $55 > 1$ and $55 > 25$, bidder B gets the object. Bidder A's payoff $= 0$; bidder B's payoff $=$ the value -55; the auctioneer's payoff $= 55$.

- There will be 30 periods. There will be no practice periods. From the first period, you will be paid for each decision you make.
- Your total payoff is the sum of your payoffs in all periods.
- Bidders: the exchange rate is CHF 0.20 per positive payoff point.
- Auctioneers: the exchange rate is CHF 0.015 per positive payoff point.

We encourage you to earn as much cash as you can. Are there any questions?

Review Questions

Please answer the review questions below. If you have any questions or have finished the review questions, please raise your hand. The experimenter will check each participant's answers individually.

1. Suppose the value is 60 and you bid 62.
   If you get the object, your payoff =
   If you don't get the object, your payoff =

2. Suppose the value is 60 and you bid 60.
   If you get the object, your payoff =
   If you don't get the object, your payoff =

3. Suppose the value is 60 and you bid 58.
   If you get the object, your payoff =
   If you don't get the object, your payoff =

4. The minimum selling price is 30 and your bid is 25, your payoff =

5. True or false:

   (a) If a bidder's value is 25, it must have been drawn from the low distribution.
   (b) If a bidder's value is 70, it must have been drawn from the high distribution.
   (c) You will be playing with the same two participants for the entire experiment.
   (d) A bidder's payoff depends only on his/her own bid.
   (e) If you are an auctioneer and your minimum selling price is higher than both bids, your payoff will be zero.

Appendix II.2: Experimental Instructions for the Rumor Setting with a Batch Auction (Experiments 3 and 4)

The first part of the instructions up to and including '1. Individual experiment' is the same as in the experimental instructions in Appendix I.1.

2. Market experiment

- You have each drawn a laminated slip, which corresponds to your PC terminal number. In this experiment you will hold the roles of a bidder as well as a vendor.
- The experiment will go for 30 periods. All periods follow the same procedure.

  - You will be endowed each period with 10 shares and 1,000 'cash' points. In each period you are given the possibility of submitting bids and asking prices for buying and selling shares. At the end of the period the positions will be closed. For every period you will be endowed with the same number of shares and 'cash' points. Your gains and losses will be counted for each period and summed up in the end.
  - You are requested to give asking prices and bids for the shares you hold or would like to purchase. Type your bids and asking prices into the corresponding fields on your screen. First, remember that you can only make as many bids for shares as you have cash for. Second, you are allowed ask offers for up to the 10 shares you have (no short selling allowed).

- In each of the 30 periods, the object's **value** for all bidders will be randomly drawn from one of two distributions:

  — **High value distribution**: If the value of the share is drawn from the high value distribution, then

    — it is randomly drawn from the set of integers between 70 and 80, where each integer is equally likely to be drawn.

  — **Low value distribution**: If the value of the share is drawn from the low value distribution, then

    — it is randomly drawn from the set of integers between 0 and 80, where each integer is equally likely to be drawn.

  — Therefore, if the value is drawn from the high value distribution, it can take on any integer value between 70 and 80. Similarly, if the value is drawn from the low value distribution, it can take on any integer value between 0 and 80.

In each of 30 periods, the value of the share will be randomly and independently drawn from the high value distribution with a predetermined chance of $x\%$, and from the low value distribution with $(100 - x)\%$ chance. There is only one value per period for the share, which is the same for all participants.

Comment: In experiment 4, the 'x%' is replaced by 70% and '(100 − x)%' by 30%.

You are **not** told: — the value of x.
                             — which distribution the value is drawn from.

You are told: — the value of the share at the end of each period.

1. Example:
1st Bid: 3 shares for 45
2nd Bid: 1 share for 50

1st Asking price: 4 shares for 65
2nd Asking price: 3 shares for 60

Checks: Your bids sum up to 185 (3*45 + 1*50) < 1000: ✓
        Your asking prices sum up to 7 shares: ✓

2. Example:
1st Bid: 12 shares for 35
2nd Bid: 7 shares for 40
3rd Bid: 6 shares for 45
4th Bid: 4 shares for 60

1st Asking price: 8 shares for 80
2nd Asking price: 5 shares for 75

Checks: Your bids sum up to 1, 210 (12*35 + 7*40 + 6*45 + 4*60): **Too much!** You are allowed to give asking prices up to 1,000 points (that's all the cash you have).

Your asking prices sum up to 13 shares: **Too much!** You are allowed to give asking prices for up to 10 shares (you don't have more than 10 shares).

Remark
You have to state per period at least one bid as well as one offer (the minimal price for a bid is 1, the maximum price for an ask offer is 80). You have per period 2 minutes to state your bids and ask offers. Please note that you may state per period more than one bid and ask offer. Please state only integer values as bids and ask offers
To buy or sell shares, please state your bids or ask offers as follows:
  State your bid in the box below 'your bid' and click on the button 'bid'. The same procedure is applied for ask offers. If you would like to state another offer for the same price, please click once again on the same button. If you would like to state bids or ask offers for another price, please state the desired price in the box and click on the corresponding button. Your overall bids and ask offers are visible in the columns 'your bids' and 'your ask offers'.

Your bids:	Your bids:	Your ask offers:	Your ask offers:
	45	65	
	50	65	
	50	65	
	50	65	
		60	
		60	

Bid	**Ask**

In the case above you have stated bids for

1 share at the price of 45
3 shares at the price of 50

as well as ask offers for

4 shares at the price of 65
2 shares at the price of 60

Each period contains the following steps:

1. All participants state their bids and ask offers.
2. All bids and ask offers are collected. The order book will look something like the following:

Example of a possible order book

Order to buy		Order to sell	
Amount	Price	Amount	Price
3	35	2	80
6	40	5	75
7	45	8	65
10	50	7	60
7	60	4	55
Total: 33 $(3+6+7+10+7)$		26 $(2+5+8+7+4)$	

3. Determination of the price at which all shares are traded in this period:

Price	Possible buys	Possible sells	Possible traded volume
35	33	0	0
40	30 $(33-3)$	0	0
45	24 $(30-6)$	0	0
50	17 $(24-7)$	0	0
55	7 $(17-10)$	4 $(11-7)$	4
60	**7**	**11 $(19-8)$**	**7**
65	0	19 $(24-5)$	0
75	0	24 $(26-2)$	0
80	0	26	0

At a price of 60 the most shares can be traded. In this example the price will be set at 60 and the trades for *those* shares, for this is possible, will be executed at 60. The trading volume is 7 shares.

— The value of the share is determined according to the rules mentioned above.
— You will get the following feedback on your screen: The value of the share (in this period), the price at which the trades are executed, whether you have traded or not and, if yes, how many shares you traded, as well as your payoff.

• This process represents one period.

Example:
You have given the following orders in the example above:

1st Bid: 2 shares at a price of 40
2nd Bid: 4 shares at a price of 50

1st Asking price: 3 shares at a price of 75
2nd Asking price: 1 share at a price of 65
3rd Asking price: 2 shares at a price of 55

The ask offer for 2 shares at a price of 55 is accepted and both shares are traded at the price of 60.

The true value of the share is determined and amounts in this hypothetical example to 71. Therefore you have a payoff of -22 $[2*(60-71)=-22$, since you sold the share]. In this case you suffer a loss of 22. If you had been the counterparty and had bought two shares at the price of 60, then you would have had a payoff of $+22$ $[2*(71-60)]$.

Rules of the Auction and Payoffs

- If your bids are above or your ask offers for shares are below the traded price, your trades will be automatically executed.
- If your bids and your ask offers for shares are the same as the traded price, they will be executed according to your contingent.

Example as in the order book:
Assuming the ask offers at the price of 60 are from trader no. 1 with 3 shares and from trader no. 2 with 4 shares. Then the 4 shares offered at 55 will be executed automatically, leaving 3 shares to trade out of 7 offered at 60 (a rate of 42.8%).

There are 3 shares left to trade and 7 shares outstanding (composed of 3 shares from trader no. 1 and 4 shares from trader no. 2).

Then trader no. 1 will be able to trade 1 share ($3*0.428=1.28$) and trader no. 2 will be able to trade 2 shares ($4*0.428=1.72$ shares).

The rule is that decimal place (in this case .28 and .72) below .5 will be rounded down, above .5 rounded up.

There will be 30 periods. There will be no practice periods. From the first period on you will be paid for each decision you make.

- Your total payoff is the sum of your payoffs in all periods.
- You will receive a base salary that you can increase by making good trades. The salary, however, may get smaller when you experience losses. In any case you don't have to pay any money back to us.
- The exchange rate is CHF 0.03 per positive profit point, CHF -0.03 per negative point.

We encourage you to earn as much cash as you can. Are there any questions?

Review Questions

Please answer the review questions. If you have any questions or have finished the review questions, please raise your hand. The experimenter will check each participant's answers individually.

1. Suppose the value of the share is 60 and you have bid 1 share at 62.
   Are you able to trade the share in any case?

Assuming you are able to trade and the value of the share is 65, your payoff is =
Assuming the value of the share is 55, then your payoff is =

2. Suppose the value of the share is 60 and you have bid 1 share at 60.
   Are you able to trade the share in any case?
   Assuming you are able to trade and the value of the share is 65, your payoff is =
   Assuming the value of the share is 55, then your payoff is =

3. Suppose the value of the share is 60 and you have bid 1 share at 58.
   Are you able to trade the share in any case?
   Assuming you are able to trade and the value of the share is 65, your payoff is =
   Assuming the value of the share is 55, then your payoff is =

4. Suppose the value of the share is 60 and you have bid 3 shares at 52.
   Are you able to trade the share in any case?
   Assuming you are able to trade and the value of the share is 65, your payoff is =
   Assuming the value of the share is 55, then your payoff is =

5. True or false:
   (a) If the value of the share is 25, it must have been drawn from the low distribution.
   (b) If the value of the share is 60, it must have been drawn from the high distribution.
   (c) Your bids and ask offers are in competition with the other bids and ask offers of all other participants.
   (d) If you have stated ask offers that are all higher than the traded price, then you are not able to sell any shares.
   (e) All shares are traded at the same price within each period.

Appendix II.3: Experimental Instructions for the Rumor Setting in a Continuous Double Auction (Experiments 5 to 12)

The first part of the instructions up to and including '1. Individual experiment' is the same as in the experimental instructions as in Appendix I.1.

2. Market experiment

- You have each drawn a laminated slip, which corresponds to your PC terminal number. In this experiment you will hold the roles of a bidder as well as a vendor.
- The experiment will go for 30 periods. All periods follow the same procedure:

  - You will be endowed each period with 10 shares and 1,000 'cash' points. Each period you are given the opportunity to submit bids and ask offers for buying and selling shares. At the end of the period the positions will be closed. For every period you will be endowed with the same numbers of shares and 'cash' points. Your gains and losses will be counted for each period and summed up in the end.
  - You are requested to give ask offers and bids for the shares you hold or would like to purchase. Type your bids and ask offers into the corresponding fields on your screen. First, remember that you can only give as many bids for shares as you have cash for. Second, you are allowed ask offers up to the 10 shares you have (no short selling allowed).

- In each of 30 periods, the share's **value** will be randomly drawn from one of two distributions:

  — **High value distribution**: If the value of the share is drawn from the high value distribution, then

    — it is randomly drawn from the set of integers between 70 and 80, where each integer is equally likely to be drawn.

  — **Low value distribution**: If the value of the share is drawn from the low value distribution, then

    — it is randomly drawn from the set of integers between 0 and 80, where each integer is equally likely to be drawn.

  — Therefore, if your value is drawn from the high value distribution, it can take on any integer value between 70 and 80. Similarly, if your value is drawn from the low value distribution, it can take on any integer value between 0 and 80.

In each of 30 periods, the value of the share will be randomly and independently drawn from the high value distribution with a predetermined chance of $x\%$, and from the low value distribution with $(100 - x)\%$ chance. There is only one value per period for the share, which is the same for all participants.

Comment: The instructions of experiment 7 are exactly the same as above. In experiment 6, the 'x%' is replaced by 70% and '(100 − x)%' by 30%. Experiment 8 replaces the probabilities of 70%/30% with 50%/50%. In experiments 9 and 11, the values of 70 and 80 are replaced by 160 and 200. In experiment 10, both the 'x%' and '(100 − x)%' as well as the absolute values (70, 80) are replaced with 70%/30% and 160/200 correspondingly. In comparison to experiment 10, the probabilities of 70%/30% in experiment 12 are replaced with 50%/50%.

You are **not** told: — the value of x.
                     — which distribution the value is drawn from.

You are told: — the value of the share at the end of each period.

Each period consists of the following steps:

1. The trading phase

In each period you have 90 seconds to trade the share. Check the trade screen below. On top is the current period and time remaining. In the middle of the screen, you see the number of shares in your share account and the cash in your trade account.

In the lower part of the screen, you trade:

(a) You make **offers to sell** to the other participants in the window on the very left. Enter the price you are asking in the blue field and click on 'ask'. This price appears then on the screen of all participants right next to this field, in the field '**offers to sell**'. You can only enter positive integer amounts, and your offer must be lower than the currently lowest offer.

(b) The next window contains the offers to sell of all participants. You can **buy** one share at one of these prices. The currently best offer is highlighted. When you hit 'buy', you automatically buy a share from the participant who made this offer. The respective amount is debited from your **trade account**.

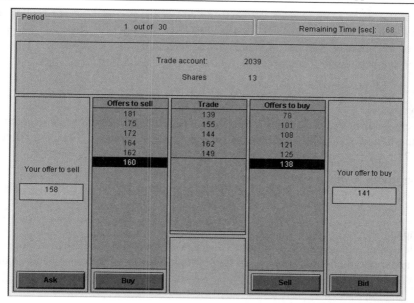

Note: The action screen is representative for experiments 9 to 12 only.

(c) The window in the centre of the lower part of the screen lists all prices at which shares were traded in this period.

(d) The fourth window contains the price bids of all participants. You can **sell** one of your shares at one of these prices. The best bid is highlighted. When you hit 'sell', you sell one of your shares to the participant who made this offer. The resulting cash amount is credited to your **trade account**.

(e) You can make an **offer to buy** in the window on the very right. Enter the amount at which you are willing to buy a share in the blue field and click on 'bid'. This price subsequently appears on all screens in the field '**offers to buy**'. You can only enter positive integer amounts and your offer must be higher than the currently highest offer.

Some trade rules for shares:

- Do not sell shares that you do not own yet.
- Do not sell shares to yourself.
- Do not buy shares with debt, i.e. you are not allowed to offer more for a share than you currently have in your trade account.

The computer will enforce these rules automatically. If you are ever astonished about problems with the execution of one of your orders, please check first whether you followed the rules just mentioned.

1. After the trading period (90 seconds per period) has expired, the **value** of the share is determined according to the rules mentioned above.
2. You receive the following feedback on your screen: The value (determined in this period) of the share as well as your profit.

Your profit in each period is calculated as follows:

[(Value of the share * Number of shares at the end of the period) + Your trading account at the end of the period)] –
[(Value of the share * Number of shares at the beginning of the period) + Your trading account at the beginning of the period)]

- This process represents one period.

1. Example:
At the beginning of the period you hold 10 shares and 1,000 in your trade account. At the end of the period you hold 7 shares and have a trade account of 1,145. The value of the share is 73.

Then your profit in this period is:
$[(73*7) + 1,145] − [(73*10) + 1,000] = −74$. You have therefore suffered a loss of 74 in this period.

2. Example:
At the beginning of the period you hold 10 shares and 1,000 in your trade account. At the end of the period you hold 12 shares and have a trade account of 980. The value of the share is 53.

Then your profit in this period is:
$[(53*12) + 980] − [(53*10) + 1,000] = +86$. You have therefore realized a gain of 86 in this period.

30 periods will be played. There will be no trial periods. From the first period on you will be paid for your decisions.

- Your total profit is the sum of the profits of all periods played.
- You will receive a base salary that you can increase by making good trades. The salary, however, may get smaller when you experience losses. In any case you don't have to pay any money back to us.
- The exchange rate is CHF 0.03 per positive profit point, CHF 0.03 per negative point. *(CHF 0.01 and CHF −0.01 respectively in experiments 9–12.)*

We would like to remind you that the better your decisions are, the more you can earn. Are there any questions?

Review Questions

Please answer the review questions. If you have any questions or have finished the review questions, please raise your hand. The experimenter will check each participant's answers individually.

1. When you buy a share, what happens to your trade account?

2. When you sell a share, what happens to your trade account?

3. Are you able to buy a share when you don't have sufficient cash in your trading account?

4. Are you able to sell a share when the number of shares you own is zero?

5. How do you state offers to buy a share?

6. How do you state offers to sell a share?

7. What happens when you click on the button 'sell'?

8. What happens when you click on the button 'buy'?

9. True or false:
   (a) If the value of the share is 54, it must have been drawn from the low distribution.
   (b) If the value of the share is 71, it must have been drawn from the high distribution.
   (c) The determined value of the share of each period is the same for all participants.
   (d) All shares are traded at the same price within each period.

APPENDIX III

Appendix III.1: Second Stage Experimental Instructions

The experimental instructions for the second stage follow the instructions of the continuous double auction (experiments 5 to 12) with the following modifications:

2. Market experiment

- You have each drawn a laminated slip, which corresponds to your PC terminal number. In this experiment you will hold the roles of a bidder as well as a seller.
- The experiment will go for 12 periods. All periods follow the same procedure.
- You will be endowed each period with 10 shares of company X and 2,500 'cash' points. In each period you are given the opportunity to submit bids and ask offers for buying and selling shares. At the end of the period the positions will be closed. For every period you will be endowed with the same number of shares and 'cash' points. Your gains and losses will be counted for each period and summed up in the end.
- You are requested to give ask offers and bids for the shares you hold or would like to purchase. Type your bids and ask offers into the corresponding fields on your screen. First, remember that you can only give as many bids for shares as you have cash for. Second, you are allowed ask offers up to the 10 shares you have (no short selling allowed)
- In each of the 12 periods the value of the share of company X will be between 0 and 200. In addition you will receive during each period on your screen further news about the value of the share. All messages are communicated to you via newsticker.

    Attention! The news that you will receive during each period can, but does not have to be truthful. If, though, probability measures are specified in the messages, then these are in any case correct.

    At the end of each period you are informed about the value of the share.

The following text messages are communicated to the participants in each session randomly, though for all at the same time.

1. Rumor! Company X will publish an earnings warning. A share of company X would only be worth at most 40.

2. Rumor! Company X will publish an earnings warning. You estimate the probability at 50% that the rumor will turn out to be true.

3. Rumor! Company X will publish an earnings warning. A share of company X would only be worth at most 40. You estimate the rumor's source to be credible.

4. Rumor! Company X will publish an earnings warning. A share of company X would only be worth at most 40. You estimate the rumor's source to be non-credible.

5. Rumor! Company X will publish an earnings warning. A share of company X would only be worth at most 40. You estimate the rumor's content to be plausible.

6. Rumor! Company X will publish an earnings warning. A share of company X would only be worth at most 40. You estimate the rumor's content to be non-plausible.

7. Rumor! Company X is in merger talks with company Y. A share of company X would be worth at least 160.

8. Rumor! Company X is in merger talks with company Y. A share of company X would be worth at least 160. You estimate the probability at 50% that the rumor will turn out to be true.

9. Rumor! Company X is in merger talks with company Y. A share of company X would be worth at least 160. You estimate the rumor's source to be credible.

10. Rumor! Company X is in merger talks with company Y. A share of company X would be worth at least 160. You estimate the rumor's source to be non-credible.

11. Rumor! Company X is in merger talks with company Y. A share of company X would be worth at least 160. You estimate the rumor's content to be plausible.

12. Rumor! Company X is in merger talks with company Y. A share of company X would be worth at least 160. You estimate the rumor's content to be non-plausible.

The underlying distributions and the probabilities that determine the value of the share are as follows:

1. Uniform distribution from 0 to 200 with 50%; uniform distribution from 0 to 40: 50%

2. Uniform distribution from 0 to 200 with 50%; uniform distribution from 0 to 40: 50%

3. Uniform distribution from 0 to 200 with 30%; uniform distribution from 0 to 40: 70%

4. Uniform distribution from 0 to 200 with 70%; uniform distribution from 0 to 40: 30%

5. Uniform distribution from 0 to 200 with 30%; uniform distribution from 0 to 40: 70%

6. Uniform distribution from 0 to 200 with 70%; uniform distribution from 0 to 40: 30%

7. Uniform distribution from 0 to 200 with 50%; uniform distribution from 160 to 200: 50%

8. Uniform distribution from 0 to 200 with 50%; uniform distribution from 160 to 200: 50%

9. Uniform distribution from 0 to 200 with 30%; uniform distribution from 160 to 200: 70%

10. Uniform distribution from 0 to 200 with 70%; uniform distribution from 160 to 200: 30%

11. Uniform distribution from 0 to 200 with 30%; uniform distribution from 160 to 200: 70%

12. Uniform distribution from 0 to 200 with 70%; uniform distribution from 160 to 200: 30%

APPENDIX IV

Appendix IV.1: Third Stage Experimental Instructions

The experimental instructions for the third stage follow the second stage instructions, with the following modifications

2.   Market experiment

• You have each drawn a laminated slip, which corresponds to your PC terminal number. In this experiment you will hold the roles of a bidder as well as a vendor.
• The experiment will go for 12 periods. All periods follow the same procedure.
• You will be endowed each period with 10 shares of company X and 2,500 'cash' points. In each period you are given the opportunity to submit bids and ask offers for buying and selling shares. At the end of the period the positions will be closed. For every period you will be endowed with the same number of shares and 'cash' points. Your gains and losses will be counted for each period and summed up in the end.
• You are requested to give ask offers and bids for the shares you hold or would like to purchase. Type your bids and ask offers into the corresponding fields on your screen. First, remember that you can only give as many bids for shares as you have cash for. Second, you are allowed to offer up to the 10 shares you have (no short selling allowed).
• In each of the 12 periods the value of the share of company X will between 0 and 200. In addition you will receive during each period further news about the value of the share on your screen.

Attention! There are two different groups of participants. One group will receive during each period more precise news than the other concerning the value of the share. It is, however, not known what the ratio of the corresponding groups is. Please note that the news you will receive during each period can be, but does not have to be, truthful. If, though, within the messages probability measures are specified, then these are in any case correct. All messages are communicated to you via newsticker.

In addition it is possible that after each period you might change from one group to the other. This is not communicated to you.

At the end of each period you are informed about the value of the share.

The following text messages are communicated to the participants in each session randomly, though for all at the same time.

First group:

1. Rumor! Company X will publish an earnings warning. A share of company X would only be worth at most 40.

2. Rumor! Company X will publish an earnings warning. You estimate the probability at 50% that the rumor will turn out to be true.

3. Rumor! Company X will publish an earnings warning. A share of company X would only be worth at most 40. You estimate the rumor's source to be credible.

4. Rumor! Company X will publish an earnings warning. A share of company X would only be worth at most 40. You estimate the rumor's source to be non-credible.

5. Rumor! Company X will publish an earnings warning. A share of company X would only be worth at most 40. You estimate the rumor's content to be plausible.

6. Rumor! Company X will publish an earnings warning. A share of company X would only be worth at most 40. You estimate the rumor's content to be non-plausible.

7. Rumor! Company X is in merger talks with company Y. A share of company X would only be worth at least 160.

8. Rumor! Company X is in merger talks with company Y. A share of company X would be worth at least 160. You estimate the probability at 50% that the rumor will turn out to be true.

9. Rumor! Company X is in merger talks with company Y. A share of company X would be worth at least 160. You estimate the rumor's source to be credible.

10. Rumor! Company X is in merger talks with company Y. A share of company X would be worth at least 160. You estimate the rumor's source to be non-credible.

11. Rumor! Company X is in merger talks with company Y. A share of company X would be worth at least 160. You estimate the rumor's content to be plausible.

12. Rumor! Company X is in merger talks with company Y. A share of company X would be worth at least 160. You estimate the rumor's content to be non-plausible.

Second group:

1. Rumor! Company X will publish an earnings warning. With a probability of 50% the share of company X will be worth at most 40.

2. Rumor! Company X will publish an earnings warning. With a probability of 50% the share of company X will be worth at most 40.

3. Rumor! Company X will publish an earnings warning. With a probability of 70% the share of company X will be worth at most 40.

4. Rumor! Company X will publish an earnings warning. With a probability of 30% the share of company X will be worth at most 40.

5. Rumor! Company X will publish an earnings warning. With a probability of 70% the share of company X will be worth at most 40.

6. Rumor! Company X will publish an earnings warning. With a probability of 30% the share of company X will be worth at most 40.

7. Rumor! Company X is in merger talks with company Y. With a probability of 50% the share of company X will be worth at least 160.

8. Rumor! Company X is in merger talks with company Y. With a probability of 50% the share of company X will be worth at least 160.

9. Rumor! Company X is in merger talks with company Y. With a probability of 70% the share of company X will be worth at least 160.

10. Rumor! Company X is in merger talks with company Y. With a probability of 30% the share of company X will be worth at least 160.

11. Rumor! Company X is in merger talks with company Y. With a probability of 70% the share of company X will be worth at least 160.

12. Rumor! Company X is in merger talks with company Y. With a probability of 30% the share of company X will be worth at least 160.

APPENDIX V

Appendix V.1: Fourth Stage Experimental Instructions

The experimental instructions for the fourth stage follow the third stage instructions, with the following modifications:

2. Market experiment

- You have each drawn a laminated slip, which corresponds to your PC terminal number. In this experiment you will hold the roles of a bidder as well as a vendor.
- The experiment will go for 12 periods. All periods follow the same procedure.
- You will be endowed each period with 10 shares of company X and 2,500 'cash' points. In each period you are given the opportunity to submit bids and ask offers for buying and selling shares. At the end of the period the positions will be closed. For every period you will be endowed with the same numbers of shares and 'cash' points. Your gains and losses will be counted for each period and summed up in the end.
- You are requested to give ask offers and bids for the shares you hold or would like to purchase. Type your bids and ask offers into the corresponding fields on your screen. First, remember that you can only give as many bids for shares as you have cash for. Second, you are allowed to ask for up to the 10 shares you have (no short selling allowed).
- In each of the 12 periods the value of the share of company X will between 0 and 200. In addition you will receive during each period further news about the value of the share on your screen.

    Attention! There are two different groups of participants. One group will receive during each period more precise news than the other concerning the value of the share. It is, however, not known what the ratio of the corresponding groups are. Please note that the news you will receive during each period can be, but does not have to be, truthful. If, though, within the messages probability measures are specified, then these are in any case correct. All messages are communicated to you via newsticker.

    In addition it is possible that after each period you might change from one group to the other. This is not communicated to you.

    At the end of each period you are informed about the value of the share.

Each period contains the following steps:

1. At the beginning of each period there is a trading phase. This phase lasts until the first message is communicated via newsticker. The trading rules follow the same instructions as in the other experiments.

2. After the first trading phase is over and the first message has been communicated over the newsticker, the first communication phase follows. For the rules of communication please consult the screen below. The first communication phase lasts for 45 seconds. During this time it is <u>not</u> possible to trade. In addition, it is not possible to state new sell and buy orders. The offers to sell and the offers to buy that have been stated before the communication phase starts, however, stay in place.

   The communication can, for example, serve to find out what other market participants know, to receive insights on their trading strategy or to convince them of your own strategy. Click within the e-mail area on the number of the participant in the field 'participants' you would like to contact and click on 'dial'. A line to that participant is now open. You can choose from the messages in the box 'possible messages' by clicking on one of them. Click then on 'Send message', and the message is sent to the corresponding participant.

   When you receive a message, you can either respond to the other market participant or hang up. If you would like to respond, choose one among the possible answers and click on 'Send message'. If you do not want to answer, click on 'disconnect'. The line is then disconnected.

   Within the e-mail area at the top left you can see the actual 'Status of communication'. In the middle you see which participant you are connected with. If you are in communication with another market participant, you can see within the e-mail area on your right-hand side the previous communication structure within that period.

   For your information: You can communicate with at most two participants at the same time, though there is no limit during one period. You can also communicate with the same participants over several periods.

3. After the first communication phase is over, another trading phase follows. The trading phase lasts for 45 seconds as well. The rules for trading are the same as stated above. During this time it is <u>not</u> possible to communicate with each other. The communication status already existent before the trading phase starts, however, stays in place.

4. After the second trading phase another communication phase follows. This communication phase lasts for 30 seconds. The rules for communication follow the stated instructions as stated above.

5. After the second communication phase another trading phase follows until the complete time of one period (3 minutes) has elapsed.

Your profit for each period is calculated as follows:

[(Value of the share * Amount of shares at the end of the period) + Your trading account at the end of the period)] −
[(Value of the share * Amount of shares at the beginning of the period) + Your trading account at the beginning of the period)]

• This process represents one period.

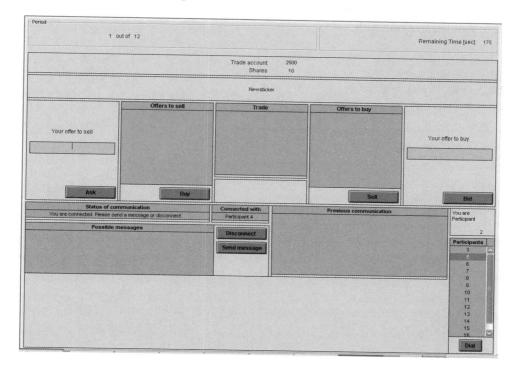

Appendix V.2: First Two Message Levels

1.
1.1 Have you seen the rumor, what do you think of it?
1.2 Have you seen the rumor, do you know more?
1.3 Have you seen the rumor, you have to buy this share!
1.4 Have you seen the rumor, you have to sell this share!

2.
2.1
2.1.1 You have to buy this share!
2.1.2 You have to sell this share!
2.1.3 I don't have a clue, and you?
2.1.4 I don't care, and you?
2.1.5 I don't know, do you know more?
2.1.6 There could be something to it.

2.2
2.2.1 No, I don't know more.
2.2.2 Sounds plausible.
2.2.3 Sounds not plausible.

2.2.4 Seems to be a credible source.
2.2.5 Seems not to be a credible source.
2.2.6 Will become true with . . . %.

2.3
2.3.1 Are you sure?
2.3.2 O.K., if you think so.
2.3.3 Sounds convincing.

Notes

Chapter 1: Introduction

1. Cf. Kapferer (1996a) pp. 11–12.

Chapter 2: Definitions and Characteristics of Rumors

1. Allport and Postman (1947), p. ix.
2. Knapp (1944), p. 22.
3. Peterson and Gist (1951), p. 159.
4. See DiFonzo and Bordia (1997) and Rosnow (1991).
5. See Rosnow (1974) and Shibutani (1966).
6. See Rosnow and Fine (1976), p. 11.
7. See Gluckman (1963) and Rosnow and Fine (1976).
8. See Kapferer (1996a), p. 15.
9. Shibutani (1966), p. 17.
10. See Kapferer (1996a), p. 19.
11. See Kapferer (1996a), p. 23.
12. Kapferer (1996a), p. 24.
13. See Kapferer (1996a), p. 25.
14. See Schlieper-Damrich (2003), p. 5.
15. Kimmel (2003), p. 22.
16. See Kimmel (2003), p. 30, adapted from Kimmel et al. (1992), own supplements.
17. See Neubauer (1999), p. 15.
18. See Neubauer (1999), p. 11.
19. See Neubauer (1999), p. 27 ff.
20. Shibutani (1966), pp. 215–226.
21. See Koenig (1985), p. 3.
22. See Allport and Postman (1947), Knopf (1975) and Odum (1943).
23. See Koenig (1985), p. 5.
24. Allport and Postman (1947), p. ix.
25. Knapp (1944), pp. 35–36.
26. Allport and Postman (1947), p. 502.
27. Koenig (1985), p. 4.
28. Koenig (1985), p. 5.
29. Rosnow (1980), p. 582.

30. Rosnow (1980), p. 582.
31. Rosnow (1980), p. 582.
32. Kerner et al. (1968), p. 326.
33. Allport and Postman (1946), p. 505.
34. Rosnow (1980), p. 582.
35. Rosnow (1991), p. 485, see also Chorus (1953), Ojha (1973).
36. Rosnow (1980), p. 586.
37. Anthony (1973), Anthony, Jaeger and Rosnow (1980), Esposito (1987) and Kimmel and Keefer (1989).
38. Rosnow, Esposito and Gibney (1988), Rosnow, Yost and Esposito (1986) and Walter and Beckerle (1989).
39. See Rosnow (1991), pp. 493–494.
40. Rosnow (1991), p. 493.
41. See Cooper (1982), Esposito and Rosnow (1983), Rosnow and Fine (1976) and Sheffey (1982).
42. Rosnow (1991), p. 494.

Chapter 3: Rumors and the Theory of Finance

1. The foundations laid for the concept of Efficient Markets can be found in Fama (1970, 1976).
2. See Barberis and Thaler (2003), Fama (1998), Rubinstein (2000) and Shiller (2002).
3. See Barberis and Thaler (2003).
4. Shleifer (2000), pp. 2–5.
5. See Shleifer (2000).
6. Ricciardi and Simon (2000), p. 27.
7. For the EMH and the concept of arbitrage, see Fama (1970, 1976).
8. Koenig (1985), p. 154.
9. See Kapferer (1996a), pp. 253–255.
10. See Schweizer Touristik, May 16, 2003, own translation.
11. See Shibutani (1966), p. 114.
12. See Kapferer (1990), p. 37.
13. See Koenig (1985), p. 153.
14. Eatwell, Milgate and Newman (1990) and Mas-Colell, Whinston and Green (1995).
15. The concept of bounded rationality is also discussed in, for example, Gigerenzer and Selten (2001).
16. More on procedural rationality can be found in Rizzello (1999).
17. A truly philosophical approach to rationality can be found in Rescher (1993).
18. Shiller (2000) also deals explicitly with rationality in financial markets.
19. Rose (1951), p. 468.
20. http://www.fool.com/Features/1998/sp981015InsideBusinessWeek01.htm
21. Kimmel (2003), p. 80.
22. DeBondt and Thaler (1985, 1987), Lo and MacKinlay (1990), Seyhun (1990), Stein (1989) and Zarowin (1989, 1990).
23. Liu (1992) and Syed, Liu and Smith (1989).
24. Beneish (1991), Liu, Smith and Syed (1990) and Lloyd-Davies and Canes (1978).
25. Cited in Bruhn and Wunderlich (2004), p. 212, own translation.
26. Allport and Postman (1946), p. 502.
27. Bruckner (1965) p. 65.
28. Bruckner (1965) p. 63.
29. Bruckner (1965) p. 65.
30. Bikhchandani, Hirshleifer and Welch (1992), Ellison and Freudenberg (1995), Kirman (1993) and Vettas (1997, 1998), cited in Kosfeld (2005).

31. Brunnermeier (2003); originally the paper was entitled 'Buy on rumors – sell on news'.
32. Van Bommel (2003), p. 1500.
33. According to the Securities Exchange Commission (SEC), insider trading generally refers to buying or selling a security, in breach of a fiduciary duty or other relationship of trust and confidence, while in possession of material, nonpublic information about the security. Insider trading violations may also include 'tipping' such information, securities trading by the person 'tipped' and securities trading by those who misappropriate such information.
34. Brügger (1999), pp. 218–219.
35. Goldinger (2002), pp. 98–102.
36. Goldinger (2002), p. 99, own translation.
37. Goldinger (2002), p. 99.

Chapter 4: Legal Aspects of Rumors in Financial Markets

1. See http://www.sec.gov/divisions/enforce/insider.htm
2. United States vs. O'Hagan (1997), 521 U.S. 642, 651–652.
3. Fleming (2002), p. 1432.
4. SEC vs. Mayhew, 121 F.3d 44, 49 (2d Cir. 1997).
5. SEC v. Monarch Fund, 608 F.2d 938, 942 (2d Cir. 1979).
6. United States vs. Mylett, 97, F.3d 663, 667 (2d Cir. 1996), quoted in Fleming (2002), p. 1432.
7. http://www.sec.gov/litigation/admin/33-7891.htm
8. SEC press release on March 1, 2001: 'SEC Charges 23 Companies and Individuals in Cases Involving Broad Spectrum of Internet Securities Fraud'.
9. http://www.sec.gov/litigation/aljdec/id214jtk.htm
10. Rundschreiben der Eidg. Bankenkommission: Aufsichtsrechtliche Regeln zur Vermeidung von Marktmissbrauch, Entwurf vom 15. Dezember 2003, http://www.ebk.ch/d/aktuell/20031216/rs031216_01d.pdf
11. See Rundschreiben der Eidg. Bankenkommission: Aufsichtsrechtliche Regeln zur Vermeidung von Marktmissbrauch, Entwurf vom 15. Dezember 2003, p. 4, own translation.
12. See Bainbridge (2000).
13. Refer to Figure 4.2 for the explanation of the word 'inefficiency' in this context.
14. In reference to Fama's (1970) three forms of market efficiency (weak, semi-strong and strong), it is here used as making a statement for comparison purposes only. In this case the term 'market efficiency' would be somewhere between semi-strong and strong. It does not fulfill the strong market efficiency hypothesis, since on inside information no excess returns should be possible. However, it is a stronger form than the semi-strong form, because the insider is able to earn excess returns, though the inside information as such is not publicly available yet.
15. See Manne (1966b), p. 116.
16. See Carlton and Fischel (1983), pp. 869–871, Manne (1966a), pp. 116–119 and Manne (1970).
17. Bainbridge (2000), p. 784.
18. Bainbridge (2000), p. 785.
19. Bainbridge (2000), p. 785.
20. http://www.sec.gov/rules/final/33-7881.htm
21. http://www.sec.gov/rules/final/33-7881.htm
22. See Dooley (1980), pp. 35–36, Manne 1966b, p. 114.
23. Bainbridge (2000), p. 787.
24. See Bainbridge (1993), Dooley (1995), Easterbrook (1981) and Padilla (2002).
25. See Bainbridge (2000), p. 792.
26. Padilla (2002), p. 7.
27. Rothbard (2001), p. 538.
28. Bainbridge (2000), p. 794.

29. See Easley and O'Hara (1987), Glosten and Milgrom (1985) and Kyle (1985, 1989). O'Hara (1995) provides a comprehensive review of these models.
30. Quoted in Fridson (1996), p. 169.
31. http://www.sec.gov/answers/tmanipul.htm
32. Allen and Gale (1992), p. 505.
33. Allen and Gale (1992), p. 505.
34. Allen and Gale (1992), p. 505.
35. http://www.sec.gov/answers/tmanipul.htm
36. Allen and Gale (1992), p. 505.
37. Allen and Gale (1992), p. 506.
38. Section from the NZZ am Sonntag, December 7, 2003, p. 27, own translation.
39. http://www.sec.gov/answers/tmanipul.htm
40. *Wall Street Journal Europe*, January 19, 2005, p. M1 and p. M5.
41. From the press release of the NASD, January 14, 2005.

Chapter 5: Survey of Rumors in Financial Markets

1. Interview in the *Finanz und Wirtschaft*, December 17, 2005, p. 17, own translation.
2. Keynes (1936), p. 156.
3. *Wall Street Journal*, 'Making Book on the Buck', Sept. 23, 1988, p. 17.
4. Kostolany (1998), p. 23, own translation.
5. Rosnow and Kimmel (2000), cited in Kimmel (2003), p. 21.
6. See Oberlechner and Hocking (2003), p. 9.
7. Oberlechner and Hocking (2003), p. 11.
8. Soros (1987), p. 29.
9. See also Allen, Morris and Shin (2003) and Morris and Shin (1998).
10. Oberlechner and Hocking (2003), p. 15.
11. See Rizzello (1999) and Slovic (1986).
12. Oberlechner and Hocking (2003), p. 16.

Chapter 6: Rumor Experiments

1. See Cunningham, Anderson and Murphy (1974) and Friedman and Sunder (1994).
2. See Anderson and Sunder (1995), King et al. (1992) and Smith, Suchanek and Williams (1988).
3. See Oehler (1995), p. 132.
4. See, for example, Beattie and Loomes (1997) and Jamal and Sunder (1991).
5. The authors refer to Andreassen (1984) for a detailed discussion on the price series development.
6. Ajzen (1977), Kahneman and Tversky (1973), Tversky and Kahneman (1980); cited in DiFonzo and Bordia (1997), p. 332.
7. See Tversky and Kahneman (1982b), Michotte (1963).
8. Matthews and Sanders (1984), cited in DiFonzo and Bordia (1997), p. 333.
9. DiFonzo and Bordia (1997), p. 346.
10. DiFonzo and Bordia (1997), p. 346.
11. DiFonzo and Bordia (2002), p. 786.
12. DiFonzo and Bordia (2002), p. 787.
13. DiFonzo (1994), cited in DiFonzo and Bordia (2002), p. 798.
14. DiFonzo and Bordia (2002), p. 798.
15. For two of the original works see Kahneman and Tversky (1973) and Tversky and Kahneman (1982a).

16. See also Friedman and Sunder (1994), pp. 132–134.
17. See Ellsberg (1961).
18. Howard (1988), p. 682.
19. Ellsberg (1961), p. 652.
20. See Camerer and Weber (1992), pp. 329–330.
21. See, for example, Marschak (1988).
22. E.g. Howard (1992).
23. Frisch and Baron (1988), p. 153.
24. See Einhorn and Hogarth (1985).
25. See Knight (1921).
26. See Camerer and Weber (1992), p. 331.
27. See Camerer and Weber (1992), p. 332.
28. See Camerer and Weber (1992), pp. 332–341.
29. From Camerer and Weber, 1992, p. 334.
30. See Tversky and Kahneman (1992).
31. Camerer and Weber (1992), p. 342.
32. See Sarin and Winkler (1992) and Smith (1969).
33. See Becker and Sarin (1990), Kahn and Sarin (1988) and Segal (1987).
34. See Ellsberg (1961), Gilboa and Schmeidler (1989), Hodges and Lehmann (1952) and Nehring (1997).
35. See Einhorn and Hogarth (1985).
36. See Gilboa (1987), Schmeidler (1986, 1989) and Wakker (1989b).
37. See Dempster (1967), Levi (1984) and Shafer (1976).
38. Kogan and Wang (2002), Ludwig and Zimper (2004), Mukerji and Tallon (2000, 2001), Routledge and Zin (2001) and Uppal and Wang (2003).
39. Billot, Chateauneuf, Gilboa and Tallon (2000), Chateaneuf, Dana and Tallon (2000) and Mukerji and Tallon (2004b).
40. See Mukerji and Tallon (2004a) for an overview.
41. Fox and Tversky (1995), p. 601.
42. Fox and Weber (2002), p. 495.
43. See Tversky, Sattath and Slovic (1988).
44. See Fischbacher (1999).
45. Bossaerts, Ghirardato, Guarneschelli and Zame (2004), p. 3.
46. The state price probability ratio for ambiguous states is defined as the ratio of the state price over the probability that reflects uniform initial priors over the ambiguous states, updated to reflect the history of states drawn in the past.
47. Sarin and Weber (1993), p. 612.
48. See Cagetti et al. (2002), Epstein and Wang (1994), Maenhout (2000), and Uppal and Wang (2003).
49. Ziegler (2003), p. 174.
50. Mandelbrot and Hudson (2004), p. 85.
51. Epstein and Schneider (2004), p. 2.
52. Epstein and Schneider (2004), p. 19.
53. See Epstein and Schneider (2004), p. 19.
54. See Epstein and Schneider (2004), p. 27.
55. Epstein and Schneider (2004), p. 18.
56. See Barberis and Thaler (2003), Benos (1998), Caballé and Sákovics (2003), Daniel et al. (1998) and Odean (1998).
57. See Kapferer (1984).
58. See Chaiken (1980).
59. See Giffin (1975).

60. Kapferer (1989), pp. 83–84.
61. See Kapferer (1996a), p. 88.
62. See Kapferer (1996a), p. 103.
63. See Fischbacher (1999).
64. For reviews see, for example, Hirshleifer (2001) or Daniel et al. (2002).
65. For an overview of economic models of social learning, see Chamley (2004).
66. See Hirshleifer and Teoh (2003), p. 27.
67. See Wärneryd (2001), p. 205.
68. This text passage is based on a section of the article, 'Die Hypothese hinter der Analyse' by Alfons Cortés from Unifinanz AG.
69. See Leibenstein (1950).
70. DeBondt and Forbes (1999), p. 146.
71. See Hirschleifer and Teoh (2003), p. 28.
72. Also mentioned by Brunnermeier (2001), p. 147.
73. Smith and Sorensen (2000), p. 372.
74. Celen and Kariv (2004), p. 486.
75. The studies often first mentioned are those from Banerjee (1992), Bikhchandani, Hirshleifer and Welch (1992) and Welch (1992).
76. Bernardo and Welch (2001), Ellison and Freudenberg (1993, 1995), Hirshleifer et al. (1994), Hirshleifer and Noah (1999) and Hirshleifer and Welch (2002).
77. See Lux (1995), Lynch (2000) and Shiller (2000).
78. E.g. Garber (2000).
79. See Allen and Gale (2000), for a review, see Brunnermeier (2001).
80. For how, for example, non-perfect rational investors can influence asset prices, see Hirshleifer (2001).
81. Banerjee (1992) and Welch (1992).
82. Avery and Zemsky (1998).
83. See Avery and Zemsky (1998), p. 736.
84. Bikhchandani and Sharma (2000), p. 10.
85. See Huberman (2001).
86. See Coval and Moskowitz (2001).
87. See Lewis (1999) and Tesar and Werner (1995).
88. Bikhchandani and Sharma (2000), p. 13.
89. Exceptions are Wermers (1999) and Graham (1999).
90. See Grinblatt, Titman and Wermers (1995), Lakonishok, Shleifer and Vishny (1992) and Wermers (1999).
91. Bikhchandani and Sharma (2000), p. 18.
92. See Bikhchandani and Sharma (2000), p. 20.
93. See Anderson (2001), Celen and Kariv (2001), Allsopp and Hey (2000), Hung and Plott (2001) and Sgroi (2003).
94. See Bloomfield (1996), Libby, Bloomfield and Nelson (2001), Noeth et al. (1999) and Sunder (1995).
95. See Fischbacher (1999).
96. Cipriani and Guarino (2004) and Drehmann, Oechssler and Roider (2004).
97. Drehmann, Oechssler and Roider (2004), p. 22.
98. Drehmann, Oechssler and Roider (2004), p. 29.
99. See Kosfeld (2004) for an overview.
100. See Bavelas (1950), Leavitt (1951); experimental research on that behalf has started with Cook and Emerson (1978).
101. Brown (2004), pp. 7–8.

102. Brügger (1999), pp. 218–219, other similar studies have been conducted by Abolafia (1996), Baker (1984) and Smith (1999).
103. See Fischbacher (1999).
104. See Knorr Cetina and Brügger (2002).

Chapter 7: Conclusions and Outlook

1. See Hirshleifer (2001), p. 1577.
2. See Hirshleifer (2001), p. 1577.
3. Ziegler (2003), p. 174.
4. Mandelbrot and Hudson (2004), p. 85.
5. Arthur (1995), Arthur et al. (1997) and Arthur et al. (1999).
6. Barberis and Thaler (2003), Benos (1998), Caballé and Sákovics (2003), Daniel et al. (1998) and Odean (1998).
7. See Knorr Cetina and Brügger (2002).
8. Brügger (1999) mentions as well that certain relationships among traders are purely informative with no business relations. In that case, the relationship is reciprocal because each party provide the other with valuable information so that a certain balance is assured.

References

Abolafia, M.Y. (1996): Hyper-rational gaming, *Journal of Contemporary Ethnography*, **25** (2), 226–250.

Aboody, D., and B. Lev (2000): Information asymmetry, R&D and insider gains, *Journal of Finance*, **45** (6), 2747–2766.

Ackert, L.F., B.K. Church, J. Tompkins, and P. Zhang (2004): What's in a name? An experimental examination of investment behavior, FRB of Atlanta Working Paper no. 2003–12.

Aggarwal, R.K., and G. Wu (2004): Stock market manipulations, *Journal of Business*, **79**, 1915–1953.

Ajzen, I. (1977): Intuitive theories of events and the effects of base-rate information on prediction, *Journal of Personality and Social Psychology*, **35** (5), 303–314.

Allen, F., and D. Gale (1992): Stock price manipulation, *The Review of Financial Studies*, **5** (3), 503–529.

Allen, F., and D. Gale (2000): Bubbles and crises, *The Economic Journal*, **110**, 236–256.

Allen, F., and G. Gorton (1992): Stock price manipulation, market microstructure and asymmetric information, *European Economic Review*, **36**, 624–630.

Allen, F., S. Morris, and H.S. Shin (2003): Beauty contests, bubbles and iterated expectations in asset markets, Cowles Foundation Discussion Paper No. 1406, Yale University.

Allen, S., and R. Ramanan (1995): Insider trading, earnings changes, and stock prices, *Management Science*, **41** (4), 653–668.

Allport, G.W., and L.J. Postman (1946): An analysis of rumor, *Public Opinion Quarterly*, **10**, 501–517.

Allport, G.W., and L.J. Postman (1947): *The Psychology of Rumor*, Holt, New York.

Allsopp, L., and J. Hey (2000): Two experiments to test a model of herd behaviour, *Experimental Economics*, **3**, 121–136.

Anderson, E.W., L.P. Hansen, and T.J. Sargent (2003): Robustness, detection and the price of risk, Manuscript, University of Chicago.

Anderson, L.R. (2001): Payoff effects in information cascade experiments, *Economic Inquiry*, **39**, 690–615.

Anderson, L.R., and C.A. Holt (1997): Information cascades in the laboratory, *American Economic Review*, **87**, 847–862.

Anderson, M.J., and S. Sunder (1995): Professional traders as intuitive Bayesians, *Organizational Behavior and Human Decision Processes*, **64** (2), 185–202.

Andreassen, P.B. (1984): The effects of price variability and news on volume of trading and profits, unpublished doctoral dissertation, Columbia University.

Anscombe, F.J., and R. Aumann (1963): A definition of subjective probability, *Annals of Mathematical Statistics*, **34**, 199–205.

Anthony, S. (1973): Anxiety and rumor, *Journal of Social Psychology*, **89**, 91–98.

Anthony, S., M.E. Jaeger, and R.L. Rosnow (1980): Who hears what from whom and with what effect, *Personality and Social Psychology Bulletin*, **6** (3), 473–478.

Arthur, W.B. (1995): Complexity in economic and financial markets, *Complexity*, **1**, 20–25.

Arthur, W.B., S. Durlauf, and D. Lane (Eds) (1997): *The Economy as an Evolving Complex System II*, Addison-Wesley, Reading, MA.

Arthur, W.B., B. LeBaron, and R. Palmer (1999): Time series properties of an artificial stock market, *Journal of Economic Dynamics and Control*, **23**, 1487–1516.

Ausubel, L.M. (1990): Insider trading in a rational expectations economy, *American Economic Review*, **80** (5), 1022–1041.

Avery, C., and P. Zemsky (1998): Multidimensional uncertainty and herd behavior in financial markets, *American Economic Review*, **88** (4), 724–748.

Bagnoli, M., and B.L. Lipman (1996): Stock price manipulation through takeover bids, *Rand Journal of Economics*, **27** (1), 124–147.

Bainbridge, S.M. (1993): Insider trading under the restatement of the law governing lawyers, *Journal of Corporate Law*, **19**, 1–40.

Bainbridge, S.M. (2000): Insider trading: An overview, Working paper, UCLA School of Law.

Baker, W.E. (1984): The social structure of a national securities market, *American Journal of Sociology*, **89** (4), 775–811.

Banerjee, A.V. (1992): A simple model of herd behavior, *Quarterly Journal of Economics*, **107**, 797–817.

Banerjee, A.V. (1993): The economics of rumours, *Review of Economic Studies*, **60**, 309–327.

Barberis, N., and R. Thaler (2003): A survey of behavioral finance, in *Handbook of the Economics of Finance* ed. by G.M. Constantinides, M. Harris, and R. Stulz, pp. 1053–1123, Elsevier, Amsterdam.

Bavelas, A. (1950): Communication patterns in task-oriented groups, *Journal of Acoustical Society of America*, **22**, 725–730.

Beaudry, P., and F.M. Gonzales (2000): An equilibrium analysis of information aggregation in investment markets with discrete decisions, Working Paper, University of British Columbia.

Beattie, J., and G. Loomes (1997): The impact of incentives upon risky choice experiments, *Journal of Risk and Uncertainty*, **14**, 155–168.

Becker, J.L., and R.K. Sarin (1990): Economics of ambiguity in probability, Working paper, UCLA Graduate School of Management.

Becker, S.W., and F.O. Brownson (1964): What price ambiguity? Or the role of ambiguity in decision making, *Journal of Political Economy*, **72**, 62–73.

Benabou, R., and G. Laroque (1992): Using privileged information to manipulate markets: Insiders, gurus and credibility, *Quarterly Journal of Economics*, **107** (3), 921–958.

Beneish, M.D. (1991): Stock prices and the dissemination of analysts recommendations, *Journal of Business*, **64**, 393–416.

Benos, A.V. (1998): Aggressiveness and survival of overconfident traders, *Journal of Financial Markets*, **1**, 353–383.

Bernardo, A., and I. Welch (2001): On the evolution of overconfidence and entrepreneurs, *Journal of Economics and Management Strategy*, **10**, 301–330.

Bernhardt, D., B. Hollifield, and E. Hughson (1995): Investment and insider trading, *The Review of Financial Studies*, **8** (2), 501–543.

Bikhchandani, S., D. Hirshleifer, and I. Welch (1992): A theory of fads, fashion, custom and cultural change as informational cascades, *Journal of Political Economy*, **100**, 992–1026.

Bikhchandani, S., and S. Sharma (2000): Herd behavior in financial markets: A review, IMF Working Paper WP/00/48.

Billot, A., A. Chateauneuf, I. Gilboa, and J.-M. Tallon (2000): Sharing beliefs: Between agreeing and disagreeing, *Econometrica*, **68** (3), 685–694.

Bloomfield, R. (1996): Quotes, prices and estimates of value in a laboratory market, *Journal of Finance*, **51**, 1791–1808.

Bossaerts, P. (2003): The physiological foundations for the theory of financial decision making, Working Paper, Caltech.

Bossaerts, P., P. Ghirardato, S. Guarneschelli, and W.R. Zame (2004): Ambiguity and asset markets, Working Paper, Caltech.

Brown, M. (2004): Relational contracts in competitive markets – an experimental analysis, unpublished PhD thesis, Institute for Empirical Research in Economics, University of Zurich.

Brown, M., A. Falk, and E. Fehr (2004): Relational contracts and the nature of market interactions, *Econometrica*, **72** (3), 747–780.

Bruckner, H.T. (1965): A theory of rumor transmission, *Public Opinion Quarterly*, **29** (1), 54–70.

Brudney, V. (1979): Insiders, outsiders, and the informational advantages under the Federal Securities Law, *Harvard Law Review*, **93**, 322–376.

Brügger, U. (1999): Wie handeln Devisenhändler: Eine ethnographische Studie über Akteure in einem globalen Markt, Dissertation der Universität St. Gallen.

Bruhn, M., and W. Wunderlich (Eds) (2004): *Medium Gerücht, Studien zu Theorie und Praxis einer kollektiven Kommunikationsform*, Haupt Verlag, Bern.

Brunnermeier, M.K. (2001): *Asset Pricing under Asymmetric Information: Bubbles, Crashes, Technical Analysis, and Herding*, Oxford University Press, Oxford.

Brunnermeier, M.K. (2003): Information leakage and market efficiency, *Review of Financial Studies*, **18** (2), 417–457.

Caballé, J., and J. Sákovics (2003): Speculating against an overconfident market, *Journal of Financial Markets*, **6**, 199–225.

Cagetti, M., L. Hansen, T. Sargent, and N. Williams (2002): Robustness and pricing with uncertain growth, *Review of Financial Studies*, **15**, 363–404.

Camerer, C., and T.-H. Ho (1991): Isolation effects in compound lottery reductions, Working Paper, University of Pennsylvania Department of Decision Sciences.

Camerer, C., and M. Weber (1992): Recent developments in modeling preferences: uncertainty and ambiguity, *Journal of Risk and Uncertainty*, **5**, 325–370.

Carlton, D.W., and D.R. Fischel (1983): The regulation of insider trading, *Stanford Law Review*, **35**, 857–895.

Celen, B., and S. Kariv (2001): An experimental test of observational learning under imperfect information, *Economic Theory*, **26** (3), 667–699.

Celen, B., and S. Kariv (2004): Distinguishing informational cascades from herd behavior in the laboratory, *American Economic Review*, **94** (3), 484–498.

Chaiken, S. (1980): Heuristic versus systemic information processing and the use of source versus message cues in persuasion, *Journal of Personality and Social Psychology*, **39** (5), 752–766.

Chakraborty, A., and B. Yilmaz (2000): Informed manipulation, Working Paper, Wharton School, University of Pennsylvania.

Chakravarty, S., and J.J. McConnell (1997): An analysis of prices, bid/ask spreads, and bid and ask depths surrounding Ivan Boesky's illegal trading in Carnation stock, *Financial Management*, **26**, 18–34.

Chakravarty, S., and J.J. McConnell (1999): Does insider trading really move stock prices?, *Journal of Financial and Quantitative Analysis*, **34** (2), 191–209.

Chamley, Ch. P. (2004): *Rational Herds: Economic Models of Social Learning*, Cambridge University Press, Cambridge.

Chateauneuf, A., R. Dana, and J.-M. Tallon (2000): Optimal risk sharing rules and equilibria with Choquet-expected-utility, *Journal of Mathematical Economics*, **34**, 191–214.

Chen, Y., P. Katuscak, and E. Ozdenoren (2003). Sealed bid auctions with ambiguity: Theory and experiments, Working Paper, University of Michigan.

Chen, Z, and L.G. Epstein (2002): Ambiguity, risk and asset returns in continuous time, *Econometrica*, **70**, 1403–1443.

Chipman, J.S. (1960): Stochastic choice and subjective probability, in *Decisions, Values and Groups*, Vol. I, pp. 70–95, Pergamon Press, Oxford.

Choquet, G. (1953): Theory of capacities, *Annales de l'Institut Fourier*, **5**, 131–295.

Chorus, A. (1953): The basic law of rumor, *Journal of Abnormal and Social Psychology*, **48**, 313–314.

Chow, C.C., and R.K. Sarin (2001): Comparative ignorance and the Ellsberg Paradox, *Journal of Risk and Uncertainty*, **22** (2), 129–139.

Christie, W.G., and R.D. Huang (1995): Following the Pied Piper: Do individual returns herd around the market?, *Financial Analysts Journal* (July–August), 31–37.

Cipriani, M., and A. Guarino (2001): Herd behavior and contagion in financial markets, mimeo, New York University.

Cipriani, M., and A. Guarino (2004): Herd behavior in a laboratory financial market, mimeo, University College London.

Cohen, M., J.-Y. Jaffray, and T. Said (1985): Individual behavior under risk and under uncertainty: An experimental study, *Theory and Decision*, **18**, 203–228.

Cook, K.S., and R.M. Emerson (1978): Power, equity, and commitment in exchange networks, *American Sociological Review*, 43, 721–739.

Cooper, R.E. Jr. (1982): Libel and the reporting of rumor, *Yale Law Review*, **92**, 85–105.

Cornell, B., and E. Sirri (1992): The reaction of investors and stock prices to insider trading, *Journal of Finance*, **47**, 1031–1059.

Coval, J.D., and T.J. Moskowitz (2001): The geography of investment: informed trading and asset prices, *Journal of Political Economy*, **109**, 811–841.

Cunningham, W.H., W.T. Anderson, and J.H. Murphy (1974): Are students real people?, *Journal of Business*, **47**, 399–409.

Curley, S.P., and F.J. Yates (1985): The center and range of the probability internal as factors affecting ambiguity preferences, *Organizational Behavior and Human Decision Processes*, **36**, 272–287.

Curley, S.P., and F.J. Yates (1989): An empirical evaluation of descriptive models of ambiguity reactions in choice situations, *Journal of Mathematical Psychology*, **33**, 397–427.

Curley, S.P., F.J. Yates, and R.A. Abrams (1986): Psychological sources of ambiguity avoidance, *Organizational Behavior and Human Decision Processes*, **38**, 230–256.

Damodaran, A., and C.H. Liu (1993): Insider trading as a signal of private information, *The Review of Financial Studies*, **6** (1), 79–119.

Daniel, K., D. Hirshleifer and S.H. Teoh (2002): Investor psychology in capital markets: evidence and policy implications, *Journal of Monetary Economics*, **49**: 139–209.

Daniel, K., D. Hirshleifer, and A. Subrahmanyam (1998): Investor psychology and security market and overreactions, *Journal of Finance*, **53** (5), 1839–1886.

DeBondt, W.F.M., and W.P. Forbes (1999): Herding in analysts' earnings forecasts: Evidence from the United Kingdom, *European Financial Management*, **5** (2), 141–163.

DeBondt, W.F.M., and R. Thaler (1985): Does the stock market overreact?, *Journal of Finance*, **40**, 793–805.

DeBondt, W.F.M., and R. Thaler (1987): Further evidence on investor overreaction and the stock market seasonality, *Journal of Finance*, **42**, 557–581.

DeBondt, W.F.M., and R. Thaler (1995): Financial decision-making in markets and firms: A behavioral perspective, in *Handbook of Finance* ed. by R. Jarrow et al., Elsevier, Amsterdam.

de Finetti, B. (1977): Probabilities of probabilities: A real problem or a misunderstanding?, in *New Directions in the Application of Bayesian Methods* ed. by A. Aykac and C. Brumat, pp. 1–10, North-Holland, Amsterdam.

DeGrauwe, P., and M. Grimaldi (2003): Bubbling and crashing exchanges rates, CESIfo Working Paper 1045.

DeMarzo, P.M., M. Fishman, and K.M. Hagerty (1998): The optimal enforcement of insider trading regulations, *Journal of Political Economy*, **106** (3), 602–632.

Dempster, A.P. (1967): Upper and lower probabilities induced by a multivalued mapping, *Annals of Mathematical Statistics*, **38**, 325–339.

De Quervain, D., U. Fischbacher, V. Treyer, M. Schellhammer, U. Schnyder, A. Buck, and E. Fehr (2004): The neural basis of altruistic punishment, *Science*, **305**, 1254–1258.

Dewey, J. (1997): *How We Think*, Dover Publications, Mineola.

DiFonzo, N., P. Bordia, and R.L. Rosnow (1994): Reining in rumors: *Organizational Dynamics*, **23** (1), 47–62.

DiFonzo, N., and P. Bordia (1997): Rumor and prediction: Making sense (but losing dollars) in the stock market: *Organizational Behavior and Human Decision Processes*, **71** (3), 329–353.

DiFonzo, N., and P. Bordia (2002): Rumors and stable-cause attribution in prediction and behavior, *Organizational Behavior and Human Decision Processes*, **88** (2), 785–800.

Dolan, P., and M. Jones (2004): Explaining attitudes towards ambiguity: An experimental test of the comparative ignorance hypothesis, *Scottish Journal of Political Economy*, **51** (3), 281–301.

Dooley, M.P. (1980): Enforcement of insider trading restrictions, *Virginia Law Review*, **66**, 1–89.

Dooley, M.P. (1995): *The Fundamentals of Corporation Law*, Foundation Press. Mineola, NY.

Dow, J., and R. Werlang (1992): Uncertainty aversion, risk aversion, and the optimal choice of portfolio, *Econometrica*, **60**, 197–204.

Drehmann, M., J. Oechssler, and A. Roider (2004): Herding and contrarian behavior in financial markets – an internet experiment, University of Bonn Economics Discussion Papers 25/2002.

Drudi, F., and M. Massa (2002): Asymmetric information and trading strategies: testing behavior on the primary and secondary T-bond markets around auction days, Working Paper, INSEAD.

Easley, D., and M. O'Hara (1987): Price, trade, size, and information in securities markets, *Journal of Financial Economics*, **19**, 69–90.

Easterbrook, F.H. (1981): Insider trading, secret agents, evidentiary privileges, and the production of information, *Supreme Court Review*, 309–365.

Eatwell, J., M. Milgate, and P. Newman (1990): *Utility and Probability*, Macmillan Press, London.

Eguíluz, V.M., and M.G. Zimmermann (2000): Transmission of information and herd behavior: An application to financial markets, *Physical Review Letters*, **85** (26), 5659–5662.

Einhorn, H.J., and R.M. Hogarth (1985): Ambiguity and uncertainty in probabilistic inference, *Psychological Review*, **92**, 433–461.

Einhorn, H.J., and R.M. Hogarth (1986): Decision making under ambiguity, *Journal of Business*, **59**, 225–250.

Ellison, G., and D. Freudenberg (1993): Rules of thumb for social learning, *Journal of Political Economy*, **101**, 612–643.

Ellison, G., and D. Freudenberg (1995): Word-of-mouth communication and social learning. *The Quarterly Journal of Economics*, **110**, 93–125.

Ellsberg, D. (1961): Risk, ambiguity and the Savage axioms, *Quarterly Journal of Economics*, **75**, 643–669.

Epstein, L.P., and M. Schneider (2003): Recursive multiple priors, *Journal of Economic Theory*, **113**, 32–50.

Epstein, L.P., and M. Schneider (2004): Ambiguity, information quality and asset pricing, Working Paper, University of Rochester.

Epstein, L.P., and T. Wang (1994): Intertemporal asset pricing and Knightian uncertainty, *Econometrica*, **62**, 283–322.

Esposito, J.L. (1987): Subjective factors and rumor transmission: A field of investigation of the influence of anxiety, importance, and belief of rumor mongering (Doctoral dissertation, Temple University, 1986), Dissertation Abstracts International, 48, 596B.

Esposito, J.L., and R.L. Rosnow (1983): Corporate rumors: How they start and how to stop them, *Management Review*, 44–49.

Estrada, J. (1995): Insider trading: Regulation, securities markets and welfare under risk aversion, *Quarterly Review of Economics and Finance*, **35**, 421–445.

Falk, A., and U. Fischbacher (2000): A theory of reciprocity, Working Paper no. 6, Institute for Empirical Research in Economics, University of Zurich.

Fama, E.F. (1970): Efficient capital markets: A review of theory and empirical work, *Journal of Finance*, **May**, 383–417.

Fama, E.F. (1976): *Foundations of Finance*, Basic Books, New York.

Fama, E.F. (1998): Market efficiency, long-term returns and behavioral finance, *Journal of Financial Economics*, **49**, 286–306.

Farmer, D. and A. Lo (1999): Frontiers of finance: Evolution and efficient markets, *Proceedings of the National Academy of Sciences*, **96**, 9991–9992.

Fehr, E., and U. Fischbacher (2003): The nature of human altruism, *Nature*, **425**, 785–791.

Fehr, E., and S. Gächter (2000): Fairness and retaliation: The economics of reciprocity, *Journal of Economic Perspectives*, **14** (3), 159–181.

Festinger, L. (1954): A theory of social comparison processes, *Human Relations*, **7**, 117–140.

Finnerty, J.E. (1976): Insiders and market efficiency, *Journal of Finance*, **31**, 1141–1148.

Fischbacher, U. (1999): z-Tree: Experimental software, University of Zurich.

Fishman, M.J., and K.M. Hagerty (1992): Insider trading and the efficiency of stock prices, *Rand Journal of Economics*, **23** (1), 106–122.

Fishman, M.J., and K.M. Hagerty (1995): The mandatory disclosure of trades and market liquidity, *Review of Financial Studies*, **8**, 637–676.

Fleming, T. (2002): Telling the truth slant – defending insider trading claims against legal and financial professionals, *William Mitchell Law Review*, **28** (4), 1422–1442.

Fox, C.R., and A. Tversky (1995): Ambiguity aversion and comparative ignorance, *The Quarterly Journal of Economics*, **110** (3), 585–603.

Fox, C.R., and M. Weber (2002): Ambiguity aversion, comparative ignorance, and decision context, *Organizational Behavior and Human Decision Processes*, **88** (1), 476–498.

Fridson, M. (Ed.) (1996): Wiley Investment Classics reprints of Charles Mackay, *Extraordinary Popular Delusions and the Madness of Crowds*, and Joseph de la Vega, *Confusion de Confusions* (1688), John Wiley & Sons, New York.

Friedman, D., and S. Sunder (1994): *Experimental Methods: A Primer for Economists*, Cambridge University Press, Cambridge.

Frisch, D., and J. Baron (1988): Ambiguity and rationality, *Journal of Behavioral Decision Making*, **1**, 149–157.

Garber, P.M. (2000): *Famous First Bubbles: The Fundamentals of Early Manias*. MIT Press, Cambridge, MA.

Gardenfors, P., and N.-E. Sahlin (1982): Unreliable probabilities, risk taking, and decision making, *Synthese*, **53**, 361–386.

George, T. (1989): The impact of public and private information on market efficiency, Working Paper, University of Michigan.

Gerard, B., and Nanda, V. (1993): Trading and manipulation around seasoned equity offerings, *Journal of Finance*, **48**, 213–245.

Gervais, S. (1996): Market microstructure with uncertain information precision: A multiperiod analysis, Working Paper, Wharton School, University of Pennsylvania.

Giffin, G. (1975): The contribution of studies of source credibility to a theory of interpersonal trust in the communication process, *Psychological Bulletin*, **68** (2), 104–120.

Gigerenzer, G., and R. Selten (2001): *Bounded Rationality*, The MIT Press, Cambridge, MA.

Gigerenzer, G., U. Hoffrage, and H. Kleinbölting (1991): Probabilistic mental models: A Brunswikian theory of overconfidence, *Psychological Review*, **98**, 506–528.

Gigliotti, G., and B. Sopher (1990): The testing principle: A resolution of the Ellsberg Paradox, Working Paper, Department of Economics, Rutgers University.

Gilboa, I. (1987): Expected utility with purely subjective non-additive probabilities, *Journal of Mathematical Economics*, **16**, 65–88.

Gilboa, I., and D. Schmeidler (1989): Maxmin expected utility with a non-unique prior, *Journal of Mathematical Economics*, **18**, 141–153.

Gilson, R.J., and R.H. Kraakman (1984): The mechanisms of market efficiency, *Virginia Law Review*, **70**, 549–644.

Glosten, L.R. (1989): The insider, liquidity, and the role of monopolist specialists, *Journal of Business*, **62**, 211–236.

Glosten, L.R., and P.R. Milgrom (1985): Bid, ask, and transaction prices in a specialist market with heterogeneously informed traders, *Journal of Financial Economics*, **14** (1), 71–100.

Gluckman, M. (1963): Gossip and scandal, *Current Anthropology*, **4**, 307–316.

Goldinger, H. (2002): *Rituale und Symbole an der Börse: Eine Ethnographie*, Lit Verlag, Münster.

Goldsmith, R.W., and N.-E. Sahlin (1983): The role of second-order probabilities in decision making, in *Analysing and Aiding Decision Processes*, ed. by P. Humphreys, O. Svenson, and A. Vari, pp. 455–467, North-Holland, Amsterdam.

Goldstein, I., and A. Guembel (2003): Manipulation and the allocational role of prices, Working Paper, Duke University.

Gorodsinsky R. (2003): Empirische Untersuchung über die Auswirkung von Gerüchten auf den Kapitalmarkt am Beispiel des deutschen Aktienmarktes, Diploma thesis at the Technische Universität Chemnitz, Chemnitz.

Graham, J.R. (1999): Herding among investment newsletters: Theory and evidence, *Journal of Finance*, **54**, 237–268.

Grinblatt, M., S. Titman, and R. Wermers (1995): Momentum investment strategies, portfolio performance, and herding: a study of mutual fund behaviour, *American Economic Review*, **85**, 1088–1105.

Haddock, D.D., and J.R. Macey (1987): Regulation on demand: A private interest model, with an application to insider trading regulation, *Journal of Law and Economics*, **30**, 311–352.

Hannerz, U. (1967): Gossip, networks and culture in a Black American ghetto. *Ethnos*, **32**, 35–60.

Hansen, L.P., T.J. Sargent, and D. Tallarini, Jr. (1999): Robust permanent income and pricing, *Review of Economic Studies*, **66**, 873–907.

Heath, Ch., and A. Tversky (1991): Preference and belief: Ambiguity and competence in choice under uncertainty, *Journal of Risk and Uncertainty*, **4**, 5–28.

Hens, Th., and K.R. Schenk-Hoppé (2005): Evolutionary stability of portfolio rules, *Journal of Mathematical Economics*, **41** (1–2), 43–66.

Hirshleifer, D. (2001): Investor psychology and asset pricing, *Journal of Finance*, **56** (4), 1533–1597.

Hirshleifer, D., and G. Luo (2001): On the survival of overconfident traders in a competitive securities market, *Journal of Financial Markets*, **4**, 73–84.

Hirshleifer, D., and R. Noah (1999): Misfits and social progress, Working Paper, Ohio State University.

Hirshleifer, D., Subrahmanyam, A., and S. Titman (1994): Security analysis and trading patterns when some investors receive information before others, *Journal of Finance*, **49**, 1665–1698.

Hirshleifer, D., and S.H. Teoh (2003): Herd behaviour and cascading in capital markets: A review and synthesis, *European Financial Management*, **9** (1), 25–66.

Hirshleifer, D., and I. Welch (2002): An economic approach to the psychology of change: amnesia, inertia, and impulsiveness, *Journal of Economics and Management Strategy*, **11** (3), 379–421.

Hodges, J.L., and E.L. Lehmann (1952): The use of previous experience in reaching statistical decisions, *Annals of Mathematical Statistics*, **23**, 396–407.

Hodgson, G. (1995): *Economics and Biology*, Edward Elgar Publishing, Cheltenham.

Hogarth, R.M., and H.J. Einhorn (1990): Venture theory: A model of decision weights, *Management Science*, **36**, 780–803.

Howard, R.A. (1988): Decision analysis: Practice and promise, *Management Science* **34** (6), 679–695.

Howard, R.A. (1992): The cogency of decision analysis, in *Utility: Theories, Measurement, Applications*, ed. by W. Edwards, Kluwer Academic Publishers, Dordrecht, Holland.

Huberman, G. (2001): Familiarity breeds investment, *Review of Financial Studies*, **14**, 659–680.

Huddart, S., J.S. Hughes, and C. Levine (2001): Public disclosure and dissimulation of insider trades, *Econometrica*, **69** (3), 665–681.

Huddart, S., and B. Ke (2004): Information asymmetry and cross-sectional determinants of insider trading, Working Paper, Pennsylvania State University.

Hung, A., and C.A. Plott (2001): Information cascades: replication and an extension to majority rule and conformity rewarding institutions, *American Economic Review*, **91**, 1508–1520.

Jaffe, J.F. (1974): Special information and insider trading, *Journal of Business*, **47** (3), 410–428.

Jamal, K., and S. Sunder (1991): Money vs. gaming: Effects of salient monetary payments in double oral auctions, *Organizational Behavior and Human Decision Processes*, **49**, 151–166.

Jarrow, R.A. (1992): Market manipulation, bubbles, corners and short squeezes, *Journal of Financial and Quantitative Analysis*, **27**, 311–336.

Jarrow, R.A. (1994): Derivative security markets, market manipulation, and option pricing theory, *Journal of Financial and Quantitative Analysis*, **29**, 241–261.

John K., and R. Narayanan (1997): Market manipulation and the role of insider trading regulations, *Journal of Business*, **70**, 217–247.

Kahn, B.E., and R.K. Sarin (1988): Modeling ambiguity in decisions under uncertainty, *Journal of Consumer Research*, **15**, 265–272.

Kahneman, D., and A. Tversky (1973): On the psychology of prediction, *Psychological Review*, **80**, 237–251.

Kapferer, J.-N. (1984): *Les Chemins de la Persuasion*, Dunod, Paris.

Kapferer, J.-N. (1987): *Les Rumeurs: Le Plus Vieux Média du Monde*, Editions du Seuil, Paris.

Kapferer, J.-N. (1996a): *Gerüchte: Das älteste Massenmedium der Welt*, Gustav Kiepenheuer Verlag, Leipzig.

Kapferer, J.-N. (1996b): Investor psychology in capital markets: Evidence and policy implications, with David Hirschleifer and Siew Hong Tesh, *Journal of Monetary Economics*, **49**, 139–209.

Keppe, H.-J., and M. Weber (1991): Judged knowledge and ambiguity aversion: Working Paper no. 277, Christian-Albrechts-Universität, Kiel, Germany.

Keppe, H.-J., and M. Weber (1995): Judged knowledge and ambiguity aversion, *Theory and Decision*, **39**, 51–77.

Kerner, O., et al. (1968): *Report of the National Advisory Commission on Civil Disorders*, Bantam, New York.

Keynes, J.M. (1936): *The General Theory of Employment, Interest, and Money*, Harcourt, Brace & World, New York.

Kimmel, A.J. (2003): Rumors and rumor control: A manager's guide to understanding and combating rumors, Lawrence Erlbaum Associates, Mahwah, NJ.

Kimmel, A.J., et al. (1992): Mass mediated rumor and gossip, unpublished manuscript, Fitchburg State College, Fitchburg, MA.

Kimmel, A.J., and R. Keefer (1989): Psychological correlates of the acceptance and transmission of rumors about AIDS, unpublished manuscript, Fitchburg State College, Department of Behavioral Science, Fitchburg, MA.

King, R.R., V.L. Smith, and A.W. Williams, and M. Van Boening (1992): The robustness of bubbles and crashes in experimental stock markets, in *Evolutionary Dynamics and Nonlinear Economics – A Transdisciplinary Dialogue* ed. by I. Prigogine, R.H. Day, and R. Chen, Oxford University Press, Oxford.

Kirman, A. (1993): Ants, rationality, and recruitment, *The Quarterly Journal of Economics*, **108**, 137–156.

Kiymaz, H. (2001): The effects of stock market rumors on stock prices: Evidence from an emerging market, *Journal of Multinational Financial Management*, **11**, 105–115.

Knapp, G.H. (1944): A psychology of rumor, *Public Opinion Quarterly*, **8**, 22–37.

Knight, F.H. (1921): *Risk, Uncertainty and Profit*, Houghton Mifflin, Boston.

Knopf, T. (1975): *Rumors, Race and Riots*, Transaction Books, New Brunswick, NJ.

Knorr Cetina, K., and U. Brügger (2002): Global microstructures: The virtual societies of financial markets, *American Journal of Sociology*, **107** (4), 905–950.

Kodres, L.E., and M. Pritsker (1997): Directionally similar position taking and herding by large futures market participants, Risk Measurement and Systemic Risk – Proceedings of a Joint Central Bank Research Conference, Board of Governors of the Federal Reserve Systems, Washington, DC.

Koenig, F.W. (1985): Rumor in the marketplace: The social psychology of commercial hearsay, Auburn House, Dover, MA.

Kogan, L., and T. Wang (2002): A simple theory of asset pricing under model uncertainty, Working Paper, University of British Columbia.

Kosfeld, M. (2004): Economic networks in the laboratory: A survey, *Review of Network Economics*, **3**, 20–41.

Kosfeld, M. (2005): Rumours and markets, *Journal of Mathematical Economics*, **41** (6), 646–664.

Kostolany, A. (1998): *Kostolanys Börsenpsychologie*, 2nd edn, Econ Verlag, München.

Kumar, P., and D. Seppi (1992): Futures manipulation with 'cash settlement', *Journal of Finance*, **47**, 1485–1502.

Kuran, T., and C. Sunstein (1999): Availability cascades and risk regulation, *Stanford Law Review*, **51**, 683–768.

Kyle, A.S. (1984): A theory of futures markets manipulation, in *The Industrial Organization of Futures Markets* ed. by R.W. Anderson, D.C Heath, Lexington, MA.

Kyle, A.S. (1985): Continuous auctions and insider trading, *Econometrica*, **53**, 1315–1335.

Kyle, A.S. (1989): Informed speculation with imperfect competition, *Review of Economic Studies*, **56**, 317–356.

Laffont, J.-J., and E.S. Maskin (1990): The efficient market hypothesis and insider trading on the stock market, *Journal of Political Economy*, **98** (1), 70–93.

Lakonishok, J., A. Shleifer, and R.W. Vishny (1992): The impact of institutional trading on stock prices, *Journal of Financial Economics*, **32**, 23–43.

Larson, J.R. Jr. (1980): Exploring the external validity of a subjectively weighted utility model of decision making, *Organizational Behavior and Human Performance*, **26**, 293–304.

Lauriola, M., and I.P. Levin (2001): Relating individual differences in attitude toward ambiguity to risky choices, *Journal of Behavioral Decision Making*, **14**, 107–122.

Leavitt, H.J. (1951): Some effects of certain communication patterns on group performance, *Journal of Abnormal and Social Psychology*, **46**, 38–50.

Lee, I.H. (1998): Market crashes and informational avalanches, *Review of Economic Studies*, **65**, 741–759.

Leibenstein, H. (1950): Bandwagon, snob, and Veblen effects in the theory of consumers' demand, *Quarterly Journal of Economics*, **64** (2), 183–207.

Leland, H.E. (1992): Insider trading: Should it be prohibited?, *Journal of Political Economy*, **100** (4), 859–887.

Levi, I. (1984): *Decisions and Revisions*, Cambridge University Press, Cambridge.

Lewis, K.K. (1999): Trying to explain home bias in equities and consumption, *Journal of Economic Literature*, **37**, 571–608.

Libby, R., R. Bloomfield, and M. Nelson (2001): Experimental research in financial accounting, Cornell University.

Liu, P. (1992): The impact of the insider trading scandal on the information content of the *Wall Street Journal's* 'Heard on the Street' column, *Journal of Financial Research*, **15**, 181–188.

Liu, P., S.D. Smith, and A.A. Syed (1990): Stock price reactions to the Wall Street Journal's securities recommendations, *Journal of Financial and Quantitative Analysis*, **25**, 399–410.

Liu, Z., J. Luo, and Ch. Shao (2001): Potts model for exaggeration of a simple rumor transmitted by recreant rumormongers, *Physical Review E*, **64**, 046134-1–9.

Lloyd-Davies, P., and M. Canes (1978): Stock prices and the publication of second-hand information, *Journal of Business*, **51**, 43–56.

Lo, A.W. (2004): The adaptive market hypothesis: Market efficiency from an evolutionary perspective, *Journal of Portfolio Management*, **30**, 15–29.

Lo, A.W., and A.C. MacKinlay (1990): When are contrarians profits due to stock market overreaction?, *Review of Financial Studies*, **3**, 175–206.

Ludwig, A., and A. Zimper (2004): Investment behavior under ambiguity: The case of pessimistic decision makers, Working Paper, University of Mannheim.

Luo, G. (1998): Market efficiency and natural selection in a commodity futures market, *Review of Financial Studies*, **11**, 647–674.

Lux, T. (1995): Herd behavior, bubbles and crashes, *Economic Journal*, **105**, 881–896.

Lynch, A. (2000): Thought contagions in the stock market, *Journal of Psychology and Markets*, **1**, 10–23.

MacCrimmon, K.R. (1968): Descriptive and normative implications of the decision-theory postulates, in *Risk and Uncertainty* ed. by K. Borch and J. Mossin, Macmillan, London.

Maenhout, P. (2000) Robust portfolio rules and asset pricing, INSEAD Working Paper.

Mandelbrot, B. and R.L. Hudson (2004): *The (Mis)Behavior of Markets: a Fractal View of Risk, Ruin, and Reward*, Basic Books, New York.

Manne, H.G. (1966a): *Insider Trading and the Stock Market*, Free Press, New York.

Manne, H.G. (1966b): In defense of insider trading, *Harvard Business Review*, **44**, 113–122.

Manne, H.G. (1970): Insider trading and the law professors, *Vanderbilt Law Review*, **23**, 547–590.

Manove, M. (1989): The harm from insider trading and informed speculation, *The Quarterly Journal of Economics*, **104** (4), 823–845.

Marschak, J. (1988): Personal probabilities of probabilities, *Theory and Decision*, **6**, 121–153.

Mas-Colell, A., M.D. Whinston, and J.R. Green (1995): *Microeconomic Theory*, Oxford University Press, Oxford.

Matthews, L., and W. Sanders (1984): Effects of causal and noncausal sequences of information on subjective prediction, *Psychological Reports*, **54**, 211–215.

Merrick, J.J., N.Y. Naik, and P.K. Yadav (2004): Strategic trading behaviour and price distortion in a manipulated market: Anatomy of a squeeze, *Journal of Financial Economics*, **77** (1), 171–218.

Meulbroeck, L. (1992): An empirical analysis of illegal insider trading, *Journal of Finance*, **47**, 1661–1699.

Michotte, A. (1963): *The Perception of Causality*, Basic Books, New York.

Morris, S., and H.S. Shin (1998): Unique equilibrium in a model of self-fulfilling currency attacks, *American Economic Review*, **88** (3), 587–597.

Mukerji, S., and J.-M. Tallon (2000): Ambiguity aversion and the absence of indexed debt, *Economic Theory*, **24** (3), 665–685.

Mukerji, S., and J.-M. Tallon (2001): Ambiguity aversion and incompleteness of financial markets, *Review of Economic Studies*, **68** (4), 883–904.

Mukerji, S., and J.-M. Tallon (2004a): An overview of economic applications of David Schmeidler's models of decision making under uncertainty, in *Uncertainty in Economic Theory: A Collection of Essays in Honor of David Schmeidler's 65th Birthday*, Chapter 13, ed. by I. Gilboa, Routledge, London.

Mukerji, S., and J.-M. Tallon (2004b): Ambiguity aversion and the absence of wage indexation, *Journal of Monetary Economics*, **51** (3), 653–670.

Nehring, K. (1997): A theory of rational choice under complete ignorance, Working Paper, University of California, Davis.

Neubauer, H.-J. (1999): *The Rumour: A Cultural History*, Free Association Books, London.

Noeth, M., C.F. Camerer, R. Plott, and M. Weber (1999): Information aggregation in experimental asset markets: Traps and misaligned beliefs, Working Paper, University of Mannheim.

Oberlechner, Th., and S. Hocking S. (2003): Information sources, news, and rumors in financial markets: Insights into the foreign exchange market, *Journal of Economic Psychology*, **25**, 407–424.

Odean, T. (1998): Volume, volatility, price, and profit when all traders are above average, *Journal of Finance*, **53**, 1887–1934.

Odum, H.W. (1943): *Race and Rumors of Race*, University of North Carolina Press, Chapel Hill.

Oehler, A. (1995): *Die Erklärung des Verhaltens privater Anleger: Theoretische Ansätze und empirische Analysen*, Schäffer-Poeschel, Stuttgart.

O'Hara, M. (1995): *Market Microstructure Theory*, Blackwell Publishers, Cambridge, MA.

Ojha, A.B. (1973): Rumour research: An overview, *Journal of the Indian Academy of Applied Psychology*, **10**, 56–64.

Padilla, A. (2002): Can agency theory justify the regulation of insider trading?, *The Quarterly Journal of Austrian Economics*, **5** (1), 3–38.

Peterson, W.A., and N.P. Gist (1951): Rumor and public opinion, *American Journal of Sociology*, **45**, 159–167.

Pound, J., and R. Zeckhauser (1990): Clearly heard in the street: The effect of takeover rumors on stock prices, *Journal of Business*, **63** (3), 291–308.

Rescher, N. (1993): *Rationalität: eine philosopische Untersuchung über das Wesen und Rechtfertigung von Vernunft*, Verlag Königshausen & Neumann, Würzburg.

Ricciardi, V., and H.K. Simon (2000): What is behavioral finance?, *The Business Education and Technology Journal*, **2** (1), 26–34.

Richards, A. (1999): Idiosyncratic risk: An empirical analysis, with implications for the risk-relative-value trading strategies, IMF Working Paper.

Rizzello, S. (1999): *The Economics of the Mind*, Edward Elgar Publishing, Cheltenham.

Rose, A.M. (1951): Rumor in the stock market, *Public Opinion Quarterly*, **15** (3), 461–468.

Rosnow, R.L. (1974): On rumor: *Journal of Communication*, **24** (3), 26–38.

Rosnow, R.L. (1980): Psychology of rumor reconsidered, *Psychological Bulletin*, **87** (3), 578–591.

Rosnow, R.L. (1991): Inside rumor: A personal journey: *American Psychologist*, **46** (5), 484–496.

Rosnow, R.L. (2001): Rumor and gossip in interpersonal interaction and beyond: A social exchange perspective, in *Behaving Badly: Aversive Behaviors in Interpersonal Relationships* ed. by R.M. Kowalski, pp. 203–232, American Psychological Association, Washington, DC.

Rosnow, R.L., J.L. Esposito, and L. Gibney (1988): Factors influencing rumor spreading: Replication and extension, *Language and Communication*, **8**, 29–42.

Rosnow, R.L., and G.A. Fine (1976): *Rumor and Gossip: The Social Psychology of Hearsay*, Elsevier, New York.

Rosnow, R.L., and A.J. Kimmel (2000): Rumors, *Encyclopaedia of Psychology* (Vol. 7 pp. 122–123), Oxford University Press, Oxford.

Rosnow, R.L., J.H. Yost, and J.L. Esposito (1986): Belief in rumor and likelihood of rumor transmission, *Language and Communication*, **6**, 189–194.

Rothbard, M.N. (2001): *Man, Economy and State*, Ludwig von Mises Institute, Auburn, AL (first published in 1962).

Rozeff, M.S., and M.A. Zaman (1998): Overreaction and insider trading: Evidence from growth and value portfolios, *Journal of Finance*, **53** (2), 701–716.

Routledge, B., and S. Zin (2001): Model uncertainty and liquidity, NBER Working Paper 8683, Carnegie Mellon University.

Rubinstein, M. (2000): Rational markets: Yes or no? The affirmative case, Working Paper RPF-294, Haas School of Business, University of California, Berkeley.

Sarin, R.K., and P. Wakker (1990): Incorporating attitudes towards ambiguity in Savage's setup, Working Paper, Anderson Graduate School of Management, UCLA.

Sarin, R.K., and M. Weber (1993): Effects of ambiguity in market experiments, *Management Science*, **39** (5), 602–615.

Sarin, R.K., and R.L. Winkler (1992): Ambiguity and decision modeling: A preference-based approach, *Journal of Risk and Uncertainty*, **5** (4), 389–407.

Savage, L.J. (1954): *The Foundations of Statistics*, John Wiley & Sons, New York.

Schlieper-Damrich, R. (2003): Gerüchtekommunikation, http://www.perspektivenwechsel.de/perspektivenwechsel/link05/docs/geruechtekommunikation.pdf.

Schmeidler, D. (1986): Integral representation without additivity, *Proceedings of the American Mathematical Society*, **97**, 255–261.

Schmeidler, D. (1989): Subjective probability and expected utility without additivity, *Econometrica*, **57**, 571–587.

Schneider, E. (2003): Verarbeitung und Verbreitung von Gerüchten an Finanzmärkten, Diploma thesis at the Technische Universität Chemnitz, Chemnitz.

Segal, U. (1987): The Ellsberg Paradox and risk aversion: An anticipated utility approach, *International Economic Review*, **28**, 175–202.

Seyhun, H.N. (1986): Insiders, profits, costs of trading and market efficiency, *Journal of Financial Economics*, **16**, 189–212.

Seyhun, H.N. (1990): Overreaction or fundamentals: Some lessons from insiders' response to the market crash of 1987, *Journal of Finance*, **45**, 1363–1388.

Seyhun, H.N. (1992): Why does aggregate insider trading predict future stock returns?, *The Quarterly Journal of Economics*, **107** (4), 1303–1331.

Seyhun, H.N. (1998): *Investment Intelligence from Insider Trading*, MIT Press, Cambridge, MA.

Sgroi, D. (2003): The right choice at the right time: A herding experiment in endogenous time, *Experimental Economics*, **6** (2), 159–180.

Shafer, G. (1976): *A Mathematical Theory of Evidence*, Princeton University Press, Princeton.

Sheffey, J.M. (1982): Securities law responsibilities of issuers to respond to rumors and other publicity: Reexamination of a continuing problem, *Notre Dame Lawyer*, **57**, 755–796.

Shibutani, T. (1966): *Improvised News: A Sociological Study of Rumor*, Bobbs-Merrill, Indianapolis.

Shiller, R. (2000): *Irrational Exuberance*, Princeton University Press, Princeton.

Shiller, R. (2002): From efficient markets theory to behavioral finance, Cowes Foundation Discussion Paper no. 1385, Yale University.

Shiller, R. (2003): From efficient markets theory to behavioral finance, *Journal of Economic Perspectives*, **17** (1), 83–104.

Shleifer, A. (2000): *Inefficient Markets: An Introduction to Behavioral Finance*, Oxford University Press, Oxford.

Simon, H. (1982): *Models of Bounded Rationality*, MIT Press, Cambridge, MA.

Slovic, P. (1986): Psychological study of human judgment: Implications for investment decision making, in *Judgment and Decision Making: An Interdisciplinary Reader* ed. by H.R. Arkes and K.R. Hammond, pp. 173–193, Cambridge University Press, New York.

Slovic, P., and A. Tversky (1974): Who accepts Savage's axiom? *Bahavioral Science*, **19**, 268–373.

Smith, C.W. (1999): *Success and Survival on Wall Street: Understanding the Mind of the Market*, Rowman & Littlefield, New York.

Smith, L., and P. Sorensen (2000): Pathological outcomes of observational learning, *Econometrica*, **68** (2), 371–398.

Smith, V.L. (1969): Measuring nonmonetary utilities in uncertain choices: The Ellsberg urn, *Quarterly Journal of Economics*, **83**, 324–329.

Smith, V.L., G.L. Suchanek, and A.W. Williams (1988): Bubbles, crashes, and endogenous expectations in experimental spot asset markets, *Econometrika*, **56** (5), 1119–1151.

Soros, G. (1987): *The Alchemy of Finance: Reading the Mind of the Market*, John Wiley & Sons, New York.

Stein, J. (1989): Overreaction in the options market, *Journal of Finance*, **44**, 1011–1024.

Sunder, S. (1995): Experimental asset markets: A survey, in *The Handbook of Experimental Economics* ed. by J.H. Kagel and A.E. Roth, pp. 445–500, Princeton University Press, Princeton.

Syed, A.A., P. Liu, and S.D. Smith (1989): The exploitation of inside information at the Wall Street Journal: A test of strong form efficiency, *Financial Review*, 24, 567–579.

Taylor, K.A. (1991): Testing credit and blame attributions as explanations for choices under ambiguity, Working Paper, Department of Decision Sciences, University of Pennsylvania.

Tesar, L., and I.M. Werner (1995): Home bias and high turnover, *Journal of International Money and Finance*, **14**, 467–492.

Trojani, F., and P. Vanini (2004): Robustness and ambiguity aversion in general equilibrium, *Review of Finance*, **2**, 279–324.

Tversky, A., and C.R. Fox (1995): Weighing risk and uncertainty, *Psychological Review*, **102** (2), 269–283.

Tversky, A., and D. Kahneman (1980): Causal schemes in judgements under uncertainty, in *Progress in Social Psychology* ed. by M. Fishbein, pp. 49–72, Erlbaum, Hillsdale, NJ.

Tversky A., and D. Kahneman (1982a): Belief in the law of small numbers, in *Judgement under Uncertainty: Heuristics and Biases* ed. by D. Kahneman, P. Slovic, and A. Tversky, pp. 23–31, Cambridge University Press, Cambridge.

Tversky, A. and D. Kahneman (1982b): Causal schemes in judgements under uncertainty, in *Judgement under Uncertainty: Heuristics and Biases* ed. by D. Kahneman, P. Slovic, and A. Tversky, pp. 117–128, Cambridge University Press, Cambridge.

Tversky, A., and D. Kahneman (1992): Advances in prospect theory: Cumulative representation of uncertainty, *Journal of Risk and Uncertainty*, **5**, 297–323.

Tversky, A., Sattath, S., and P. Slovic (1988): Contingent weighting in judgment and choice, *Psychological Review*, 371–384.

Uppal, R., and T. Wang (2003): Model misspecification and under-diversification, *Journal of Finance*, **58** (6), 2465–2486.

Van Bommel, J. (2003): Rumors, *The Journal of Finance*, **58** (4), 1499–1519.

Vettas, N. (1997): On the informational role of quantities: Durable goods and consumers' word-of-mouth communication, *International Economic Review*, **38**, 915–944.

Vettas, N. (1998): Demand and supply in new markets: Diffusion with bilateral learning, *Rand Journal of Economics*, **19**, 215–233.

Von Mises, L. (1996): *Human Action*, 4th revd edn, Fox & Wilkes, San Francisco.

Von Neumann, J., and O. Morgenstern (1947): *Theory of Games and Economic Behavior*, 2nd edn, Princeton University Press, Princeton.

Wakker, P. (1984): Cardinal coordinate independence for expected utility, *Journal of Mathematical Psychology*, **28**, 110–117.

Wakker, P. (1989a): Continuous subjective expected utility with non-additive probabilities, *Journal of Mathematical Economics*, **18**, 1–27.

Wakker, P. (1989b): *Additive Representation of Preferences: A New Foundation for Decision Analysis*, Kluwer Academic Publishers, Dordrecht, Holland.

Walter, G.L., and C.A. Beckerle (1989): The virulence of dread rumors: A field experiment, Poster presented at the meeting of the Eastern Psychological Association, Boston, MA.

Wärneryd, K.-E. (2001): *Stock-Market Psychology, How People Value and Trade Stocks*, Edward Elgar Publishing, Cheltenham.

Watzlawick, P. (1985): *Wie wirklich ist die Wirklichkeit? Wahn Täuschung Verstehen*, Piper, München.

Welch, I. (1992): Sequential sales, learning and cascades, *Journal of Finance*, **47**, 695–732.

Wermers, R. (1999): Mutual fund herding and the impact on stock prices, *Journal of Finance*, **54**, 581–622.

Yates, J.F., and L.G. Zukowski (1976): Characterization of ambiguity in decision making, *Behavioral Science*, **21**, 19–25.

Zarowin, P. (1989): Does the stock market overreact to corporate earnings information?, *Journal of Finance*, **44**, 1385–1400.

Zarowin, P. (1990): Size, seasonality, and stock market overreaction, *Journal of Financial and Quantitative Analysis*, **25**, 113–126.

Zhou, C., and J. Mei (2003): Behavior based manipulation. Unpublished Working Paper 03028, NYU Stern School of Business.

Ziegler, A. (2003): *Incomplete Information and Heterogeneous Beliefs in Continuous-time Finance*, Springer Finance, Berlin.

Zivney, T.L., W.J. Bertin, and K.M. Torabzadeh (1996): Overreaction to takeover speculation, *The Quarterly Review of Economics and Finance*, **36** (1), 89–115.

Index